Praise for *Marcion*

David Litwa's book provides a fresh start with Marcion. The author offers for the first time an investigation of Marcion that breaks with reliance on the polemical remarks of his opponents and lets go of the questionable project of trying to reverse-engineer those polemical distortions to arrive at reliable information. For those who thought that was our only option, Litwa's book will be eye-opening. He assembles a portrait based primarily on material traceable to Marcion himself, as either author or authorizer. Building on recent advances in reconstructing the Marcionite scriptures, Litwa gives a careful reading of the theology they support. His close analysis of the remains of Marcion's *Antitheses* is unparalleled in previous scholarship for its depth and insight. The result is a major contribution to the current renaissance of work on Marcion. At the same time, it is a lesson in the difference a disciplined methodology can make in a field where the "church fathers" all too often still set the terms of our understanding of early Christianities.

—Jason BeDuhn, professor of the comparative study of religions, Northern Arizona University

In attempting to remove Marcion from the long shadow of Adolf von Harnack, Litwa aims to undermine any and all heresiologically inflected interpretations of Marcion on the grounds that they are inescapably reductionistic. In addition to offering an interesting reconstruction of Marcion's life and thought, Litwa provocatively proposes that present-day Christians would do well to carry on Marcion's legacy by rejecting any hint of divine terror or violence. The Old Testament and biblical passages containing any trace of divine violence, Litwa argues, should be "decanonized." That is, they should by no means be received as divinely inspired. Litwa suggests further that Christians' attempts to account for divine violence in the Bible must be supplanted in favor of Marcion's Gospel of the wholly good God according to which Jesus's Father cannot be identified with the God of Israel in the Old Testament. In short, Litwa reinvigorates Marcion in order to venerate him and the legacy he putatively ought to have among Christians today.

—Alexander H. Pierce, assistant professor of historical theology, North American Lutheran Seminary

In the last four or five decades, Marcion has been the focus of much innovative and intense research that has challenged many of the assumptions of previous scholarship, in particular that of Adolf von Harnack. David Litwa's new book is a welcome and bold attempt at formulating a new interpretation of Marcion for the twenty-first century. It is comprehensive and circumspect in its handling of the sources, well informed in its critical dialogue with the whole range of previous scholarship, cautious regarding the many methodical problems besetting its subject matter, and precise in its proposals of new interpretations. Readers—be they experts on the topic or new to it—will find their views of Marcion and the theological and philosophical context of the second century enriched and challenged at every turn. Moreover, Litwa's perceptive exploration of Marcion's theology and the ancient controversies triggered by it is constantly alive to their modern resonance. This monograph will surely inform future debates on the shape of early Christian theological discourse and one of its most controversial protagonists.

—Winrich Löhr, University of Heidelberg

If you have ever questioned the stories about the violence of God found in the Old Testament, Litwa's reexamination of the early Christian theologian Marcion offers some answers. This book is a much-needed corrective to two thousand years of mistreatment and mischaracterization of Marcion as the archenemy of Christianity when, in fact, Marcion was the original framer of the New Testament as the gospel of the wholly good God. Read on!

—April DeConick, Rice University, author of *Comparing Christianities: An Introduction to Early Christianity*

MARCION

MARCION

THE GOSPEL OF A WHOLLY GOOD GOD

M. DAVID LITWA

FORTRESS PRESS
Minneapolis

MARCION

The Gospel of a Wholly Good God

30 29 28 27 26 25 2 3 4 5 6 7 8 9

Library of Congress Control Number: 2024054567 (print)

Cover image: A meeting of the first Christians in Rome - a letter from Paul is read. Wood engraving, published in 1886, from ZU_09/Getty Images; and Defocused sunrise or sunset - stock photo from Olga Siletskaya/Getty Images
Cover design: Kris E. Miller

Print ISBN: 979-8-8898-3487-8
eBook ISBN: 979-8-8898-3488-5

To all spiritual seekers

CONTENTS

PREFACE

Years ago at a session of the Society of Biblical Literature Annual Meeting, I listened to a book review on Judith Lieu's *Marcion: The Making of a Heretic* (2015) by Michael Bird. In his inimitable Australian accent, Bird dubbed Lieu's book "the new Harnack." "The new Harnack?" I thought. "We don't need a new Harnack. We need a book on Marcion that completely replaces Harnack's paradigm, that makes us no longer need to read Harnack except to understand the history of Marcion's twentieth-century reception." The present work aims to do just that. It amasses all the evidence against Harnack's paradigm—all the anomalies—to forge a new paradigm and to stimulate a new wave of Marcion research in the twenty-first century.

The secret is this: Harnack's paradigm has already collapsed, though most people don't seem to know it. Imagine an ironclad warship, a destroyer. Once it sailed the high seas with speed. But over the course of its century-long voyage, it has been hit by half a dozen small torpedoes. The torpedoes all came at different times and produced what only seemed like pockmarks in the hull. Now the ship is halfway under water—but the sailors still go about their tasks, and everyone on shore assumes that she'll come to port. Such is Harnack's paradigm. It has died the death of a thousand pinpricks, from many criticisms over the course of a century. Yet people still talk as if his model for understanding Marcion reigns.

A few points on language and word usage in this book. It seems that Marcionites, including perhaps Marcion himself, were not entirely strict in their theological language. They could refer to a Judean "god" just like Christians today can speak of Greco-Roman "gods." This book however, will endeavor to be strict, only referring to the Judean lord as "the (lower) creator," while leaving the title "God" to Marcion's supreme Father. In general, when "God" is capitalized, it refers to the high God or Father; but when the *g* is lowercase, it refers to a lower being which for Marcionites includes the (lower) creator. Furthermore, this work refers to Marcion's Gospel as the Evangelion or simply as "the Gospel," abbreviated as "G." Lastly, it calls Ephesians by the Marcionite title "Laodiceans" (abbreviation: "Laod"). This letter should not be confused with the apocryphal epistle to the Laodiceans preserved in Latin.

All translations of ancient texts, unless otherwise noted, are freshly made. Hebrew Bible passages are translated from the Septuagint (LXX), with LXX versification.

Readers are encouraged to engage with this book in tandem with its online companion course on Marcion, which you can find at: https://mdavidlitwa.com/courses.

ABBREVIATIONS

Abbreviations for citations of ancient texts employed in this work are taken from *The SBL Handbook of Style for Biblical Studies and Related Disciplines*, 2nd ed. (Atlanta: SBL Press, 2014). Other abbreviations are as follows:

AAH	Pseudo-Tertullian, *Against All Heresies*
AM	Tertullian, *Against Marcion*
BeDuhn-Bilby	Jason D. BeDuhn and Mark G. Bilby, "Greek Edition of the First New Testament: ΕΥΑΓΓΕΛΙΟΝ," version 1.2, deposited 2023-10-19; *idem*, "Greek Edition of the First New Testament: ΑΠΟΣΤΟΛΟΣ," version 1, deposited 2023.
Klinghardt	Matthias Klinghardt, *The Oldest Gospel and the Formation of the Canonical Gospels*, 2 vols. (Leuven: Peeters, 2021).
Pan.	Epiphanius, *Panarion* (*Refutation of All Heresies*)
Ref.	*Refutation of All Heresies.* Edited by M. David Litwa. WGRW 40. Atlanta: SBL Press, 2016
Roth	Dieter Roth, *The Text of Marcion's Gospel* (Leiden: Brill, 2015).
Schmid	Ulrich Schmid, *Marcion und sein Apostolos: Rekonstruktion und historische Einordnung der Marcionitischen Paulusbriefausgabe* (Berlin: de Gruyter, 1995).

Introduction

> It is dangerous to be right in matters on which the established authorities are wrong.
>
> —Voltaire

To some, Marcion of Pontus is a heretic; to others a hero; and to a few, what made Marcion a hero was the fact that he was a heretic. A great reformer, arguably, is simply a heretic who won. Some heretics become heroes with good postmortem public relations. Jesus died condemned by the Sanhedrin for blasphemy, but rose with angels in a blaze of glory. Paul of Tarsus was beaten five times in the synagogues, but his mission to the gentiles was successful and scalable—there are over two billion Christians today.

Enter Marcion: a Christian theologian with perhaps the worst postmortem PR in history. His opponents, mostly churchmen and heresy writers (or heresiologists), made all sorts of claims about him.[1] They said that he mutilated Scripture, that he took canonical Luke, still in its infancy, and like a rabbi fulfilling the covenant with Abraham, "circumcised it."[2] But perhaps canonical Luke—a book much larger than Marcion's Gospel—did not exist in the Pontian's early days. Perhaps it was the expansion of Marcion's Gospel, or of its archetype, and the heresiologists—who attributed their Gospels to "apostolic" persons—simply assumed that Luke was earlier than Marcion's version without careful attention to its history or language.

1. The best introduction to Marcion's opponents is Judith M. Lieu, *Marcion and the Making of a Heretic: God and Scripture in the Second Century* (Cambridge: Cambridge University Press, 2015). A briefer summary can be found in M. David Litwa, *Found Christianities: Remaking the World of the Second Century CE* (London: Bloomsbury, 2022), 13–17. The present book updates and expands this summary.

2. Irenaeus, *Haer.* 1.27.2 (*circumcidens*)

Maybe Marcion did not exclude canonical texts. Maybe he was the very first canon maker, the first to make a list of authoritative Christian books with a line drawn in the sand: *these and no others.* There were no second-century church councils defining the canon—and there would not be for centuries. Even Martin Luther supposed he had the power to relegate James—that "epistle of straw"—to an appendix, and this reformer succeeded in ousting the deuterocanonical books (for instance, Judith, Tobit, and the Maccabees) from Protestant Bibles.[3] If this internal housecleaning of sacred—but not quite canonical—texts, could be performed in the sixteenth century, then how much more in the second?

Heresiologists said that Marcion excluded the "Old" Testament, rejecting Hebrew prophecies about Christ. Perhaps, however, the "Old" Testament had not yet been invented because Christians did not yet have a "New" Testament. Perhaps Jewish scriptures such as the books of Moses were not systematically read in churches of Marcion's day. Perhaps the master idea of Jesus fulfilling Hebrew Bible prophecies was a development based on decades of reflection, as Christians in competition with Jews claimed the Jewish heritage and prestige? Maybe Marcion was the only Christian to let Jews be Jews, and to let Jewish understandings of their own messiah remain theirs, with no accusation that they somehow misunderstood their own sacred literature, their own cultural heritage. Maybe he did not reject the Hebrew scriptures as such, but only as sacred texts normative for Christians and read in their liturgies. Maybe Marcion read and reflected on Jewish scriptures more than most of his contemporaries—more than even most Christians today.

Heresiologists said that Marcion was a ditheist. Yet perhaps he was the only Christian after Jesus to taste the pure sweetness of divine goodness. Perhaps he was the only Christ follower with the courage to call the god of this world an inconsistent, bloodthirsty tyrant. Euripides said that "if the gods do evil, they are not gods,"[4] and Nietzsche could not believe in a god who couldn't dance.[5] Marcion could not believe in a god who was not good—*wholly*

---

3. Jason D. Lane, *Luther's Epistle of Straw: The Voice of St. James in Reformation Preaching* (Berlin: de Gruyter, 2018), 1–3.

4. Euripides as quoted by Plutarch, *Stoic Self-Contradiction* 1049f.

5. Friedrich Nietzsche, "On Reading and Writing," in *Thus Spake Zarathustra*, in *The Portable Nietzsche*, ed. and trans. Walter Kaufmann (London: Penguin, 1954).

good—with no exception, excuses, or special pleading. This meant that the creator who confessed to making "evils" (Isa 45:7) was not in fact God most high, but something more like a renegade subordinate to the true king, an upper-middle management functionary in a bigger bureaucracy of superhuman beings.

Of course, the creator claimed to be a god—even the only one—but the pride of local potentates sometimes needed to be humbled by the true emperor. And if the true emperor did not come in person, he would send his Son, endowed with plenipotentiary power. Marcion believed in scriptures that spoke of one God, one Lord of heaven, one faith, one Father of us all. He created a Christian church—a denomination, of sorts—that lasted nine centuries (and has recently been revived). He preached to gentiles, ever aiming to dislodge them from polytheistic thinking. The last thing Marcion would say about himself was, "I'm a ditheist."

Heresiologists said that Marcion's Jesus was a glorified ghost, a phantom unborn, without father or mother—a simulated, seeming Savior. But each Sunday Marcion consumed the eucharistic bread, biting down on the figure of Christ's doughy—though quite tangible—flesh. A woman in Marcion's Scriptures wiped the feet of Jesus with her hair and kissed them with tender lips. Christ was solid to the touch, so solid he could be whipped, punched, and nailed fast to a rough beam of wood. True, Jesus tried to create a new fellowship of spiritual kin, but his mother and brothers were still asking for him outside. According to surviving evidence, Marcion never denied Jesus's birth, and never questioned Jesus's humanity. He believed in a Scripture that spoke of Christ coming in the likeness of sinful flesh and appearing in human form (Rom 8:3; Phil 2:6–8). If Christ's humanity was different, that was because he was an incarnate god, and the heightened quality of his flesh was manifest on the Mount of Transfiguration, where the body of Jesus demonstrated its higher quality by glowing like the sun.

Heresiologists said that Marcion denied the world, along with the human body, and that he hated the material creation. But how then did he drink water, eat bread, and bask in the noonday sun? Why did he make his living transporting people and goods on the wine dark sea? Why did he call the Father "Lord of heaven" (G 10:21) and "creator of everything" (Laod 3:8)? How could Marcion's Lord stop wind and waves with a word, heal lepers and restore sight to the blind? Was this not the Lord of matter—of soil, sun, and sea? If the law of Marcion's God was to reject creation, "he would have prescribed not to eat or drink, to see nothing, to not get up or be seated, not to hear or stand up."[6]

Marcion did discipline his body, as jealous enemies noticed, but that does not mean he hated it. The Pontian enjoined celibacy for baptized members of his community. But his Scriptures said that the children of God are—in this present life—not married or given in marriage, but are equal to angels (G 20:36). The apostle Paul recommended celibacy with force and clarity (1 Cor 7), and if other Christians smiled, nodded, and found a way to dodge this advice, Marcion refused to find an excuse. He was out to make a holy church, the bride of Christ, and never asked Christians to make a commitment greater than he himself had made. There is a pattern here, a true imitation of Christ: Jesus was celibate; the great apostle was celibate; and so was Marcion.

All this is more than a thought experiment, of course—a "perhaps" followed by a few "maybes." No, this book is a set of arguments aiming to do no less than transform how people think about Marcion. The old paradigm cannot survive a thousand anomalies. For a century, Marcion has stood under the shadow of Adolf von Harnack. In one way or another, every study after Harnack's *Marcion: Gospel of an Alien God*—even those who resisted it—has reinscribed some element of its presentation. In itself, that would not be bad if Harnack had managed not to reinscribe the heresiologists. But time and time again in that great historian's book, the heresiological portrait of the Pontian is raised to the level of scholarly prestige.

A series of six *d*'s summarizes the default Harnackian (which is now the encyclopedia) portrait of the Pontian: Marcion the *d*itheist, the *d*ocetist, the *d*etester of Jews, the *d*enier of the world, the *d*eleter of Scripture, and the *d*emiurgist. A ditheist is a believer in two gods (a kind of polytheist); a docetist denies that Christ was human or had true flesh; a detester of Jews attacks not just Judaism but Jews themselves; a world-denier lives ascetically out of hatred for matter and its creator; a deleter of Scripture cuts out passages that don't suit one's ideology; and a demiurgist removes creative power from God, bestowing it on a lower being (sometimes called "god").

These six *d*'s are demolished by one single rule—a rule as simple as it is underused—that Marcion's beliefs are defined by the touchstone of his

6. Ephrem, *Hymnes Contre les Hérésies (Hymns against Heresy)* 45.2.

Scriptures. Of course the testimony of Marcion's enemies remains data, but it is secondary. It has always been secondary. The heresiologists don't have the final say, and when they contradict Marcion's Scriptures, the Scriptures prevail. The goal here is to stop representing heresiological rhetoric and speculation about Marcion as the truth of history.

To be sure, Marcion's Scriptures must be reconstructed, but reliable reconstructions are available, and readers will learn here how reliable reconstructions are made (chapter 5). Marcion's interpretation of his Scriptures is sometimes lacking or confused with the reports of his enemies. But if his Scriptures are largely reconstructable, then these Scriptures still become the primary source that controls every heresiological claim, that trumps every heresiological dogma, no matter how firmly entrenched.

In himself, Marcion was neither a heretic nor a hero. He should be treated as a person in the mighty river of history, a Christian theologian who lived some nineteen centuries ago when Christianity lacked creeds, confessions, and ecumenical councils; when it had no papacy, prelates, or political power. Marcion lived in the laboratory in which Christianity was synthesized. Or rather, he lived in the jungle of competing discourses, trying to define the faith, the story, and the organization of an institution so simply—yet so deceptively—called "the" church.

In the tender years of the Christian movement, Marcion made his mark. As an asteroid crashing into Earth creates a gigantic crater, the enormity of Marcion's impact is clear from those who responded to him. At least fifteen elite Christian writers wrote treatises against him in the first fifty years after his death.[7] At least one epistle, 3 Corinthians, was produced in Paul's name to oppose Marcion.[8] Some argue that the Pastoral Epistles and Acts were written

---

7. Adolf von Harnack, *Marcion: The Gospel of the Alien God*, trans. John E. Steely and Lyle D. Bierma (Durham: Labyrinth, 1990), 99–103. For Harnack's main text, I cite this English translation. Starred pages (*) refer to the appendices in the German text: *Marcion: Das Evangelium vom fremden Gott: Eine Monographie zur Geschichte der Grundlegung der katholischen Kirche*, 2nd ed. (Darmstadt: Wissenschaftliche Buchgesellschaft, 1985), 314*–341*. See also Peter Lampe, *From Paul to Valentinus: Christians at Rome in the First Two Centuries*, ed. Marshall Johnson, trans. Michael Steinhauser (Minneapolis: Fortress, 2003), 250–251.

8. Martin Rist, "III Corinthians as a Pseudepigraphic Refutation of Marcionism," *Iliff Review* 26 (1969): 40–58.

with Marcion in mind.[9] And a few voices see the Latin letter to the Laodiceans as a Marcionite text.[10] One scholar even claimed that Marcion wrote the initial draft of his (quite different) letter to the Laodiceans (now called Ephesians).[11]

Marcion did not just create a school, or a school of thought. The Pontian was a man of action, an ecclesial entrepreneur. He organized churches in different lands; he published a particular Bible; he set up strict rules for his community, an order of worship, and a way of life. If he failed, he failed forward. Yet by any measure of success, he did not fall flat. He created an ecclesiastical network that survived until the tenth century—and Christians claiming to be Marcionites exist today.

While he yet lived, Marcion's enemies looked askance at his global success. A Christian poet of late antiquity called him "the Pontic plague" and "a miraculous monstrosity."[12] To this day, Marcion is still introduced as the greatest threat to Christendom, serving as the pastor's whipping boy, and the foil of theologians. To boil down the anti-Marcion refrain, it often sounds like this: "read the Bible with Marcion's diligence, though not with his eyes." Such a perspective might recognize the importance of Marcion, but it assumes the viewpoint of his enemies, and does not foster a critical and historical approach to his life and work.[13]

Even good scholars have chosen to replace neutral research with value judgments. It was once popular to quote, for instance, the catchy dictum of

---

9. Joseph Tyson, *Marcion and Luke Acts: A Defining Struggle* (Columbia: University of South Carolina Press, 2006); Martina Janßen, "'Wider die Antithesen der fälschlich so genannten Gnosis': 1 Tim 6,20 und die Antithesen Markions," in *Frühes Christentum und Religionsgeschichtliche Schule: Festschrift zum. 65 Geburtstag von Gerd Lüdemann*, ed. Martina Janßen (Göttingen: Vandenhoeck & Ruprecht, 2011), 96–109.

10. Enrico Norelli, "La Lettre aux Laodicéens: Essai d'interprétation," *Archivum Bobiense* 23 (2001): 45–90.

11. R. Joseph Hoffman, *Marcion: On the Restitution of Christianity: An Essay on the Development of Radical Paulinist Theology in the Second Century* (Missoula: Scholars Press, 1984), 275–276.

12. *Carmen adversus Marcionitas* 3.299, 302 (*Pontica pestis, mirabile monstrum*).

13. Marcion as threat or danger is a common trope in the secondary literature (e.g., J. Woltmann "Der geschichtliche Hintergrund der Lehre Markions vom Fremden Gott," in *Wegzeichen: Festgabe zum 60. Geburtstag von Prof. Dr. M. H. Biedermann*, ed. E. Suttner and C. Patak [Würzburg: Augustinus Verlag, 1971], 30).

Franz Overbeck that, "No one has understood Paul; and the only person who did understand him—Marcion—misunderstood him."[14] This is certainly a backhanded compliment if there ever was one. In the context of the Lutheran reading of Marcion, Marcion came close to understanding Paul because Marcion's Paul resembled Luther's; nevertheless, Marcion failed to hold together the dialectical tensions of the Lutheran reading (a God hidden and revealed, just and good, and so on).

The obvious question here is why the Lutheran (or any other later) tradition is held up as a criterion for judging the thought of Marcion, a man of the second century? There is creative anachronism, perhaps, but one should have the charity to treat Marcion as a man of his own times and on his own terms.

One would have thought that in recent times comments like Overbeck's would have lost their cachet. Yet one still finds remarks to the effect that Marcion, that great Paulinist, misunderstood Paul.[15] This overgeneralizing judgment—apart from being a potential reinscription of ancient polemic—is out of place in a scholarly study of Marcion. Upon what criteria, after all, could one judge that an interpreter—nearly two millennia closer to Paul than modern people, with his own presuppositions governed by a different historical context—misunderstood Paul?[16] More humility is required here, along with a

---

14. *Niemand hat Paulus je verstanden und der einzige, der ihn verstand, Marcion, hat ihn missverstanden.* According to Albert Schweitzer, *The Mysticism of Paul the Apostle* (New York: Seabury, 1931), 38n1 the original dictum was first spoken of Hegel's pupils. Overbeck applied it to Paul during a conversation with Harnack sometime in the 1880s. Harnack then popularized it. For more recent quotations of the Overbeck dictum, see Gerd Lüdemann, *Heretics: The Other Side of Early Christianity*, trans. John Bowden (Louisville: Westminster John Knox, 1996), 148; Richard Pervo, *The Making of Paul: Constructions of the Apostle in Early Christianity* (Minneapolis: Fortress, 2010), 205.

15. For example, J. Christiaan Beker, "Christologies and Anthropologies of Paul, Luke-Acts and Marcion," in *From Jesus to John: Essays on Jesus and New Testament Christology in Honour of Marinus de Jonge*, ed. Martinus C. De Boer (Sheffield: Sheffield Academic Press, 1993), 179–181; Schmid, 260; Todd D. Still, "Shadow and Light: Marcion's (Mis)Construal of the Apostle Paul," in *Paul and the Second Century*, ed. Michael F. Bird and Joseph R. Dodson (London: T&T Clark, 2011), 107. Scholars often conclude that Marcion misunderstood Paul because they assume a heresiological or Harnackian view of Marcion.

16. Maurice Wiles, *The Divine Apostle: The Interpretation of St. Paul's Epistles in the Early Church* (Cambridge: Cambridge University Press, 1967), 132; Andreas Lindemann, *Paulus im ältesten Christentum: Das Bild des Apostles und die Rezeption der paulinischen Theologie in der frühchristlichen Literatur bis Marcion* (Tübingen: Mohr Siebeck, 1979), 3, 72.

method that remains sympathetic to ancient readers of all types. This is especially true given that Marcionite thinkers, beliefs, and documents have been mocked, pilloried, and in some cases buried by an opposing (self-proclaimed "straight-thinking") tradition.[17]

It may be true that one can only understand the past through one's own interpretive horizon. At the same time, the disciplined historical imagination has the ability to reenvision the past through the lens of its subject(s). The goal is not to promote the viewpoint of these subjects (as if "Marcionism" could be applied today without adjustment), but to walk a mile in Marcion's shoes in order to obtain a new picture of the world—or in this case, of church history.

The benefits of this approach are manifold, for Marcion is indispensable. Anyone interested in the New Testament and early Christian history should know Marcion in order to understand the Synoptic problem, the construction of the New Testament, the spread of early Christianity, its earliest rites, its ethics, the development of its scriptures, the means of their interpretation, the evolution of biblical theology, the earliest interaction of theology and philosophy, the so-called parting of the ways with Judaism, the church's (primeval) story about itself, and how so-called gnostics are a part of this tale.

One should not exaggerate Marcion's importance, though one ought not minimize it either. The Pontian probably did not write the first Gospel, which became a model for the four Gospels best known today. He did, however, compile a scriptural collection that established the basic structure of the New Testament still surviving today. Without Marcion, distinctly Christian scriptures would eventually have been canonized, but the final product might have looked measurably less Pauline than it does today. Without Marcion, there would probably have been a version of "according to Mark, Matthew, and John," but there might not have been the Gospel of Luke as we know it. Moreover, the church "history" told in Acts might not have needed to lionize Paul, or talk up his union with Peter and the other apostles. Without Marcion, there would have been an "Old" Testament, but it might not have been made

17. R. Joseph Hoffmann, "How Then Know This Troublous Teacher? Further Reflections on Marcion and his Church," *Second Century* 6 (1987–88): 189. See also Stanley K. Stowers, "What Does Unpauline Mean?" in *Paul and the Legacies of Paul*, ed. William S. Babcock (Dallas: Southern Methodist University Press, 1990), 70–77.

a measuring rod for Christian doctrine and practice.[18] At least the contours of canonical Christian literature, if not Christian history, would have looked significantly different if Marcion's star had not risen so high.

To understand Marcion's life and contribution to church history, one must first examine his historical context. The initial step in this journey, then, is to lift the veil on the Roman Empire of the early second century CE—when it stood at the pinnacle of its glory and at the height of its power.

18. See John Barton, *Holy Writings, Sacred Text: The Canon in Early Christianity* (Louisville: Westminster John Knox, 1997), 58.

Part I

Setting the Scene

CHAPTER ONE

The Roman Empire in Marcion's Time

> If a man were called to fix the period in the history of the world during which the condition of the human race was most happy and prosperous, he would, without hesitation, name that which elapsed from the death of Domitian to the accession of Commodus.
>
> —Edward Gibbon, *The History of the Decline and Fall of the Roman Empire*, 108.

EDWARD GIBBON'S RATHER rosy picture of the early second-century empire is focused almost entirely on manifestations of high culture.[1] However happy and prosperous this era might have been for the elite—it was rife with misery for the masses. Slaves, day-laborers, women, and disabled peoples were largely deprived of basic human rights, nutritious food, and health services. If one agrees that the second century was an era of noteworthy cultural and scientific achievement, relative political stability, and religious diversity, this says very little about the happiness and prosperity of the average person. Christianity—and in particular Marcionite Christianity—could never have succeeded the way it did if thousands—if not millions—of people in the empire did not crave salvation *from* this world, the vale of tears.

The Imperial Engine

In Marcion's day, the Roman Empire achieved the height of its strength and the furthest extent of its expansion. The government had long devolved into a monarchy in which only a small minority of the subjects were citizens who could avoid burdensome taxes. The emperor stood at the pinnacle of a gigantic

1. The present chapter adapts Litwa, *Found Christianities*, 19–31.

bureaucracy of provincial governors, their retainers, generals, imperial slaves, secretaries, tax collectors (and so on) who ensured that money and goods pumped into and out of the imperial capital.

To control other cities in the empire, Rome made alliances with local elites (kings, noblemen, members of civic assemblies) to keep the peace and to maintain the supply chains. The major industry was farming, and most of the wealth was generated by cultivating land. There was no official Roman police force. Provinces that were distant and difficult to manage had large armies (legions) permanently stationed in the vicinity. Local rebellions might have temporary success, but when the Romans unleashed the full force of their military machine, few of their enemies were left standing.

Emperors

The following whirlwind history focuses entirely on the four men who claimed the imperial purple during Marcion's adult life (between 96 and 161 CE). The story opens with the emperor Nerva (reigned 96–98 CE), the elderly aristocrat chosen to replace the assassinated and tyrannical emperor Domitian. Nerva was remembered fondly by the Roman elite for restoring their sense of respect as well as their ancient privileges. Among many small changes in the administration and the completion of a few building projects, Nerva either discontinued the infamous Jewish tax or, more likely, reformed it. His most important political act was the choice of an accomplished heir in his prime, Marcus Ulpius Trajan.

Trajan (reigned 98–117 CE) was a successful general from the Spanish provinces, a good-natured leader, not enthralled with the trappings of authority. He was the first to expand the empire since Caesar Augustus by carving out the province of Dacia (much of modern Romania) after a double invasion. Late in life, Trajan enjoyed military success in the western section of the Parthian empire (modern Iraq), but he, like Alexander the Great, died soon after obtaining these victories, and the lands won were mostly abandoned by his successor, Hadrian (117–138 CE).

Hadrian was a man of culture, not of campaigns. He policed the empire's boundaries, but focused his efforts investing in its cities. In the course of his perambulations, Hadrian founded several cities himself, including one named for his perished boy lover, Antinous, in Egypt. Fiercely pro-Hellenic, Hadrian clashed with nationalist Jews in Palestine, and ruthlessly suppressed them when they revolted there (132–135 CE). Months before his death, Hadrian chose the next three emperors to succeed him.

His immediate successor was Antoninus Pius (reigned 138–161 CE), an unassuming, careful governor in his early fifties. Through his generals, Pius pushed the Roman empire deep into Scotland and had diplomatic success with client kings in the East. He was known for his restoration of buildings and public munificence. (A temple dedicated to his deified wife was later dedicated to him and still stands in the Forum at Rome.) Pius distinguished circumcision from castration, allowing Jews to circumcise their sons. He carefully and responsibly steered the empire through its longest period of relative peace.

Cultural High Points

Although chaos could always break out on the margins of the empire, the center (modern Italy, Greece, Turkey, and North Africa) enjoyed a renaissance in the fields of literature and oration. It was the age of the so-called Second Sophistic, when intellectuals of all sorts competed in tight social markets for prestige, wealth, and honor, parading their wisdom for a fee. This wisdom was consummately Greek, constantly appealing to the heritage of the "classical" past, its imagination centered on Athens in the fifth century BCE. Even those of "barbarian" (non-Greek) heritage could still do well in this world if they learned the codes and modes of classicizing ("Attic") Greek speech and learning.

Philosophy

Philosophers—who traditionally pitted themselves against orators ("sophists")—enjoyed a share of their prosperity.[2] They served as the empire's conscience, as its moral exemplars and advisors. It was the new fashion, beginning with Hadrian, for men to sport a philosophic beard.[3] Philosophic education was the "higher ed" of the era. If one could not find a teacher, one could

2. Lucian, *The Runaways* 10–11.

3. Paul Zanker, *The Mask of Socrates: The Image of the Intellectual in Antiquity* (Berkeley: University of California Press, 1995).

buy a digest version of philosophy presenting the opinions of key philosophers (a doxography).

A notable philosopher of the time was the Stoic Epictetus (about 50–135 CE). Epictetus was a former slave from Phrygia (what is now southeastern Turkey). He was bought in Rome by a secretary of the emperor Nero, but allowed to pursue advanced education. Epictetus was disabled with a maimed leg, apparently due to his master's abuse. He obtained his freedom and taught in the capital until 95 CE. Epictetus sailed to Nicopolis on the coast of western Greece and set up his school. There, until his death, he taught high-profile Romans like Arrian, an aristocrat from Bithynia and later governor of Cappadocia (regions sandwiching Pontus). It was Arrian who transcribed Epictetus's discourses, imitating his teacher's punchy pedagogical style.

Epictetus preached freedom—a freedom that did not depend on one's external circumstances, but on one's internal choices to accept reality and to love it as the expression of divine goodness. Epictetus advocated freedom from negative emotions (the "passions"), inward disturbances that he thought were based on faulty judgments. He did not promote the sheer absence of emotion; rather, he encouraged the use of positive emotions like joy, caution, and well-wishing.[4]

A key representative of the Epicurean school was Diogenes of Oenoanda (in modern southwestern Turkey). This wealthy patron funded a rectangular piazza on whose walls he had carved one of the largest inscriptions of antiquity—originally a hundred meters long with some 25,000 words chiseled into stone. Diogenes believed that people were infected by a plague—not of germs, but of false opinions. In his old age, therefore, Diogenes wanted to exhort his fellow citizens to exemplify the virtues by which he had lived, among them justice and mutual love. So Diogenes chiseled his own words on rock, as well as those of his master Epicurus, founder of the school that pursued the higher pleasures of life: friendship, serenity, and the acceptance of death.[5]

4. Epictetus, *The Discourses, The Handbook, Fragments*, ed. and trans. Christopher Gill and Robin Hard (London: Everyman, 1995). See further A. A. Long, *Epictetus: A Stoic and Socratic Guide to Life*. (Oxford: Oxford University Press, 2002), esp. 7–37, 244–254.

5. See further Martin Ferguson Smith, *Diogenes of Oinoanda: The Epicurean Inscription* (Naples: Bibliopolis, 1993); Diskin Clay, "The Philosophical Inscription of Diogenes of Oenoanda," *Bulletin of the Classical Studies* 1 (2007): 283–291.

Cynic philosophers like Demonax and Peregrinus Proteus castigated the complacent in the tradition of Diogenes of Sinope (about 410–322 BCE).[6] Diogenes was called "Cynic" ("dog-like") because of his radical shamelessness and rejection of material comforts. Reportedly, he lived in a tub and refused even a bowl and spoon since he could eat without them.[7] He is reported to have masturbated publicly, to have castigated rich people and philosophers (notably, Plato), and in general to have performed a whole series of antics demonstrating how someone could live self-sufficiently without the need of material or social goods that fed human pride. His mission, in short, was to "deface the coinage," meaning "to overthrow all custom and convention."[8]

Despite debate among the schools, Platonism was slowly edging toward dominance in the field. The most popular Platonic dialogue was the *Timaeus*, Plato's "likely story" of creation, put in the mouth of an ancient Pythagorean from South Italy. Plato took over and adapted several ideas attributed to Pythagoras, the famous sage and mathematician. Some of Plato's heirs continued this trend, to such an extent that they formed a Neopythagorean revival in the first century BCE, which flourished for the next two centuries.

The Platonist Plutarch (about 40–125 CE), for instance, showed interest in Pythagorean numerology and was inclined toward vegetarianism.[9] He studied in Athens and Alexandria before becoming a philosopher, orator, and diplomat. Living in Rome for more than a decade, he rubbed shoulders with several leading lights and won Roman citizenship. As an older man, Plutarch served as priest of Apollo at Delphi and perfected the genre of comparative biography.[10]

---

6. Lucian, *Demonax*; *The Passing of Peregrinus*.

7. Diogenes Laertius, *Lives of Eminent Philosophers* 6.37.

8. See further Luis E. Navia, *Diogenes the Cynic: The War Against the World* (Amherst: Humanity Books, 2005); Ansgar Allen, *Cynicism* (Cambridge, MA: MIT Press, 2020); Louisa Shea, *The Cynic Enlightenment: Diogenes in the Salon* (Baltimore: Johns Hopkins University Press, 2010), 1–20.

9. Plutarch, *E at Delphi* 387f.

10. For Plutarch, see further John Dillon, *The Middle Platonists 80 BCE to AD 220*, 2nd ed. (Ithaca: Cornell University Press, 1996), 185–192; Tomas Hägg, *The Art of Biography in Antiquity* (Cambridge: Cambridge University Press, 2012), 239–281; Frederick E. Brenk, *On Plutarch: Religious Thinker and Biographer* (Leiden: Brill, 2017), 10–24.

Apuleius (about 125–190 CE) was another imperial Platonist. Born in Madauros (in modern-day Algeria), he received the finest education in rhetoric at the provincial capital of Carthage. The orator then moved to Athens to pursue studies in poetry, music, and geometry. Though once put on trial for being a magician, he represented himself as a philosopher. He grew wealthy as a public speaker in Greece and attained high office in Africa. His novel *Metamorphoses*—the adventures of a man turned into a donkey—evince the comic, playful side of his personality as well as his interest in Eastern religions.[11]

Apuleius's work *On Plato and His Teachings* is a handy introduction to second-century Platonism and is complimented by the *Handbook of Platonism* written by an otherwise unknown man called Alcinous. Both handbooks represent a particular phase of Platonism called "Middle Platonism," whose theological doctrines can here be summarized: a transcendent, bodiless deity—sometimes called "the Good"—abides in eternal peace and self-contemplation far above the heavens. A lower being, the creator, made the heavens and the earth after the model existing in the mind of the Good.[12] This world is the best of all possible worlds governed by good mediating deities called "daimones" who flitted between stars and planets, between kindly and arbitrary emotions.[13] The soul is naturally deathless. Suffering is necessary to train the soul for virtue. Virtue is the domination of "the passions"—raging emotions like fear, anger, jealousy, and greed.[14] The purest part of the soul is the mind (*nous*), considered to be the true, bodiless self, the thing most like unto God and daily called to become more divine.[15]

---

11. See further Stephen Harrison, ed., *Apuleius: Rhetorical Works* (Oxford: Oxford University Press, 2001), 185–194; Harrison, *Apuleius: A Latin Sophist* (Oxford: Oxford University Press, 2004); Richard Fletcher, *Apuleius's Platonism* (Cambridge: Cambridge University Press, 2014), 111–172; Dillon, *Middle Platonists*, 306–338.

12. Atticus was an exception by identifying the creator with the Good (Dillon, *Middle Platonists*, 254).

13. See further M. David Litwa, *Posthuman Transformation: Becoming Angels and Demons* (Cambridge: Cambridge University Press, 2021), 9–14.

14. See further Simo Knuuttila, *Emotions in Ancient and Medieval Philosophy* (Oxford: Oxford University Press, 2010); Francesco Becchi, "The Doctrine of the Passions: Plutarch, Posidonius and Galen," in *Plutarch in the Religious and Philosophical Discourse*, ed. Lautaro Roig Lanzillotta and Israel Munoz Gallarte (Leiden: Brill, 2012), 43–53.

15. On second-century Platonism, see Alcinous, *Handbook of Platonism*, trans. John Dillon (Oxford: Clarendon, 1993), esp. chaps. 10, 12, 15–17, 25–32, 35. See further Dillon, *Middle Platonists*, 267–304.

One can see why early Christian intellectuals came to favor Platonism. Plato's "Good," though technically beyond being and deity, closely conformed to their summodeistic ideal.[16] Some Christians identified the Platonic creator (or "demiurge") with the God who spoke in the book of Genesis. Angels fulfilled the function of daimones.[17] The soul is immortal—by God's grace. Life is a battle against the passions, passions that rage until the soul, envelope of the mind, finds release from the body.

Literature, Medicine, Astronomy

The second century was the heyday of the romantic novel with the appearance of works like Xenophon's *Ephesian Tale*, *Leucippe and Clitophon* by Achilles Tatius, and Longus's *Daphnis and Chloe*.[18] The novel had a significant influence on Christian fiction, mostly in Acts literature (for instance, the *Acts of Paul* and *Acts of John*), which related romantic—or rather anti-romantic—tales about apostles travelling into new territory and detaching wives from high-profile husbands.[19]

Lucian, a Syrian from what is now eastern Turkey (about 125–190 CE), wrote mostly in the genre of satire. His works were aimed to burst the proverbial bubble of schmoozing politicians, local religious leaders, and pompous philosophers. This Syrian had an interest in religious cults, criticized animal sacrifice, and thrilled in pointing out the oddity of local customs. His exposition of the Syrian goddess sounds respectfully like a Herodotean disquisition, but one never knows when his tongue lay against his cheek.[20]

---

16. See further Stephen Mitchell and Peter van Nuffelen, eds, *Monotheism between Pagans and Christians in Late Antiquity* (Leuven: Peeters, 2010).

17. Philo, *On Giants* 6.

18. These novels are translated in B. P. Reardon, *Collected Ancient Greek Novels*. (Berkeley: University of California Press, 2008). See further G. Schmeling, ed., *The Novel in the Ancient World* (Leiden: Brill, 2003); Tim Whitmarsh, ed., *The Cambridge Companion to the Greek and Roman Novel* (Cambridge: Cambridge University Press, 2008).

19. See J. K. Elliott, *The Apocryphal New Testament* (Oxford: Oxford University Press, 1993), 229–590.

20. On Lucian's biography, see Simon Swain, *Hellenism and Empire: Language, Classicism, and Power in the Greek World, AD 50–250* (Oxford: Clarendon, 1996), 298–329; Daniel Richter, "Lives and Afterlives of Lucian of Samosata," *Arion* 13:1 (2005): 75–100.

In Alexandria, Claudius Ptolemy (flourished 125–160 CE) composed his handbook of mathematical astronomy, the *Almagest.* In this work, Ptolemy proved earth's spherical shape and argued for a geocentric cosmos with seven revolving planets. Ptolemy also published his *Tetrabiblos,* which sought to place astrology (the influence of stars and planets on human life) on what was considered to be scientific footing.

The medical doctor Galen (about 129–215 CE) astonished crowds in Rome with dissections revealing his detailed knowledge of anatomy. He traced the nerves back to the brain and identified this organ as the center of human thought, motion, and feeling. He argued that knowledge was only certain when it stemmed from empirical premises and that only keen observation, not outdated theories, led to the right diagnoses. He explained the order of the human body and the purpose of its organs with the idea of a benign creator.[21]

Religious Movements

Peoples of the ancient Mediterranean believed that "all things are full of gods" (a quote attributed to the ancient philosopher Thales).[22] These gods wanted to be known and worshiped according to ancient customs. Gods and daimones were not all-powerful. They protected and privileged certain locales where they received praise. Gods could be known by different names in different places. In the great family of Gods, there were central ones (the twelve Olympians led by Zeus) and peripheral daimones (like Pan and Priapus). The central ones were Panhellenic—universally recognizable among Greeks and Hellenized peoples. In many areas outside Greece, local deities were assimilated to the Olympians (as happened early on in Rome where the king god Jupiter was traditionally identified with Zeus).

Gods were worshiped primarily through sacrifice, from the cutting of the throats of blood-filled beasts, to the sprinkling of humble grain seeds on

21. On Galen, see Swain, *Hellenism and Empire,* 357–379; J. Rocca, *Galen on the Brain: Anatomical Knowledge and Physiological Speculation in the Second Century AD* (Leiden: Brill, 2003); Susan P. Mattern, *The Prince of Medicine: Galen in the Roman Empire* (Oxford: Oxford University Press, 2013); Rebecca Flemming, "Demiurge and Emperor in Galen's World of Knowledge," in *Galen and the World of Knowledge,* ed. Christopher Gill, Tim Whitmarsh, and John Wilkins (Cambridge: Cambridge University Press, 2009), 59–83.

22. Aristotle, *On the Soul* 1.5, 411a7.

a fire. Larger offerings of cattle were typical of state festivals. Lesser offerings were made at home—like libations (a tipping of the goblet to a god presiding over a banquet). Sacrifices were typically accompanied by formulaic prayers and gestures. In times of need, prayers were often accompanied by vows—promises to perform some action to proclaim the god's glory if events turned out well.

Gods were active and present in the lives of their worshipers through dreams, visions, and oracles. Oracles were big business in antiquity. Artemidorus, a dream interpreter in the vicinity of Ephesus, mentioned "dice-diviners, cheese-diviners, sieve-diviners, figure-readers, palm readers, dish-diviners, and necromancers" all offering their services in the streets of big cities.[23] Richer customers could visit official oracle shrines run by priests in gleaming temples.[24] Dreams and healings were sought in "sleep overs" (incubations) within temple chambers.[25]

Imperial Cult

The imperial cult was one of the few empire-wide forms of worship; it was state run, well-funded, and carefully organized. Cities competed with each other in order to house imperial temples, and one of the greatest privileges of the day was to become the priest of a particular emperor.[26] Thousands would gather at the imperial festivals, games, and spectacles held on the emperor's birthday. The emperor was believed to be a god—though one of the lesser ones—worshiped with distinctive rites and he was often made a partner with a main god in gleaming temples.[27]

---

23. Artemidorus, *Dream Interpretation (Oneirocritica)* 2.69.

24. The province of Asia was famous for two large oracle shrines: Claros (near the city of Colophon) and Didyma (near Miletus).

25. See Aelius Aristides's "Sacred Tales," in *P. Aelius Aristides: The Complete Works*, vol. 2, trans. Charles A. Behr (Leiden: Brill, 1981), 278–353.

26. Steve Friesen, *Twice Neokoros: Ephesus, Asia, and the Cult of the Flavian Imperial Family.* (Leiden: Brill, 1993); Barbara Burrell, *Neokoroi: Greek Cities and Roman Emperors* (Leiden: Brill, 2004), 270–287, 331–342.

27. The classic work here is S. R. F. Price, *Rituals and Power: The Roman Imperial Cult in Asia Minor* (Cambridge: Cambridge University Press, 1984).

Translocal Cults

Although the Romans generally looked askance at cults not under their control, they could not halt their spread. The native cults of Egypt in honor of Isis and Serapis spread widely during this period. Converts shaved their heads and abstained from meat in preparation for expensive initiations. The initiations involved the vision of the gods, a newfound sense of privilege, and hope for the afterlife. Here is an account from Lucius, main character in Apuleius's *Metamorphoses*: "I approached the border of Death, tread the threshold of Proserpina [queen of the Underworld]; I travelled through every element; at midnight I saw the sun shimmering in clear light; I approached the gods below and the gods above face to face, and I worshiped them close by."[28]

The cult of Cybele, mother of the gods, and Attis the Phrygian shepherd had long been established in Rome. Although few men followed the priests of Attis in their ritual of self-castration, people of all kinds gawked at their raucous processions during their spring festival in late March (often overlapping with Easter).

Judaism was a foreign, but recognized religion, one that had long been transplanted into several Greco-Roman cities. With one terrible exception between 115–117 CE, Jews in the "Diaspora," or wider world beyond Judea, proved to be loyal and productive subjects. They built ornate synagogues in many Mediterranean cities, added to the economic vibrancy of major centers, and became local benefactors. Jewish intellectuals like Philo of Alexandria (about 20 BCE–50 CE) offered a philosophical variant of Judaism featuring an imageless, transcendent God and a clear code of ethics (the Mosaic Law). New translations of this Law were being made as the old, standard translation (called "the Seventy" or "Septuagint") was increasingly abandoned to the Christians. Jews boasted of being older than the Greeks and closer to the wellsprings of divine wisdom. They succeeded in attracting (some prominent) converts (or proselytes) who could attend synagogue services without undergoing full initiation through circumcision.

Emerging Religious Currents

The cult of Mithras, taken to be a Persian deity related to the sun, gained traction especially among Roman soldiers in the second century. It also provided

---

28. The key source here is Apuleius, *Metamorphoses* 11.23. See the commentary in W. H. Keulen and Ulrike Egelhaaf-Gaiser, *Apuleius Madaurensis Metamorphoses Book XI: The Isis Book*. (Leiden: Brill, 2015).

those of middling social status (freedmen, slaves, shopkeepers) with a new sense of identity. Seven grades of initiation led to the holy office of "father." Communal meals in a "cave" or underground chamber fostered a sense of comradery. The secrets of the cult remain buried because no theological treatises were written (at least none survive). Mithraic iconography (most famously the tauroctony, a depiction of Mithras slaying a bull) is relatively abundant, however, and continues to inspire a rich crop of speculation.[29]

In Egypt, treatises associated with the god Thoth, or Hermes Thrice Great, began to appear. At one time, these treatises were considered purely literary products of Greek philosophy, spiced up with a few Egyptian characters and local color. Today, Egyptian emphases and inspiration in the literature are more widely accepted.[30] References to "pure food,"[31] a ritual embrace,[32] and formal prayers[33] suggest to some scholars both a ritual and community life. Some theorize more boldly about a Hermetic "way" that involved "a sequence of concrete ritual practices, some regular, some occasional, some temporary, others developing as a consequence of the disciple's formation."[34] Under the guidance of a teacher, Hermetic initiates progressed from a dualistic view of the world to a monistic one in which God, often depicted as a cosmic mind, was all in all.[35]

---

29. On Mithras, see Roger Beck, *The Religion of the Mithras Cult in the Roman Empire: Mysteries of the Unconquered Sun* (Oxford: Oxford University Press, 2006); Richard Gordon, "Ritual and Hierarchy in the Mysteries of Mithras," in *The Religious History of the Roman Empire: Pagans, Jews, and Christians*, ed. J.A. North and S. R. F. Price (Oxford: Oxford University Press, 2011), 325–365; Luther H. Martin, *The Mind of Mithraists: Historical and Cognitive Studies in the Roman Cult of Mithras* (London: Bloomsbury, 2015); Olympia Panagiotidou, *The Roman Mithras Cult: A Cognitive Approach* (London: Bloomsbury, 2017).

30. Thomas McAllister Scott, "Egyptian Elements in Hermetic Literature" (PhD diss., Harvard Divinity School, 1987); Christian Bull, *Tradition of Hermes: The Egyptian Priestly Figure as a Teacher of Hellenized Wisdom*. RGRW 186 (Leiden: Brill, 2018), 33–190, 427–455.

31. *Prayer of Thanksgiving* VI,7 65.6.

32. *Disc. 8–9* VI,6, 57.26–27; *Prayer of Thanksgiving* VI,7, 65.4.

33. For example, *The Prayer of Thanksgiving* VI,7, parallel to *Asclepius* 41.

34. Anna Van den Kerchove, *Le voie d'Hermès: Pratiques rituelles et traités hermétiques*. Nag Hammadi and Manichaean Studies 77 (Leiden: Brill, 2012), 374–375. See further S. Giversen, "Hermetic Communities?" in *Rethinking Religion: Studies in the Hellenistic Process*, J. P. Sorensen, ed. (Copenhagen: Museum Tusculanum, 1989), 49–54.

35. Bull, *Tradition of Hermes*, 191–243.

For an example of a new religious movement with a known founder, one can highlight the prophet Alexander. Alexander settled in Abonouteichos, a small city in the Pontic region. He had the skill and audacity to establish a new oracle, and he was able to convince the locals that the healing god Asclepius had been reborn in the form of a snake. This snake—a large python named Glycon—Alexander wrapped underneath his robes and outfitted with a human-like head poking out at the neckline. In this fashion, Alexander became the god's spokesman. People sent him sealed slips of paper that Alexander read, resealed, and responded to in poetic verse. The answers convinced a great number of people, including a Roman governor who ended up marrying Alexander's daughter. Other people—Epicureans and Christians especially—scorned the new rites and were debarred from Glycon's sanctuary.

Christianity was the daughter or sister of Judaism, depending on one's perspective. Only in the second century, it seems, did Roman elites begin to take note of it as a separate and threatening "superstition." Christians, though some claimed that their piety was ancient, seemed novel and curious to ancient Romans. Christians worshiped a man executed as a criminal by the Roman state during the reign of a known emperor (Tiberius). They had communal meals in private settings only open to initiates. In time, there arose rumors of terrible crimes—group orgies and baby-killing—all thought to take place in secret.[36] Early Christians—who ate the body and blood of a crucified Judean—had a hard time making themselves understood.

Pliny the Younger described what he knew about Christianity in the region of Bithynia-Pontus around 110 CE. He learned that they gathered before dawn to sing an antiphonal hymn to Christ, as to a god. After the workday, they met again for a meal. Their food was harmless (no human meat, that is). Interestingly, Pliny does not mention the reading of Jewish or Christian scripture. In fact, he does not connect Christians to Judaism in any significant way. Christianity was for him a newfangled cult spreading like a malignant disease.

In Hadrian's reign Christian intellectuals (so-called Apologists) began to compose tracts explaining Christian beliefs and practices to outsiders. Despite their efforts, followers of Jesus continued to be distrusted and occasionally

---

36. See further Jennifer Knust, *Abandoned to Lust: Sexual Slander and Ancient Christianity* (New York: Columbia University Press, 2005); Litwa, *Carpocrates, Marcellina, and Epiphanes: Three Early Christian Teachers of Alexandria and Rome* (London: Routledge, 2021), 113–119.

arrested, mostly in reaction to natural disasters and jealous informers (who were sometimes fellow Christians).[37] A budding class of intellectuals labored to prove the respectability of Christian thought and morals. They struggled to obtain the scarce resource of symbolic capital. If some forms of Christianity could be depicted as subaltern and bizarre, the apologists aimed to show the positive distinctiveness of other—supposedly more rational and moral—forms of Christianity. In the constant struggle to be tolerated and understood, a whole crop of Christians came to be attacked by their own kind. Arguably, the greatest of these was Marcion.

37. See further Candida R. Moss, *Ancient Christian Martyrdom: Diverse Practices, Theologies, and Traditions* (New Haven: Yale University Press, 2012).

CHAPTER TWO

Marcion's Life

I love to sail forbidden seas, and land on barbarous coasts.

—Herman Melville, *Moby-Dick; or, The Whale*

MARCION'S HOMELAND WAS Pontus—modern North Central Turkey, on the south coast of the Black Sea. Pontus, conquered by Pompey the Great (66 BCE), became a Roman province about the same time as Syria Palestine (the Israelite homeland). Lying north of Galatia, east of Bithynia, and west of Armenia, Pontus was culturally and ethnically diverse, home to Greeks, Roman veterans, several different kinds of Anatolians, and peoples of Persian descent. It is not clear whether Marcion was ethnically Greek, Roman, Anatolian, or some mixture of these.[1]

Various cults are attested in this region. Of Persian and Anatolian deities, there were Anaïtis, Omanus, and Anadatos in Zela, Ma in Komana, and Zeus Stratios in Amaseia. Zeus Stratios may have been a form of Ahura Mazda.[2] Here was a homegrown "god of armies" or battles—precisely the kind of god against which Marcion objected. As in most Roman provinces, the imperial cult was important in Pontus. Pliny, when he was governor, made the inhabitants swear an oath to the emperor every year.[3]

---

1. Lieu thinks that Marcion was probably of Greek parentage, the "descendants of the Greek settlers" (*Marcion* 56, 317), but exactly why is unclear.

2. Franz Cumont, "Le Zeus Stratios de Mithridate," *Revue de l'histoire des religions* 43 (1901): 47–57; Jesper Majbom Madsen, *From Trophy Towns to City-States: Urban Civilization and Cultural Identities in Roman Pontus* (Philadelphia: University of Pennsylvania Press, 2020), 204.

3. Pliny, *Ep.* 10.100–101.

Epiphanius (writing about 375 CE) says that Marcion's home city was Sinope, an ancient Greek colony founded by the Milesians around the seventh century BCE.[4] Earlier heresiologists implicitly connected Marcion to Sinope, because they likened him to the Cynic Diogenes, who came from there.[5] Apparently, they presumed that Marcion came from Sinope because it was the best-known port of Pontus. Since Marcion was a shipmaster, logically, he would have come from the most serviceable port city.[6]

Despite the continued tradition of tying Marcion to Sinope, Marcion's exact birth city is unknown.[7] Assuming he grew up on the coast, there were other coastal cities of Pontus, namely Amastris, Amisus, and Trapezous.[8] Truthfully, however, it's not even clear whether Marcion grew up on the coast, as opposed to one of the cities in the interior (such as Amaseia, home of the geographer Strabo). It is just possible that Marcion was from the Pontic *region*—not the *province* of Pontus—which could mean that he was from another area east or west of the Black Sea.

Tertullian tried to portray Pontus as a cultural backwater. Yet the Carthaginian confused Pontus with Herodotus's Scythia. By Marcion's time, the cities of Pontus would have been both Hellenized and Romanized to a considerable degree.[9] That is to say, they would have featured a mix of Greek and Roman institutions, such as theaters, assemblies, bathhouses, gymnasia, schools, and so forth. It is true that Roman Pontus could not boast of any famous schools or libraries, but it was just as Hellenized as places like Syria or Thrace. Strabo, as noted, came from Pontus. Other intellectuals and orators—men like Dio Chrysostom and Arrian (contemporaries of Marcion)—came from nearby Bithynia, a place whose cultural credentials were not in doubt.

---

4. Epiphanius, *Pan.* 42.1.3. For the founding of Sinope, see Strabo, *Geographica* 12.3.11.

5. For example, *Ref.* 7.29.1, here referring to Marcion's "cynic life" (κυνικοῦ βίου); cf. Tertullian, *AM* 1.1.4; 1.19.2; 2.5.1.

6. Eckart Olshausen, "Pontos: Profile of a Landscape," in *Space, Place and Identity in Northern Anatolia*, ed. Tønnes Bekker-Nielsen (Stuttgart: Franz Steiner, 2014), 45.

7. April D. DeConick, *Comparing Christianities: An Introduction to Early Christianity* (Hoboken: Wiley Blackwell, 2024), 28.

8. For the coastal cities and ports in Marcion's day, see Arrian, *Periplus Ponti Euxini*, trans. Aidan Liddle (London: Briston Classical Press, 2003), §§12–16 (pp.69–75).

9. Madsen, *From Trophy Towns*, 1, 8–9.

In Marcion's time, Pontus produced another writer of note: Aquila, the famous Bible translator, who flourished during the reign of Hadrian (117–138 CE). Aquila comes in for rebuke by Irenaeus because he altered Isaiah 7:14 from "a virgin" to "a *young woman* will conceive."[10] Aquila's exact aims for biblical translation are unclear, and only fragments of his translation survive, but it does seem that his more literal approach to translation was aimed to render the Hebrew text more faithfully.[11] Aquila was born a gentile, but he became a Jewish proselyte. Apparently by his time, Jewish criticisms of the Septuagint (used by Christians) were loud enough to call for a new translation. Aquila, an educated native speaker of Greek, took up the task, and was widely respected by Jewish writers for centuries to come.[12]

It is an intriguing synchronicity that Aquila and Marcion presumably came from the same area, about the same time, and exhibited a similar way of reading the Hebrew scriptures (in literal fashion). Perhaps a similar climate of thought led both figures down a similar path. One can imagine a scenario in which Jews insisted that their messiah was different from the Christ of the Christians. Aquila's literal translation would have brought out the differences between Jesus the Galilean peasant and the (still to come) Jewish political messiah. Marcion may have noticed these differences due to his connections with Jewish communities in Pontus. Perhaps he even used the first fruits of Aquila's translation.

The year of Marcion's birth is unknown. Apparently, he was still flourishing in the later reign of Antoninus Pius (138–161 CE). Clement says that Marcion was older than Valentinus and Basilides, who flourished in the reigns of Hadrian (117–138) and Antoninus. Presumably, then, Marcion's birthdate

---

10. Irenaeus, *Haer.* 3.21.1; Greek text in Eusebius, *Hist. eccl.* 5.8.10. The "history" of Aquila in Epiphanius, *Weights and Measures*, 14–16 is on the whole unreliable.

11. Jerome, *Epistulae* 57.11 (to Pammachius) in *Sancti Eusebii Hieronymi Epistulae*, ed. Isidorus Hilberg, 3 vols. (Vienna: F. Tempsky, 1910).

12. Jerome calls Aquila "most learned in the Hebrew language" (*Comm. Isa* 13.20 on Isa 49:5) in *St. Jerome: Commentary on Isaiah*, trans. Thomas P. Scheck (New York: Newman Press, 2015), 617. See further Jenny R. Labendz, "Aquila's Bible Translation in Late Antiquity: Jewish and Christian Perspectives," *Harvard Theological Review* 102.3 (2009): 353–388; Giuseppe Veltri and Alison G. Salvesen, "Aquila," in *The Oxford Handbook of the Septuagint* (Oxford: Oxford University Press, 2021), 459–465.

lay between 85–100 CE.[13] This was around the time when the first narrative gospels began to be written. When Marcion grew up, there were still those who preferred the "living and lasting" voice of oral tradition, but the gradual move toward written stories and sayings of Jesus was relentless.[14]

Education

Everything known about Marcion's education comes through inference. Since he could evidently read and write, he presumably had the rudiments of grammatical training.[15] This is different from "a standard Greek education as a grammarian."[16] Marcion probably went to grammar school, but he did not become a grammarian (someone highly trained in Greek literature). He must have been able to recognize copyist errors in a text, but there is no evidence that he was trained in text-critical techniques or in writing composition.

Although Marcion probably lacked formal philosophical training, there are hints of his philosophical learning. The author of the *Refutation of All Heresies* (or Refutator) says that Marcion was inspired by Empedocles. Irenaeus links him with Epicurean thought.[17] Tertullian suggests Stoic influence.[18] Later he attributes to Marcion Epicurean and Skeptical arguments.[19] Clement says that Marcion borrowed from Pythagoras,[20] but that the wellsprings of his

13. Sebastian Moll proposed a later dating for Marcion's birth (between 100–110 CE) (*The Arch-heretic Marcion* [Tübingen: Mohr Siebeck, 2010], 26). For chronological considerations, see Winrich Löhr, "Problems of Profiling Marcion," in *Christian Teachers in Second-century Rome: Schools and Students in the Ancient City*, ed. H. Gregory Snyder (Leiden: Brill, 2020), 125–129.

14. Papias Frag. 6 in Stephen C. Carlson, *Papias of Hierapolis: Exposition of Dominical Oracles* (Oxford: Oxford University Press, 2021), 118–119.

15. See further Lampe, *From Paul*, 252–256.

16. DeConick, *Comparing Christianities*, 28.

17. Irenaeus, *Haer.* 3.24.2.

18. Tertullian, *Praescr.* 7.3; 30.1; cf. *AM* 5.19.7.

19. Tertullian, *AM* 1.25.3; 2.5.1–2 2.16.2–3; 4.15.2; 5.19.7. See further John Gager ("Marcion and Philosophy," *VC* 26 [1972]: 53–59 at 55–56) who cites Lactantius, *De ira dei* 13.20–21; Sextus Empiricus, *Pyr. Hyp.* 3.9–11 (here arguing specifically against divine foreknowledge).

20. Clement, *Strom.* 3.3.13.1.

ideas were Platonic.[21] Of course, in making these connections, heresiologists tried to delegitimate Marcion's thought by linking it with "pagan" predecessors.

Marcion himself never seems to have used discretely philosophical terms or to have claimed allegiance to any worldly philosophy. He was an intelligent man, a close reader of texts, and probably influenced by popular philosophical currents; but he lacked an official philosophical education, and he may have been skeptical of actual philosophers. His apostle warned, after all, "let no one be defrauded . . . through philosophy, as it were empty deceit" (Col 2:4, 8).[22]

Profession

Marcion was a shipmaster (*nauclerus*), which is not the same thing as a sea captain.[23] A sea captain pilots the ship, but a shipmaster owns or leases ships, maintains their seaworthiness, cares for their freight, and entrusts them to others. In short, Marcion ran a shipping business, ferrying goods and people to many Mediterranean ports.[24] Accordingly, Marcion was more than a common sailor (*nautēs*), as he was later called (probably by way of insult).[25]

To build his shipping business, Marcion must have had some venture capital, at least enough to buy or lease one vessel. Perhaps he inherited the whole shipping business from his father. If so, this weakens the claim of Epiphanius,

21. Clement, *Strom.* 3.3.21.2.

22. According to Enrico Norelli, Marcion addressed the philosophical problems of his day, but had an anti-philosophical attitude ("Marcion: ein christlicher Philosoph oder ein Christ gegen die Philosophie?" in *Marcion und seine kirchengeschichtliche Wirkung*, 113–130 at 128–129).

23. Tertullian, *Praescr.* 30.1; *AM* 1.18.4; 3.6.3; 4.9.2; 5.1.2; 5.9.2; *Digest of Justinian* 14.1. *Pace* DeConick, *Comparing Chrisianities*, 28. See further Peter Candy, "Parallel Developments in Roman Law and Maritime Trade during the Late Republic and Early Principate," *Journal of Roman Archaeology* 33 (2020), 66.

24. Gerhard May, "Marcion in Contemporary Views: Results and Open Questions," in *Gerhard May: Markion. Gesammelte Aufsätze*, ed. Katharina Greschat and Martin Meiser (Mainz: Philipp von Zabern, 2005), 20. See further Julie Vélissaropoulos, *Les nauclères grecs: Recherches sur les institutions maritimes en Grèce et dans l'Orient hellénisé* (Paris: Libraire Minard, 1980), esp. 48–49.

25. Rhodon in Eusebius, *Hist. eccl.* 5.13.3. Cf. Julius Pollux, *Onomasticon* 6.128 (ed. Bethe 2.35), cited by Löhr, "Problems of Profiling Marcion," 110. Löhr also notes that Tertullian uses *nauclerus*, *nautici* and *nautae* in order to ridicule the Valentinian pleroma (Tertullian, *Val.* 12.2–3).

who said that Marcion's father was a Christian "bishop." It is unlikely that, in the late first-century, the leadership structure of (monarchial) bishops was in place in Pontus. If it was, Ignatius would not have to argue for it in his letters. The letter of 1 Peter—partly addressed to Pontic Christians—mentions elders (or presbyters) in the plural (5:1), not monarchial bishops.

Shipmasters did well in antiquity. They had their own associations.[26] These groups had meetings in their own "houses" throughout cities of the Mediterranean, and they set up monuments that showed off their wealth.[27] Ship owners were sometimes granted privileges or immunity from civic duties and costs if they shipped goods and grain to Rome, and shippers' associations were occasionally recognized in senatorial decrees and edicts.[28]

The Jewish Wars

Marcion came of age during the Diaspora revolt (115–117 CE). During this time, Jews in Cyrene, Cyprus, and Egypt took up arms against their Roman overlords. Jewish militias massacred their enemies, destroying public buildings and torching temples. When the legions were sent in, a virtual genocide of Jews occurred in Alexandria and throughout the Egyptian countryside.[29]

By the time of the Bar Kokhba war (132–136 CE) Marcion's hair was turning gray. In the years leading up to the war, the emperor Hadrian had announced that he was rebuilding Jerusalem at his own expense—as a Roman colony. This colony would feature temples to several gods, not just the local Jupiter of the Judeans. On top of this, Hadrian reportedly placed a ban on circumcision, apparently to limit conversions to Judaism. In the aftermath, violence broke out in Judea on a scale for which Hadrian was unprepared. It took several legions, the transfer of a general from Britain to Judea, and

26. Note the *naviculariorum collegio* in Tertullian, *AM* 5.9.2.

27. See, for example, Philip A. Harland, *Greco-Roman Associations: Texts, Translations and Commentary. II. North Coast of the Black Sea, Asia Minor* (Berlin: de Gruyter, 2014), 46–50.

28. Gaius in *Digest* 3.4.1 (Alan Watson, translator. *The Digest of Justinian*, vol. 1 (Philadelphia: University of Pennsylvania Press 1985); cf. 50.6.5.3; 50.6.5.5; 50.6.6.6; 50.6.5.9. Harland, *Greco-Roman Associations* 49. See also Ascough, Harland and Kloppenborg, ed., *Associations in the Greco-Roman World: A Sourcebook* (Waco: Baylor University Press, 2012), L43, 46.

29. See further William Horbury, *Jewish War Under Trajan and Hadrian* (Cambridge: Cambridge University Press, 2014).

the emperor's own personal presence to quell the revolt. Thousands of lives were lost, and the whole province of Judea—now renamed Syria Palaestina—became a wasteland.[30]

News of these bloody conflicts had certainly reached Pontus. If Marcion's shipping business involved trade with the cities in the war zones, his purse, at least, would have been affected. There is no direct evidence that the wars affected the Pontian's theology. At the same time, it is hard to believe that they did not inform his view of the Judean lord as a stubborn and irrational warmonger. Marcion's contemporary Basilides imagined that the god of the Judeans "wanted to subject all nations to his own." This was why the rulers of other nations resisted the armies of the Judean lord.[31]

To some extent, one can comprehend the religious motivations of Jews who were threatened by imperial policies. By declaring war on Rome, Bar Kokhba and his allies were doing what they thought their god desired. An ancient Greek or Roman could well have conceded this point. But if it was truly the Judean lord driving his nation to war, he must have been perceived as bellicose. Christians whether in Palestine or Pontus could at this point make up their minds and decide that the god of Bar Kokhba was not their deity. Certainly the messiah represented by Bar Kokhba was not the Christ worshiped by Christians. Reportedly, Bar Kokhba tortured and killed Christians for refusing to deny that Jesus was the Messiah.[32]

To be sure, Marcion could simply have read the Jewish scriptures to discover that the Judean lord incited wars. And indeed, Marcion's reading of Jewish scriptures was a primary force shaping his theology. At the same time, everyone reads scriptures in a social and historical context. The anti-Judean sentiment of Marcion's day, fostered by two Jewish wars, had filtered into his consciousness. The "Lord of armies" in the Hebrew Bible was not some distant memory. He was still active in Marcion's day, still raising the war cry, and driving his nation to battle. This was not the Christian God, and Marcion knew it.

---

30. Cassius Dio, *Roman History* 69.14. See further Peter Schäfer, ed., *The Bar Kokhba War Reconsidered: New Perspectives on the Second Jewish Revolt Against Rome* (Tübingen: Mohr Siebeck, 2003); Menahem Mor, *The Second Jewish Revolt: The Bar Kokhba War, 132–136 CE* (Leiden: Brill, 2016).

31. Irenaeus, *Haer.* 1.24.4.

32. Justin, *1 Apol.* 31.6.

A Pre-Roman Ministry?

According to Harnack, Marcion preached his understanding of Christianity in both the provinces of Pontus and Asia (western Turkey), and was rejected in both places. This reconstruction, however, is based on sources that may not refer specifically to Marcion.

A Smyrnean Christian leader named Polycarp, in a letter typically dated about 130 CE, refers to opponents who deny that Jesus has come in the flesh, who do not confess the witness of the cross, and who distort the Lord's words, saying that there is neither resurrection nor judgment.[33] These are not clear references to Marcion, even if they agree with the later heresiological tradition.[34] As will be shown in this book, Marcion did not deny Christ's cross, resurrection, or judgment. The idea that Polycarp knew an early form of Marcion's thought,[35] according to which the Pontian denied Jesus's coming in flesh, his death, resurrection, and final judgment is implausible, since Marcion's Gospel affirmed all these points and Marcion presumably believed his own scriptures.[36]

If the Pastoral Epistles (1–2 Timothy and Titus) are late enough to have Marcion in view, they are more concerned about Jewish "myths" than Marcionite teachings. True, these epistles condemn unnamed enemies for forbidding marriage and abstaining from certain foods (1 Tim 4:3). Apart from regular fasting, however, and the apparent limitation of meat during ritual meals, the Marcionite diet was not distinctive. Marcion, moreover, never outright prohibited marriage for his supporters. He required celibacy for those he baptized, but some of these believers were already married (see chapter 13). The mention of "antitheses" at the end of 1 Timothy (6:20) is not a clear reference to Marcion's work by that

33. Polycarp, *Phil.* 7.1.

34. *Pace* P. N. Harrison, *Polycarp's Two Epistles to the Philippians* (Cambridge: Cambridge University Press, 1936), 172–183; R. Joseph Hoffman, *Marcion: On the Restitution of Christianity: An Essay on the Development of Radical Paulinist Theology in the Second Century* (Missoula: Scholars Press, 1984), 51–54; Markus Vinzent, *Christ's Resurrection in Early Christianity and the Making of the New Testament* (Surrey: Ashgate, 2011), 110.

35. Harrison, *Polycarp's Two Epistles*, 172.

36. Charles M. Nielsen argues that Polycarp largely accepted Marcion's views on the canon. But a high respect for Paul does not demonstrate "the near exclusion of the OT" ("Polycarp and Marcion: A Note," *Theological Studies* 47 [1986], 299).

name (chapter 6). Heresiologists disagreed on what to call Marcion's treatise, and the author of 1 Timothy does not seem to know its contents. Probably, then, the Pastorals are not a witness to (distinctly) Marcionite thought and are not reliable witnesses to Marcion's pre-Roman activity.

According to a fourth- or fifth-century catholic prologue to John's Gospel, Marcion came to the apostle John bearing writings or letters from Christian brothers in Pontus. John disapproved of Marcion—or reproved him (the manuscripts differ)—before expelling him.[37] Nonetheless, all this is ecclesial legend from late antiquity.[38] John the apostle did not write the Fourth Gospel. Even if he did, he was not a contemporary of the adult Marcion. If "John"—representing the churches in Asia Minor more broadly—had rejected Marcion, then Marcion would not have been initially accepted into the church networks of Rome. Yet Marcion was evidently welcomed into the Roman church network in the late 130s CE.[39]

Of course, one shouldn't *exclude* the idea that Marcion was active as a Christian teacher in Asia Minor in the 120s and early 130s CE. It is simply to say that there is no strong evidence for this activity. As a young man, Marcion's shipping business may have afforded him little leisure. But when he gained enough wealth, he could turn exclusively to Christian ministry.

In a tradition attested by Jerome (about 347–420 CE), Marcion sent a female teacher to Rome ahead of him to prepare the minds of Roman Christians.[40] This is an isolated tradition, but it is not outside the realm of possibility. A different and better attested female leader represented the thought of Carpocrates, namely Marcellina. Around 155 CE, she sailed the high seas from Alexandria to Rome and began a thriving movement

---

37. Jürgen Regul, *Die antimarkionitischen Evangelienprologe* (Freiburg: Herder, 1969), 34–35.

38. Regul, *Evangelienprologe*, 196–97; Otto Zwierlein, *Die antihäretischen Evangelienprologe und die Entstehung des Neuen Testaments* (Mainz: Akademie der Wissenschaften und der Literatur, 2015), 70–77; Lieu, *Marcion*, 103. B. W. Bacon showed how the information in the prologue could be derived from Tertullian ("Marcion, Papias, and the 'Elders,'" *Journal of Theological Studies* 23 [1922]: 134–160 at 143–145). See his later discussion in "The Anti-Marcionite Prologue to John," *Journal of Biblical Literature* 49:1 (1930): 43–54, esp. 48–53.

39. Regul, *Evangelienprologe*, 177. See also Enrico Norelli, ed. *Papia di Hierapolis, Esposizione degli Oracoli del Signore: I frammenti* (Milan: Paoline, 2005), 462n4; Vinzent, *Marcion and the Dating of the Synoptic Gospels* (Leuven: Peeters, 2014), 12–26.

40. Jerome, *Ep.* 133.4.

in the capital toward the end of Marcion's life.[41] If the report of Marcion's envoy is true, it would imply that Marcion already had a sense of his own distinctive brand of Christianity before coming to settle in Rome.

The Eternal City

Some late chronicles say that Marcion settled in Rome in the late 130s CE.[42] Such a dating seems fair as a rough estimation. Tertullian remarks that there was about 115 and a half years between Tiberius and Antoninus Pius (which is actually short by about a decade), and that the Marcionites placed "the same length of time" between Christ and Marcion.[43] If Christ arose in the fifteenth year of Tiberius, as Marcion's Gospel states, then Marcion would be dated to 144 CE. There is, however, no strong reason to think that 144 CE represented a special event in Marcion's life, such as his debut in Rome or his break with the Roman church network. Ancient Marcionites never said this.[44] It was Harnack who imagined that Marcionites celebrated "Marcion Day" in mid-July to honor the Pontian's restoration of the true church.[45]

Tertullian says that Marcion came to Rome "in the first warmth of faith." Some have taken this to mean that Marcion first became a Christian in Rome.[46] This is unlikely, since it compresses Marcion's theological development into a very small space of time. Marcion's response to Christians in Rome was presumably shaped by his familiarity with other types of Christianity in other places of the empire. The Pontian knew these other types because he was himself a Christian before coming to Rome. Perhaps all that Tertullian meant to say was that Marcion, on coming to the capital, was burning with religious enthusiasm.

---

41. Litwa, *Carpocrates, Marcellina, and Epiphanes*, 224–227.

42. Löhr, "Profiling," 114. *The Chronicle of Edessa* dates Marcion's separation from the church to 138 CE, see *Chronica Minora*, ed. Guidi, CSCO 1.1, p. 3, trans. Guidi CSCO 1.2, p.4 (Latin trans.).

43. Tertullian, *AM* 1.19.2.

44. Löhr, "Profiling," 114. Cf. Moll, *Arch-heretic*, 33–35 and Lieu, *Marcion*, 296.

45. Harnack, *Marcion* 20* n.3; cf. Ernst Barnikol, *Die Entstehung der Kirche im zweiten Jahrhundert und die Zeit Marcions*, 2nd ed. (Kiel: Walter G. Mühlau, 1933), 16–18.

46. Wilson, *Marcion*, 46.

According to Tertullian, Marcion soon made a large donation to the church network in Rome.[47] There was no single unified Roman church, but enough house churches had administrative connections that established a common fund for the poor, widows, and orphans in the city.[48]

Tertullian's source for Marcion's donation may have been the Pontian's own epistle to the Roman church.[49] This epistle was perhaps an introductory letter of recommendation comparable to Paul's letter to the Romans. Tertullian—who unfortunately does not quote or summarize Marcion's letter—found it to be in accord with his own catholic faith, and so assumed that Marcion was originally catholic.[50] Yet early catholic identity would still have been fluid in the 140s CE.

It is telling, however, that Marcion could present his faith in such a way that it was acceptable to an early third-century catholic writer. Throughout his long work *Against Marcion*, Tertullian's polemic consistently exaggerates the differences between Marcionite and early catholic Christians—differences that must have seemed minuscule to outsiders, and many of them may have emerged in the roughly fifty years between Marcion's death and Tertullian's time of writing. Incipient catholic leaders at Rome were, at least, happy to receive Marcion's money.

Marcion's donation was significant. The amount—200,000 sesterces—was the price of a large house in the city of Rome.[51] There survives a late first-century CE inscription, found in Spain, telling us that a woman, Baebia Crinita, gave 200,000 sesterces "for a temple to Apollo and Diana . . . and financed a banquet to celebrate the temple's dedication."[52] Even if prices

---

47. Tertullian, *AM* 4.4.3.

48. Cf. Justin, *1 Apol.* 13.1; 14.2; 15.10; 67.6–7; cf. Shepherd of Hermas, *Parables* 101 (9.24.2–3). See further Lampe, *From Paul*, 100–101.

49. Tertullian, *AM* 4.4.3; cf. 1.1.6; *Carn. Chr.* 2.4. I reject the hypothesis of Jean-Pierre Mahé ("Tertullien et l'Epistula Marcionis," *Revue des Sciences Religieuses* 45:4 [1971]: 358–371) that the letter was an instrument of propaganda explaining why Marcion broke with the Roman church.

50. Tertullian, *AM* 4.4.3.

51. Martial, *Epigrams* 3.52.

52. Rachel Meyers, "Exceptional Female Benefactors in Roman Hispania," *Classical Journal* 117:2 (2021/22) 176–204 at 182.

had considerably changed from the late first to the mid-second century CE, 200,000 sesterces was a substantial sum.

By his initial donation to the Roman church, Marcion may have followed in Paul's footsteps. Paul tried to smooth his way into the favor of Jerusalemite Christian leaders by offering a gentile collection of money for poor Jewish followers of Jesus in Jerusalem (2 Cor 8–9). Judging by Galatians, there were theological and personality conflicts between Paul and the Jerusalem "pillars," but a healthy injection of gold could soften the hearts of even open critics. These critics could at least learn to tolerate Paul when he became a donor. And if the Jerusalem leadership accepted money from gentiles, they would have to accept—at least on some level—the legitimacy of Paul's mission.

It's unclear whether Marcion earmarked his donation, and if so, how. He probably did not want it to line the pockets of the local church leaders or to build a new church building (at the time, churches typically met in houses). It is anachronistic to assert that Marcion gave "the bishop of Rome a cash gift"—in part because there was no single bishop of Rome at the time.[53] Assuming Marcion took his own Gospel seriously, he probably wanted his money to go to the poor (the widows, orphans, and disabled) in Rome.

Naturally Marcion wanted to gain power and authority in his adopted church network. But one cannot impugn his other motives. Paul wanted to fulfill the prophecy of the gentiles bringing their treasures to Jerusalem. Marcion aimed to live by the standards of his own Gospel. Few Christians have literally followed Jesus's command to sell all and give to the poor. Such instructions appear at least three times in Marcion's Gospel:

> G 11:41: "Give your possessions as alms and everything will be pure for you."
>
> G 14:33: "The one who does not renege all possessions cannot be my disciple."
>
> G 18:22: "One thing you lack. Sell all you have and give to beggars and you will have treasure in heaven."

---

53. *Pace* Dungan, *A History of the Synoptic Problem* (New York: Doubleday, 1999), 49. See Lampe, *From Paul* 397–412.

To be sure, Marcion probably did not sell *all* his possessions. But he might have approximated the evangelical commands. As a shipmaster, Marcion was reasonably well off, and he generously endowed the Roman churches.

How then does one explain Marcion's later break with the Roman leadership and the return of his funds? There are two points to keep in mind. First of all, in his letter, Marcion did not reveal all of his theology. Like any intelligent writer, he would have kept back issues that he knew seemed controversial. The other point is that Marcion's break with other church leaders in Rome likely occurred after several months or years. During his Roman sojourn, Marcion developed elements of his theology and view of scripture. He may have been spurred to action when he observed how Roman Christians focused on the Jewish Bible as scripture, and did not sufficiently highlight the importance of Paul's single Gospel.

A Precursor?

Heresiologists said that Marcion had a teacher in Rome—a man by the name of Cerdo.[54] The earliest and best source for Cerdo is Irenaeus. The Refutator depends on Irenaeus, but invents details about Cerdo's philosophical background and teaching. Pseudo-Tertullian, and Epiphanius all depend on a tradition that attributes the supposed teaching of Marcion back to Cerdo, such that Cerdo becomes a docetist, a denier of fleshly resurrection, a curtailer of Luke and even a rejector of the books of Acts and Revelation.

According to Irenaeus, Cerdo was active in Rome during the late 130s CE.[55] His original provenance is unclear. It is Epiphanius who claim that Cerdo was from Syria. Epiphanius contends that Cerdo was intellectually linked with the Syrian theologian Saturninus. Yet perhaps Epiphanius only inferred Cerdo's homeland because he connected him to Simon of Samaria and to his claimed student Menander, who flourished in Syrian Antioch.[56]

Irenaeus reports that, according to Cerdo, "the god having been proclaimed by the Law and Prophets is not the Father of our Lord Jesus Christ. For the one is known, the other is unknown; the one is just, but the other is

54. For example, Ps-Tertullian, *AAH* 6; *Ref.* 7.10; 10.19.

55. Irenaeus, *Haer.* 3.4.3.

56. Litwa, *Found Christianities*, 71–82.

good."[57] The comment can be traced back to a saying of Jesus, according to which he declares, "no one knows the Father except the Son" (G 10:22). If no one knew the Father except Jesus, then the Father is first revealed in Jesus's teaching. This is also a Johannine idea: that no one has ever seen God, but that Jesus made him known (John 1:18). All who came before Jesus are thieves and brigands (John 10:8). No one saw the Father before they saw Jesus (John 14:9). By contrast, the God of the Hebrew Bible seems to have been visible to several of his prophets. Isaiah saw the train of his robe (Isa 6:3), and Moses beheld his backside (Exod 33:17–23).

As to the distinction between a just God of the Law and a good Father of Jesus, this may have been Cerdo's own deduction. One would like to know how he made it. It may have been his own reading of the Hebrew Bible, where the Judean lord is regularly portrayed as righteous, jealous to protect his own honor, paying back the fathers' sins even to their great grandchildren (Exod 20:5).

In later tradition, Cerdo's teaching is adjusted so that the Judean lord becomes wicked. Yet this is probably a projection of Marcion's theology back onto Cerdo—an increasingly strong tendency in heresiology. As already noted, heresiologists like Pseudo-Tertullian, Epiphanius, and Filaster attribute a host of Marcion's teachings to Cerdo. The Refutator says that Cerdo was influenced by the philosophy of Empedocles and that he taught a third principle, namely matter. But these data arise from the persistent attempt to portray so-called heretics as philosophers who create schools rather than churches. All that is reliably known from Cerdo's thought comes from Irenaeus. Its basic thrust is that the good, formerly unknown God of Jesus, is different from the righteous and well-recognized lord of Judea.

Irenaeus portrays Cerdo as coming back and forth into fellowship with the incipient catholic network in Rome. Cerdo would publicly confess in accordance with majority views, but some people would accuse Cerdo of privately teaching unacceptable doctrines. After what may have been several years of Cerdo making confession and being accused, Irenaeus says that Cerdo "refrained from the gathering of godly people."[58]

57. Irenaeus, *Haer.* 1.27.1.

58. Irenaeus, *Haer.* 3.4.3.

The language is telling. Cerdo was never banned from attending services of worship in other Roman house churches or from participating in the early catholic ecclesial network. He simply decided to carry on his own independent teaching and worship in Rome, with no one to stop him.[59] Cerdo's teaching was perhaps not so much secret as it was private, designed for higher initiates whose faith merged with gnosis. One cannot definitely say that Cerdo *only* led a school, as opposed to a church movement. Churches were also places of instruction.

By the late 130s, Marcion was a mature man, probably not on the hunt for a teacher. There is nothing implausible, however, about Marcion associating with Cerdo in Rome and learning from him. What exactly Marcion learned isn't obvious, but there is no evidence that it was a full-scale Gnostic theology or that Marcion shifted from monism to dualism. It is entirely possible that Marcion and Cerdo independently grew skeptical of the Judean lord as he was portrayed in Jewish scripture.

If Marcion was influenced by Cerdo, he ultimately set out on his own path. He agreed that there was a distinction between the God of Jesus Christ and the Judean lord. Yet he came to the conclusion that the Judean lord's "justice" was only a cover for his malice.

Excommunicated?

At some point, evidently in the 140s CE, Marcion broke with the early catholic network in Rome. Epiphanius imagines a synod in which Marcion stood before the elders of the church and posed a question about Jesus's sayings: "What is the meaning of 'They do not pour new wine into old skins' or [sew] 'a patch of an unfulled cloth on an old garment . . .'?" (G 5:37, 36). The "elders" had their own explanation of the sayings (informed, it seems, by Epiphanius's imagination), but when Marcion insisted on other explanations, they refused

59. For Cerdo, see Irenaeus, *Haer.* 1.27.1; *Ref.* 7.37.1; 10.19.1; Pseudo-Tertullian, *AAH* 6.1; Epiphanius, *Pan.* 41.1.6. See further Harnack, *Marcion* 31*–39*; G. May, "Marcion und der Gnostiker Kerdon," in *Evangelischer Glaube und Geschichte, Grete Mecenseffy zum 85. Geburtstag*, ed. A. Raddatz and K. Lüthi (Vienna: Oberkirchenrat, 1984): 233–248; David W. Deakle, "Harnack & Cerdo: A Reexamination of the Patristic Evidence for Marcion's Mentor," in May and Greschat, *Marcion und seine kirchengeschichtliche Wirkung*, 177–190; Antti Marjanen, "Cerdo," in *BEEC*.

to admit him into their assembly, and Marcion cried that he would rend the Roman church.[60]

So goes the play. But these sorts of church synods featuring exegetical wrangling, ambitions for ecclesial office, and schisms caused by jealousy, were more characteristic of Epiphanius's own day than they were of the second century. Some of these same prooftexts (G 5:36–37; 6:43) do appear on the lips of Marcionite debaters in later sources.[61] Perhaps Epiphanius or his source projected these debates back onto Marcion's time.[62]

What probably happened was less flashy. Marcion did begin to have theological disagreements with people in the Roman ecclesial network. Irenaeus indicates that what Cerdo taught in secret, Marcion proclaimed openly. If so, Marcion could not have avoided friction with fellow Christians. The Pontian went the way of Cerdo and focused on nurturing his own community. Perhaps some leaders in the Roman church network decided to stop sharing communion with the house church led by Marcion (and perhaps Cerdo). In other words, they no longer shared gifts of consecrated bread and wine with Marcion's group.[63] They did not invite him to other church meetings, or treat him as a fellow colleague.[64]

Heresiologists said that Marcion was excommunicated or expelled from the church (or churches) of Rome.[65] It is still common to repeat this charge.[66] Excommunication before the end of the second century CE was "exceptionally

60. Epiphanius, *Pan.* 42.2.1–8.

61. *Adamantius* 2.16; cf. 1.28 (821c.10–14).

62. It is odd that Sebastian Moll, who rejects the biographical traditions of Ps.-Tertullian, Epiphanius, and Filaster, still wants to retain this debate as historical ("Three against Tertullian: The Second Tradition about Marcion's Life," *Journal of Theological Studies* 59:1 [2008]: 170–180 at 179–180).

63. Justin, *1 Apol.* 65.5; 67.5; Irenaeus in Eusebius, *Hist. eccl.* 5.24.15. See further Lampe, *From Paul*, 385–386.

64. See further Gerhard May, "Markions Bruch mit der römischen Gemeinde," in *Gesammelte Aufsätze*, 75–84.

65. Ephrem, *Hymns against Heresies* 22.2.

66. For example, Peter Head, "Foreign God and Sudden Christ: Theology and Christology in Marcion's Gospel Redaction," *Tyndale Bulletin* 44:2 (1993): 307–321 at 309; Étienne Nodet, "L'évolution de Paul et ses voyages," *Revue Biblique* 128:4 (2021), 546–579 at 552; Christopher M. Hays, "Marcion vs. Luke: A Response to the *Plädoyer* of Matthias Klinghardt," *Zeitschrift für die Neutestamentliche Wissenschaft* 99 (2008): 213–232 at 228;

rare"—but Marcion, it is claimed, was the exception.[67] Marcion started an "anti-movement" against the church and was "excommunicated." This makes him the "*first actual heretic.*"[68] Marcion has even earned the title "arch-heretic" because "he is the first Christian ever to be actually outside the Church for doctrinal reasons."[69]

Such views reinscribe—and even surpass—heresiological rhetoric (it was Epiphanius who called Marcion an "arch-heretic").[70] If the assumption is that "Marcion had been a member of the 'orthodox' church"[71] and that he "turned his back" on "orthodox doctrine,"[72] one should ask what was considered "orthodox" during Marcion's time. By and large, early second-century Christians did not tout the language of "orthodoxy"; they had no set creeds, no widely-accepted systematic theology. There were no large governing agencies, regular synods, or magisterial bodies. Ecclesial tradition was a cacophony of competing voices. There were no agreed-upon Christian lists of authoritative books and no copies of canon law or manuals of discipline used by a majority. The Roman ecclesial network did not have the mechanisms or authority structure to expel Marcion. There was no pope or college of cardinals, no ecclesial courts, or Congregation for the Doctrine of the Faith.[73] Marcion was not excommunicated, though he did found his own church.

There is a story indicating that Marcion continued to seek recognition and communion with other church networks. According to Irenaeus, Marcion deliberately approached Polycarp, whether in Asia Minor or Rome.[74] Marcion

---

Lee Martin McDonald, *Before There Was a Bible: Authorities in Early Christianity* (London: T&T Clark, 2023), 52.

67. Moll, *Arch-Heretic*, 44.

68. Moll, *Arch-Heretic*, 44, emphasis original.

69. Moll, *Arch-Heretic*, 46.

70. Epiphanius, *Pan.* 42.11.7.

71. Moll, *Arch-heretic*, 126.

72. Moll, *Arch-Heretic*, 27–28, 44–46.

73. Gerd Lüdemann, "Zur Geschichte des ältesten Christentums in Rom I. Valentin und Marcion. II. Ptolemäus und Justin," *ZNW* 70 (1979): 86–114; Vinzent, *Tertullian's Preface to Marcion's Gospel* (Leuven: Peeters, 2016), 328; Löhr, "Problems of Profiling," 119.

74. Jerome, *Viris Illustribus* 17, says it took place in Rome.

either urged Polycarp to recognize him (using the imperative), or posed the question—"Do you recognize me?"[75] The use of the verb "recognize" does not mean that Marcion was trying to have Polycarp identify him. Marcion evidently meant something more like, "recognize my church movement." By recognizing Marcion, Polycarp would at least open up the possibility for communion.

At this point, it seems, Polycarp played a little game with Marcion, which might indicate a bit of schadenfreude. Polycarp replied, "Yes, I recognize you—firstborn of Satan!"[76] Here Polycarp alluded, it seems, to John 8:44, which he apparently understood to mean that liars and murderers are children of the devil (compare 1 John 3:10). He was in effect calling Marcion the chief son of Satan, a liar and murderer par excellence. Perhaps this story emerged from a reading of Polycarp's letter to the Philippians, where he said that anyone who meddles with the Lord's words is "firstborn of Satan."[77] By the time Irenaeus passed on this story, Marcion had (wrongly) gained a reputation for "mutilating" the Gospel.

The historicity of the encounter is doubtful; but it illustrates something about Marcion's perceived attitude toward other Christians. The Pontian was not intolerant.[78] He still sought their approval and wanted to make connections. But men like Polycarp would have none of it. Irenaeus, for his part, approved the Polycarpian policy because it showed that the "disciples of apostles" did "not communicate even verbally with any of those who had adulterated the truth."[79] According to the tale, however, Polycarp did communicate with Marcion, though only to engage in demonization and ridicule.

To All Nations

Writing in the mid-150s CE, Justin Martyr observed that Marcion was still active, and that his message had spread to every nation in the known world. That kind of dissemination, only about fifteen years after Marcion's debut in

75. Irenaeus, *Haer.* 3.3.4. Eusebius, *Hist. eccl.* 4.14.7 has the imperative.

76. Irenaeus, *Haer.* 3.3.4.

77. Polycarp, *Phil.* 7.1. Regul, *Evangelienprologe*, 189.

78. *Pace* John Behr, *Irenaeus of Lyon: Identifying Christianity* (Oxford: Oxford University Press, 2013), 46.

79. Irenaeus, *Haer.* 3.3.4. Irenaeus says that Polycarp sojourned in Rome "under Anicetus" (*Haer.* 3.3.4), whose leadership is typically dated between 155–166 CE.

Rome, was impressive, even if Justin was exaggerating. Despite the fact that Marcion was elderly by this time, he was evidently industrious, well-connected, and amply financed. Marcion had likely retained ownership of his shipping business and he spread his gospel along accustomed trading routes.

Yet Marcion's success could not have been due to industry and resources alone. His market audience was apparently intellectually primed and emotionally ready for his message.[80] They were "warm leads," and so joined Marcion's movement when it appeared, finding in Marcion an articulate representative of what they always believed. They might not have been able to express it, but when Marcion communicated with them, they recognized their truth. Early Marcionites claimed that Marcion alone knew the true teachings.[81]

This pre-Marcionite Christianity is testified in several early second-century sources. For instance, the Paulinist who wrote the initial ten chapters of the letter to Diognetus, strongly distinguishes Christian faith from the "superstition of the Jews" (§1), emphasizes the newness of the knowledge of God revealed in Christ (8.1) apart from the Hebrew scriptures, and underscores God's unique goodness (8.8).[82] Ignatius, for his part, criticizes those who would not believe the Gospel if it was unconfirmed by "ancient records." Most take these "ancient records" as what became known as the "Old" Testament. Ignatius replies to such people: "for me Jesus Christ is the ancient records; his cross, death, resurrection, and faith in him are the sacred and ancient records."[83] This Ignatius has been called a "three-quarter-Marcionite Paulinist."[84]

Late Career and Death

Tertullian claims that Marcion repented at the end of his life and was promised entry into the catholic church if he restored all his followers to the catholic

80. Walter Bauer, *Orthodoxy and Heresy in Earliest Christianity*, ed. Robert A. Kraft and Gerhard Krodel (Philadelphia: Fortress Press, 1971), 194; cf. Jason BeDuhn, "The Myth of Marcion as Redactor: The Evidence of 'Marcion's' Gospel against an Assumed Marcionite Redaction," *Annali di Storia dell'Esegesi* 29:1 (2012): 21–48 at 36.

81. Justin, *1 Apol.* 58.2.

82. Charles M. Nielsen, "The Epistle to Diognetus: Its Date and Relationship to Marcion," *Anglican Theological Review* 52 (1970): 77–91.

83. Ignatius, *To the Philadelphians* 8.2.

84. Vinzent, *Christ's Resurrection*, 106.

fold.[85] This is not likely. First of all, Tertullian made this claim in an early work and chose not to repeat it in his larger and more thorough work *Against Marcion*. Second, no Marcionite, it seems, was ever aware that Marcion had a change of heart later in life. Third, it was impossible—if Justin was right that Marcion convinced people from every nation—for him to bring them all into the catholic fold. (Indeed, it seems almost sadistic for early catholic leaders to make such an imposing demand before they accepted Marcion's penitence.)

When Marcion died and under what circumstances are unknown. It was probably about 160 CE or shortly thereafter. Oddly, Tertullian initially dated Marcion to the time of Eleutherus of Rome (between 174 and 189 CE), but he may have mistakenly believed that Eleutherus was active in the reign of Antoninus Pius (138–161 CE).[86] According to one proposal, Marcion died in Laodicea in Asia Minor, but there is no evidence for this.[87] Marcion might have died in Rome, or on the sea, or in any city of the Mediterranean where his ships would take him.

When Marcion died, he had established a church leadership that would continue his movement. Later Marcionites referred to Marcion as their "bishop."[88] It is unclear whether Marcion ever referred to himself in this way. (An exalted view of Marcion evidently developed among his followers, such that some said he sat at Christ's left hand, with Paul on the right.[89] But all this came later.) By the end of his life, Marcion was by all accounts a successful church organizer. He had probably consecrated other leaders and set up moral rules for his community. This community, or network of communities, outlasted the founder by several hundred years—and Marcionites have not yet perished from the earth.

85. Tertullian, *Praescr.* 30.3.

86. Tertullian, *Praescr.* 30.1–2 (*Antonini fere principatu .. sub episcopatu Eleutheri*).

87. Hoffman, *Marcion*, 248.

88. *Adamantius* 1.8.

89. Origen, *Hom. Luke* 25.5.

Part II

Marcion's Scriptures

CHAPTER THREE

The Priority of Marcion's Gospel

> "O wealth of riches! Folly, power, and ecstasy! Seeing that there can be nothing to say about it, or imagine about it, or compare it to!"
>
> — F. C. Burkitt, "The Exordium of Marcion's *Antitheses*"

THE QUOTE ABOVE, referring to Marcion's Gospel, is perhaps the only direct quote surviving from Marcion's pen. It shows that the Pontian thought that his Gospel was incomparable. Incomparability is a religious way of asserting absolute superiority. The truth is, however, one *can* compare Marcion's Gospel, and scholars have been comparing it with other gospels for hundreds of years. Comparison is necessary, for it is the engine of new knowledge.

Some have asked why Marcion chose his Gospel. But if the question assumes that he knew what are today considered the canonical Gospels, then it is wrongheaded. Marcion did not grow up in the age of the fourfold Gospel. Gospel texts were not bound together in one volume, but were transmitted in separate scrolls or (more often) booklets called codices. Accordingly, Marcion's Gospel may simply have started out as the gospel available to him in Pontus. It was the gospel that he knew, an authoritative text that he inherited. By the time Marcion began coasting around the Mediterranean, of course, he would have encountered other gospels. But at some point in his life, perhaps early on, he made the decision that there was only one gospel—Paul's (Gal 1).

Justin, the earliest surviving witness, says nothing about Marcion changing his gospel text.[1] Nevertheless, heresiologists like Irenaeus, Tertullian, and Epiphanius all contend that what is now known as Luke came prior to Marcion's Gospel, and that Marcion "mutilated" or "circumcised it." This

1. *Pace* Jennifer Knust and Tommy Wasserman, *To Cast the First Stone: The Transmission of a Gospel Story* (Princeton: Princeton University Press, 2019), 106.

viewpoint has been questioned for a long time,[2] and the tide is now again turning against the heresiological hypothesis. There are both external and internal arguments indicating that Marcion's Gospel was earlier than canonical Luke.

External Arguments

If Marcion used the Gospel according to Luke, one would expect that "Luke" was cited with relative frequency during Marcion's early life. But such is not the case. The earliest patristic author to refer to a Gospel "according to Luke" is Irenaeus (about 180 CE), about twenty years after Marcion died.[3] The earliest manuscript of Luke is apparently P^4, which is dated to the late second or third century CE, and the earliest attestation of the "according to Luke" title is P^{75}, which could be as late as the fourth century.[4] Only during the time of Justin Martyr (about 155–165 CE) do something like citations of Luke appear—that is, citations that indicate editorial tendencies that later show up in canonical Luke.[5]

One cannot call these editorial tendencies "Lukan" because some of them, at least, might have appeared before the Gospel "according to Luke," in a kind of prototype Gospel. Thus, the argument that Marcion's Gospel uses Lukan phrases (such as "to preach the Gospel of God's kingdom" in, e.g., 4:43) fails, because, when Marcion read them, these phrases were not necessarily found

2. Dieter T. Roth, "Marcion's Gospel and Luke: The History of Research in Current Debate," *Journal of Biblical Literature* 127 (2008): 513–527; David Salter Williams, "Reconsidering Marcion's Gospel," *Journal of Biblical Literature* 108 no. 3 (1989): 482; Knust and Wasserman, *To Cast the First Stone*, 106–115.

3. Andrew F. Gregory, *The Reception of Luke and Acts in the Period before Irenaeus: Looking for Luke in the Second Century*, WUNT II/169 (Tübingen: Mohr Siebeck, 2003), 190, 297.

4. Brent Nongbri, "Reconsidering the Place of Papyrus Bodmer XIV-XV (P75) in the Textual Criticism of the New Testament," *Journal of Biblical Literature* 135, no. 2 (2016): 405–437; Gregory, *Reception of Luke and Acts*, 190–191; Kurt and Barbara Aland, *The Text of the New Testament: An Introduction to the Critical Editions and to the Theory and Practice of Modern Textual Criticism*, 2nd ed., trans. Erroll F. Rhodes (Grand Rapids, MI: Eerdmans, 1989), 87.

5. John Knox, *Marcion and the New Testament: An Essay in the Early History of the Canon* (Chicago: University of Chicago Press, 1942), 123; Gregory, *Reception of Luke and Acts*, 69–298.

in a Gospel called "according to Luke." Besides, they are not distinctly Lukan, because they appear in Matthew as well (4:23; 9:35; 24:14).[6] Other phrases (such as "with desire I have desired to eat this Passover with you," in G 22:15) could have been the distinctive speech of a *pre*-Lukan author who produced a work that both Marcion and "Luke" adapted and imitated in different ways.[7] (Only someone who assumes that Luke was first can refer to all distinct phrases in canonical Luke as "Lukan.")

Other documents quote what might be called Lukan tradition, though in the later second century. An example is 2 Clement. This letter is probably sometime after 150 CE, since it responds to developments in Valentinian theology after Valentinus.[8] The Carpocratians used a passage harmonizing Matthew and Luke.[9] But the source for this tradition is probably Marcellina, who did not arrive in Rome until the late 150s or early 160s CE.[10] Theophilus of Antioch's references to Luke appear after 180 CE.[11]

6. M. G. Bilby, *The First Gospel, the Gospel of the Poor: A New Reconstruction of Q and Resolution of the Synoptic Problem Based on Marcion's Early Luke*, 120n77.

7. *Pace* Michael Wolter, *Das Lukasevangelium* (Tübingen: Mohr Siebeck, 2008), 3. Dieter Roth reasserts Wolter's argument in "The Link between Luke and Marcion's Gospel: Prolegomena and Initial Considerations," in *Luke on Jesus, Paul and Christianity: What Did He Really Know?*, ed. Joseph Verheyden and John S. Kloppenborg (Leuven: Peeters, 2017), 59–80 at 76–78. Andrew Gregory observes that the identification of redactional elements is only of limited use, especially within the Synoptics, because the redactional elements are usually derived from a particular source hypothesis ("What is Literary Dependence?" in *New Studies in the Synoptic Problem*, 87–114 at 112). Cf. also Daniel A. Smith, "Marcion's Gospel and the Synoptics: Proposals and Problems," in *Gospels and Gospel Traditions in the Second Century: Experiments in Reception*, ed. Jens Schröter, Tobias Nicklas and Joseph Verheyden (Berlin: de Gruyter, 2019), 129–174 at 149.

8. Gregory, *Reception of Luke and Acts*, 137–148. See also Wilhelm Pratscher, "Der zweite Clemensbrief als Dokument des ägyptischen Christentums," in *Das ägyptische Christentum im. 2. Jahrhundert*, ed. Wilhelm Pratscher, Markus Öhler and Markus Lang (Berlin: Lit Verlag, 2008), 81–100; James Kelhoffer, "Second Clement and Gnosticism: The *status quaestionis*," *Early Christianity* 8 (2017): 124–149; Christopher Tuckett, "1 and 2 Clement," in *Texts in Contexts: Essays on Dating and Contextualising Writings from the Second and Early Third Centuries*, ed. T. Nicklas, J. Schröter, J. Verheyden (Leuven: Peeters, 2021), 51–72.

9. Gregory, *Reception of Luke and Acts*, 153.

10. Litwa, *Carpocrates, Marcellina, and Epiphanes*, 224–227.

11. Theophilus, *Autolycus* 3.28.

The Naassene Preacher also employed Lukan phrases, but he is probably late second century as well.[12]

Earlier attestations may actually attest the more fluid traditions of the prototype rather than canonical Luke. For instance, Basilides, or his followers, attested a version of what is now Luke 3:1 (the fifteenth year of Tiberius) and to the parable of Lazarus and the rich man (16:19–31).[13] Both texts are found in Marcion's Gospel, and were likely in its prototype.[14]

The same applies to the Gospel of Thomas. The Thomasine saying "there is nothing hidden which will not be made known" was part of Marcion's Gospel (G 8:17 // Thomas 5). His Evangelion also attests the interior monologue present in the parable of the rich fool (G 12:17 // Thomas 64). The exchange between Jesus and the man who requested Jesus's adjudication is also attested in the Evangelion (G 12:13–14), though Jesus's opening reference to the "man" is not. The use of Luke 4:24 in Thomas §31 is unattested for Marcion—meaning it's unclear whether it was present in his Gospel or not. Similarly, in Thomas 79, the blessing of Jesus's mother, with its correction, is present in Marcion's text (G 11:27–28). The blessing on childless women (23:29) is unattested for Marcion; but this does not mean that it was absent from his Gospel (Marcion himself lauded celibacy).[15]

Justin, who seems to cite Luke, never refers to it as the Gospel "according to Luke." Possibly, then, Justin also used the prototype gospel available to Marcion, a gospel that formed the basis of canonical Luke. In this theory, Justin's knowledge of Lukan tradition (such as the infancy narratives), derives from other sources available to him in the 150s and early 160s CE.[16]

---

12. Gregory, *Reception of Luke and Acts*, 151; M. David Litwa, *The Naassenes: Contours of An Early Christian Identity* (London: Routledge, 2023), 94–110.

13. Gregory, *Reception of Luke and Acts*, 77–80.

14. Roland H. Bainton claims that Basilides also employed Luke 2:49, 34 (hesitantly); 4:19 and 23:40 ("Basilidian Chronology and New Testament Interpretation," *Journal of Biblical Literature* 42 (1923): 81–134. These passages are unattested in Marcion's Gospel. See further Winrich Alfried Löhr, *Basilides und seine Schule: Eine Studie zur Theologie- und Kirchengeschichte des zweiten Jahrhunderts* (Tübingen: Mohr Siebeck, 1996).

15. See the analysis of Mark Goodacre (*Thomas and the Gospels: The Case for Thomas's Familiarity with the Synoptics* [Grand Rapids: Eerdmans, 2012], 82–108), who assumes that Thomas used canonical Luke.

16. Gregory, *Reception of Luke and Acts*, 225, 291, 295–96; cf. 266.

Such evidence indicates that when Marcion and Justin were in Rome together, neither may have encountered the text now called canonical Luke. Luke was still in the process of being written (or rather, edited). When the text now known as Luke did appear, it probably came connected with a freshly-written text called the Acts of the Apostles (itself not directly attested until about 180 CE).[17] All this would mean that, when Marcion published his Gospel in the 140s, he would have felt no need to emend canonical Luke, since it did not yet exist.

Special Lukan Material

Marcion's Gospel is missing about three-fourths of the material unique to canonical Luke, but it attests to over half of the material in Luke that overlaps with Mark and Matthew. In other words, a much larger proportion of material absent from Marcion's Gospel is unique to canonical Luke. The exact numbers have been run by at least four scholars working over the past seventy years, and they are statistically significant.[18]

To explain the significance, one can imagine one of two scenarios. In the first, Marcion, when he edited his Gospel, consciously looked for and omitted most of the material distinctive to Luke. Alternatively, a Lukan editor used Marcion's Gospel or its prototype and added the material distinctive to himself.

According to the first option, Marcion would have to be an advanced synthetic reader of all three Synoptic Gospels to discover exactly which stories and sayings were distinctive to the Lukan text and eliminate most of this material. It would have been much easier, however, for a later editor ("Luke") to come along and add his own distinctive material.[19] This was the material

17. Gregory, *Reception of Luke and Acts*, 299–354.

18. Knox, *Marcion*, 108; Tyson, *Marcion and Luke Acts*, 86–87, 134; Smith, "Marcion's Gospel and the Synoptics," 173 (appendix 6; cf. his appendix 1). Bilby numbers are probably most precise: 24.8 percent of Marcion's Gospel is attested in Luke for single traditions; 54.6 percent for double traditions; and 50.8 percent for triple traditions (*The First Gospel*, 125).

19. Leland Edward Wilshire argues for a "high percentage of uniquely Lucan material that is found in Marcion's text" ("Was Canonical Luke Written in the Second Century?" *New Testament Studies* 20 [1974]: 246–253 at 251), but he never defines how he determines "uniquely Lucan material." Anachronism seems built into the argument: even if *we* define a parable or verse as "Lukan," it was not "Lukan" when Marcion adopted it.

that he alone knew and added in order to improve the story—stories like the Good Samaritan, the Prodigal Son, and Pilate's slaughter of the Galileans. These were vivid, well-written, and well-integrated stories—and Marcion had no obvious reason to omit them.[20]

Contrast the heresiological theory, according to which Marcion had all four Gospels, including the Gospel of Mark. Despite having all four to choose from, Marcion chose the longest—the Gospel according to Luke—which forced him to eliminate over a hundred verses at the beginning (the birth stories), and several of the Lukan parables (such as the Prodigal Son).[21] Assuming that Luke was also attached to its sequel, the book of Acts, Marcion would have needed to remove all of Acts as well—a maneuver that would have inspired protest—though no one in antiquity ever mentions it.

It is better to imagine a gospel prototype that had already adapted elements from Mark and Matthew.[22] This prototype was then used independently by Marcion and the author of canonical Luke. The latter author considerably enlarged the prototype, possibly gave it its canonical name, "according to Luke," and attached it to Acts, which was the first "church history" connecting Jesus to the apostolic mission(s).[23]

Internal Arguments

Marcion's Gospel does not assume or exhibit a link to Acts. The Lukan prefaces (Luke 1:1–4; Acts 1:1–3), by contrast, are designed by a sophisticated writer who wanted to link the two books now called Luke and Acts.[24] Both books are addressed to a certain Theophilus as a patron, and both give the

20. Bilby, *The First Gospel*, 134.

21. Knox, *Marcion*, 122.

22. BeDuhn points out that Marcion's Gospel contains some "minor agreements" with Matthew that are not found in canonical Luke (BeDuhn, "Myth of Marcion," 33). Presumably, Marcion would not have written a gospel that had any agreements with the most Jewish of Gospels, Matthew. This is evidence that Marcion "took up a gospel already in circulation in multiple copies that had seen varying degrees of harmonization to other gospels in their transmission" (34).

23. Knox, *Marcion*, 110.

24. Matthias Klinghardt, "Markion vs. Lukas: Plädoyer für die Wiederaufnahme eines alten Falles," *New Testament Studies* 52 (2006): 496–512; Klinghardt, *Oldest Gospel*, 1.151–53.

impression that they are written by a high-status writer devoted to historical accuracy.

At the same time, there are tensions between the books, indicating different authorship. For instance, the preface in Acts must immediately correct the impression given in Luke that Jesus rose to heaven shortly after his resurrection (Luke 24:50–51). Resurrection and ascension apparently happened, in Luke, in the space of a single day. The author of Acts extended Jesus's pre-ascension stay on earth to forty days (Acts 1:3), causing narrative friction between the two volumes. The tension is explained if one understands both prefaces as added later when Luke and Acts were combined. This would have been at a time *after* Marcion's Gospel, which never knew the tradition of Jesus's forty-day post-resurrection sojourn.

There are other signs of later editorial addition. In Luke's preface, the writer uses the first person ("it seemed also to me," 1:3), which never appears in the main body of the text.[25] Moreover, all of Luke 1:5–2:52 (the infancy narratives) has a manifestly different linguistic style than the rest of Luke. This section deploys the language of the Septuagint, imitating its vocabulary, poetic technique (parallelism), and even cadence.[26] It seems likely that a later editor added this Septuagintally styled material in order to connect the Gospel more firmly to traditions of Israelite salvation history.

The most consistent interest of the Lukan editor is "to emphasize Christianity's integral relations with Judaism."[27] And generally speaking, the treatment of the Jews and Judaism is more positive in the infancy narratives than in the rest of Luke. "We learn of the importance of the Jewish Temple, about its ritual and priesthood, and the significance of sacrifices."[28] Mary and Joseph contribute to the sacrificial system. Two doves are offered for Mary's purification (Luke 2:24). It is clear that the God of Mary and Joseph is the God of Israel, and that they were a Torah-keeping family. This is striking because, in the main narrative, Jesus is regularly accused of not obeying the Torah (chapter 11).

25. Klinghardt, "Plädoyer," 501–502.

26. Paul-Louis Couchoud, "Is Marcion's Gospel One of the Synoptics?" *Hibbert Journal* 34 (1936): 268–69.

27. Knox, *Marcion*, 111.

28. Tyson, *Defining Struggle*, 98.

There are other tensions between the Lukan infancy stories and the main narrative. In Luke 1, John the Baptist is received into the world with fanfare. He is Jesus's cousin, a great prophet sent from God, filled with Holy Spirit from the womb, a mediator of salvation.[29] In the main part of the Gospel, however, Jesus is not aware of any familial ties with John. He praises John, to be sure, but only to add that the one who is "least in God's kingdom is greater than him" (7:28). It seems likely that the tension seen in Luke is caused by the later Lukan editor creating a loftier portrait of the Baptist in Luke 1–2 than had existed in the main narrative.

In Marcion's Gospel, the first time one hears about the Baptist is in the inquiry about fasting (5:33). In Luke, however, there is a well-crafted scene of Jesus being baptized by John (3:21–22), a scene probably taken from versions of Mark and Matthew. There's no literary or theological rhyme or reason for Marcion to omit this well-attested scene of John baptizing Jesus. The Lukan author probably added it so as not to seem inferior to competing gospels, and because he felt that Jesus's life was incomplete without his baptism.[30]

The treatment of Mary in Luke 1–2 is different from her portrayal later in the book. In Luke 1–2, she is honored as the virgin "who conceived by an act of God, and as the Mother who kept in her heart the secret of the birth and boyhood of Jesus, whereas elsewhere" in the Gospel, Jesus has no kind words for her. When she pays him a visit, he publicly declares that his true mother is a doer of his word (G 8:21).[31] He does not even allow his mother to be blessed by a random bystander, but blesses rather those who hear and do God's word (G 11:28). Thus there is a tension between an exalted view of Mary in the infancy narrative and a sort of indifference in the main storyline. This tension is probably caused by the later addition of Luke 1–2.

Regarding the original opening of the Gospel, two staunchly Roman Catholic biblical scholars of the twentieth century, namely Raymond Brown and Joseph Fitzmyer—although they had no special interest in Marcion—both concluded that Luke 3:1 probably served as the original opening of the

---

29. Couchoud, "One of the Synoptics," 269.

30. The emphasis on Spirit by the Lukan editor is well known (Klinghardt, *Oldest Gospel*, 1.367).

31. Couchoud, "One of the Synoptics," 269. In this quote, I have updated the biblical reference using my translation of G 7:28.

Gospel.[32] Now, 3:1 ("In the fifteenth year of Tiberius Caesar . . .") is exactly where Marcion's Gospel begins.

According to the Evangelion, Jesus debuted at Capernaum, whereas according to Luke, Jesus had his inaugural sermon at Nazareth. Nevertheless, "Luke, who had hitherto made no mention of Capernaum, describes how Jesus imagines the men of Nazareth saying, 'What we heard done in Capernaum, do also in your country' (4:23). But up till then, nothing had happened in Capernaum," according to canonical Luke. The deeds in Capernaum indicate that Jesus's initial Capernaum debut—according to Marcion's Gospel—was more original.[33]

There are two parallel incidents in Marcion's Gospel. In the first (10:25–28), a law expert asks Jesus what must be done to obtain life, and Jesus tells him to obey the love commandment in the Law.[34] By the simple term "life," is apparently meant "life on earth," the earthly abundance and longevity promised to those who followed Mosaic rules: "the one who does them shall live by them" (Gal 3:12). In the second, analogous, episode (G 18:18–24), someone asks what must be done to obtain "*eternal* life."[35] This time, "eternal" life seems to signal a higher heavenly existence. Jesus advises him to do more than just keep the Law. He tells him, "Sell all you have and give to beggars and you will have treasure in heaven. Then come follow me."

Luke has both episodes, but makes *both* questions refer to "eternal life" (10:25; 18:18). Accordingly, Jesus's two replies, one about keeping the Law, and the other about selling all, create narrative tension. A person attains eternal life either by keeping the Law or by selling everything. The Law never requires selling all; it promises great possessions to the obedient (e.g., Deut 28:1–14). The Evangelion seems more original, because it lets different questions correspond to different answers.[36] In short, Jesus's response is fitted to two types of life: to live well on earth, obey the love commandment in the Law; to obtain celestial life, sell everything.

32. Tyson, *Defining Struggle*, 90.

33. Couchoud, "One of the Synoptics," 269. Cf. Klinghardt, *Oldest Gospel*, 1.149.

34. Tertullian, *AM* 4.25.15, 18.

35. Epiphanius, *Pan.* 42.11.6, scholion 50 on Luke 18:18.

36. Couchoud, "One of the Synoptics," 269–70.

A similar case of Marcionite consistency is as follows. Marcion records Jesus as saying, "It is easier for heaven and earth to pass away than for one stroke of *my* words to fall" (G 16:17).[37] Marcion's version is supported by Luke (and G) 21:33: "The heaven and the earth will pass away, but *my* word remains forever"—a reading also found in Luke. It is the Lukan editor who creates an inconsistency by eternalizing—not Jesus's words—but the Law in 16:17: "it is easier for heaven and earth to pass away than for one stroke of a letter in the Law to be dropped." The change creates a contradiction with Luke 16:16, which says that the Law is not eternal, but only lasts until John the Baptist. Evangelion 16:16–17 seems more consistent and frankly more honest, since for most Christians of the second century, many "strokes" of the Law—for instance, the whole law of Levitical sacrifice—had been dropped. The eternalizing of the whole Law in 16:17 is evidently an attempt by a later editor to preserve the Torah's relevance for Christians, in conformity to verses like Matthew 5:17 (Jesus fulfills the Law).

Finally, Jesus's command to sell one's cloak to buy a sword (Luke 22:36) openly contradicts his advice to turn the other cheek (6:29) and to carry nothing on the road (9:3; 10:4). In Luke, the nonviolent Jesus suddenly allows for violent self-defense, even if his response to the disciples (who already have swords) is ambiguous (22:38). The tension is resolved if the "buy a sword" command (absent from Marcion's Gospel) is a later Lukan addition.

Marcion as Bad Editor?

Heresiologists asserted that Marcion "erased everything [in his Gospel] that was contrary to his own opinion."[38] Their critique was part of a larger trend of elite writers who scorned supposedly lowbrow scribes who changed texts to fit their interpretations.[39] Even today, scholars restate the heresiological view, sometimes with more force and eloquence. Marcion "ruthlessly" cut "out that

37. It seemed odd to Alfred Loisy ("Marcion's Gospel: A Reply," *Hibbert Journal* 34 [1935/36]: 378–387 at 383) that Jesus referred to a "stroke" of his oral language, but to the reader of the Gospel, Jesus's language was no longer oral.

38. Tertullian, *AM* 4.6.2; cf. *Praescr.* 38.9.

39. Jeremiah Coogan, "Meddling with the Gospel: Celsus, Early Christian Textuality, and the Politics of Reading," *Novum Testamentum* 65 (2023): 411, with n. 30.

which did not fit in with his preconceived theories."[40] Marcion "was obsessed by a compulsion to rid the Church's Savior of every taint of 'Jewishness' and thus carved a Gospel suitable to his theological requirements out of the Gospel According to Luke."[41] Marcion "was driven by the logic of his system to edit the passages that affirmed the material world as the creation of the true God, that quoted the Old Testament, that smacked of Judaism. In a manner reminiscent of the later Jefferson Bible, Marcion removed all the passages offensive to his own views."[42] One could go on.[43]

These theories about Marcion as theological editor are inaccurate and outdated. Marcion never said, according to surviving evidence, that he wanted to cleanse an original gospel from material that "smacked of Judaism" or that he wanted to strip it of Old Testament quotations. This is what the heresiologists said. And none of these heresiologists knew the state of gospel texts in Marcion's lifetime.[44] Furthermore, they never quote Marcion or his followers as "saying anything about editing or correcting anything."[45] All the heresiologists had were their own authoritative texts, which they assumed were earlier than Marcion's texts, and had been tampered with, simply because Marcion's version was different.

If Marcion *was* a theological editor, he *would* presumably have removed from his Gospel any connection or continuity between Jesus and the Jewish tradition.[46] But this is not the case.[47] There simply is no "consistent pattern

40. Wilson, *Marcion*, 118.

41. D. L. Dungan, "Reactionary Trends in the Gospel Producing Activity of the Early Church: Marcion, Tatian, Mark," *L'Évangile selon Marc: Tradition et rédaction*, ed. M. Sabbe (Leuven: Leuven University Press, 1974), 185. Dungan later claims that Marcion had a "meat-cleaver approach to issues in Christian theology" (*A History of the Synoptic Problem*, 57).

42. Bart Ehrman, *Lost Christianities: The Battles for Scripture and the Faiths We Never Knew* (Oxford: Oxford University Press, 2003), 108.

43. Tim Carter, "Marcion's Christology and Its Possible Influence on Codex Bezae," *Journal of Theological Studies* 61 (2010): 550–82 at 552; Davinson Bohorquez, "The Cross and the Throne: The Son of Man of Mathew 25:31–46 in Light of the Passion Narrative," *Crux* 58:1 (2022): 20; Francis Watson, *What is a Gospel?* (Grand Rapids: Eerdmans, 2022), 109.

44. BeDuhn, "Myth of Marcion," 23.

45. BeDuhn, "Myth of Marcion," 23.

46. Williams, "Reconsidering Marcion's Gospel," 482.

47. Klinghardt, "Plädoyer," 486–487, 495–496.

of excising Jewish elements" anywhere in Marcion's text.[48] In his Evangelion, a woman is entitled to healing as a "daughter of Abraham" (G 13:16); the beggar Lazarus lies in "Abraham's bosom" (16:22); and Jesus instructs Jewish people to obey the Law's precepts (5:14; 10:25–28; 17:14; 18:20–22; 22:8).[49] He himself is eager to eat the Passover (22:15).

Marcion's Gospel cites or refers to Hebrew Bible passages multiple times (G 4:27; 6:3; 7:27; 9:30–33; 9:54; 10:27; 17:14; 17:26–32; 18:20–22; 20:41–44; 20:41–44; 22:8; 22:15). In fact, his Gospel contains about three-quarters of the Old Testament references found in Luke. Elisha and John the Baptist are affirmed as exemplary prophetic figures in continuity with Jesus. The Baptist is portrayed as Jesus's prophesied forerunner (7:17–28). Other Israelite worthies appear positively in Marcion's Gospel, men such as Moses (5:14; 9:30–33); Elijah (9:30–33, 54); Elisha (4:27), and David (6:3; 18:38; 20:41–44).[50] Although some competition with these figures might be implied, they are not criticized.[51]

There are at least four explicit quotations of the Hebrew Bible in Marcion's Gospel.[52] First, it explicitly quotes, "I send my messenger before you who will prepare your way" (Exod 23:20/Mal 3:1) in reference to John the Baptist (G 7:27). Second, Jesus approves of the quote, "you shall love your neighbor as yourself" (Deut 6:5/Lev 19:18) and says that it will lead to life (G 10:28). Third, Jesus favorably quotes several of the Ten Commandments in Evangelion 18:20.[53] Finally, the Sadducees summarize what Moses wrote

48. BeDuhn, "Myth of Marcion," 27.

49. John J. Clabeaux's conclusion, "Abraham meant nothing to Marcion" is overblown ("Abraham in Marcion's Gospel and Epistles: Marcion and the Jews," in *When Judaism and Christianity Began: Essays in Memory of Anthony J. Saldarini*, ed. Alan J. Avery-Peck, Daniel Harrington, and Jacob Neusner, 2 vols. [Leiden: Brill, 2004] 1.69–82 at 88).

50. All this data comes from BeDuhn, "Myth of Marcion," 30–32.

51. See further Dieter T. Roth, "Prophets, Priests, and Kings: Old Testament Figures in *Marcion's Gospel* and *Luke*," in *Connecting Gospels: Beyond the Canonical/Non-Canonical Divide*, ed. Francis Watson and Sarah Parkhouse (Oxford: Oxford University Press, 2018), 41–56.

52. Phillip Andrew Davis, "Marcion's Gospel and its Use of the Jewish Scriptures," *ZNW* 112:1 (2021): 105–129.

53. There is some dispute as to whether Jesus himself quoted the commandments. Tertullian indicates a reading "you know the commandments" (*AM* 4.36.4, 7), but Epiphanius attests

(in Deut 25:5) in Marcion's Gospel 20:28, 37, and Jesus does not reject their summary.

There are also at least seven allusions to the Hebrew Bible in Marcion's Gospel. Fusing several verses from Isaiah, Jesus says to John's messengers that "the blind see, the deaf hear, the lame walk, and the dead rise."[54] The disciples want to call down fire on the Samarians, in accord with 4 Kingdoms 1:10, 12 (LXX). In Evangelion 13:27, Jesus uses the language of Psalm 6:9: "Depart from me all you workers of lawlessness!" Jesus's exhortation to gird up the loins and to keep lamps burning alludes to Exodus 12:11. According to Gospel 21:27 (among other passages), Jesus refers to himself as the "Son of the Human," using the language of Daniel 7:13 (or Ps 8:4). He does the same in the trial scene (G 22:69), combining Daniel 7:13 with Psalm 110:1. Jesus's saying about divided family members (G 12:53) alludes to Micah 7:6. Finally, Jesus's last words (G 23:46) allude to Psalm 31:6: "Father, into your hands, I will commend my spirit."

One might assume that in making these allusions, Jesus fulfills Jewish scripture.[55] But Marcion denied that Jesus fulfilled Jewish scripture ("the prophets did not see what you see," G 10:24). One scholar has proposed that Marcion didn't recognize these allusions to Hebrew scripture in his own Gospel.[56] But such a hypothesis is unlikely. As is clear from Marcion's *Antitheses* (chapter 6), the Pontian knew the Hebrew Bible very well, referring to it and quoting from it many times. His ability to pick up on a Hebrew Bible allusion must be judged to be at least as good as ours, if not better.

The fact that Marcion's Jesus *employed* language from the Hebrew Bible does not mean that Marcion understood Jesus as *fulfilling* scripture or that the readers of Marcion's Gospel made this connection. One need not take biblical language describing divided family members, commending one's spirit, and girding up loins to be prophecies. Even in cases where Jesus apparently refers to himself as the Son of the Human, the Gospel writer might not have always been intending to allude to Daniel 7:13 or Psalm 8:4. Even if the allusion was

---

a first-person, "I know the commandments" (*Pan.* 42.11.17, schol. 50). I follow BeDuhn in taking the first-person statement as accurate.

54. Davis cites Isaiah 26:19; 29:18; 35:5–6; 42:7, 18; 61:1 ("Marcion's Gospel," 121n70).

55. Davis, "Marcion's Gospel," 120.

56. Davis, "Marcion's Gospel," 108, 120, 122, 128.

always intentional, Marcion(ites) might not have assumed that these texts were prophecies.

The basic point is this: Marcion's Gospel clearly uses both quotations and allusions from Jewish scripture. There are two ways of interpreting this evidence. The first option is to accept the heresiological view that Marcion was a theological editor, but to conclude that he did a poor job, because he only half-heartedly deleted the Jewish material. Now, any reasonable person should question this view, which makes Marcion not only (1) feel free to change his scriptures to suit his theology, but also (2) to do it in such a slovenly way. Any editor with Marcion's religious enthusiasm and theological convictions would have been more consistent in deleting Jewish elements from Luke.

It is better to take the second, more convincing (and more charitable) option: *Marcion was not a theological editor.* He either felt no need to emend his Gospel to fit his theology or he believed he lacked the authority to make such emendations.[57] The latter view is more plausible. If Marcion had his way, he *would* have eliminated any and all Jewish material, but the authority of his scriptures prevented him.

Heresiologists like Tertullian and Epiphanius thought they could trap Marcion by pointing out places where his Gospel conflicts with his theology. As it turns out, the trap was sprung on them. They were correct that Marcion's Gospel does *not* agree with his theology—at least as they construed it. But this insight itself *destroys the heresiological argument that Marcion was a theological editor.* If one assumes that Marcion took Luke and tried to edit out all the opposing ("Judaic") material, then his edition was a spectacular failure. Much of the Judaic material remains, as Epiphanius realized: "Even though he has only remnants of the Gospel and preserved letters, still from them it will be shown to the intelligent that Christ is not alien to the old covenant, that, accordingly, the prophets were not alien to the Lord's advent, that the apostle preaches a resurrection of flesh, that he calls the prophets 'righteous,' and that the families of Abraham, Isaac, and Jacob were among the saved."[58] As it turns out, Epiphanius could *easily* prove all this from Marcion's Evangelion.

57. Harry Gamble has shown that the theory of Marcion deleting Romans 15–16 due in part to the Hebrew Bible quotations in Romans 15 is implausible. Marcion probably inherited a fourteen-chapter text of Romans (*The Textual History of the Letter to the Romans: A Study in Textual and Literary Criticism* [Grand Rapids: Eerdmans, 1977] 100–114).

58. Epiphanius, *Pan.* 42.9.6–7.

Marcion's supposed carelessness and oversight simply do not explain the fact that so much Jewish material remains in his text.[59] To explain all the opposing material, it makes more sense to hypothesize that Marcion inherited a gospel with this "Judaic" material. Marcion did not remove this material because he did not feel free to do so, because he considered his Gospel to be his authoritative rule of faith.[60]

Unfortunately, today two conflicting views about Marcion still continue to be juxtaposed. On the one hand, the view that Marcion was a theological editor, and on the other, that he believed in the authority of his text.[61] Oddly, the necessary inference is rarely made—*if Marcion believed in the authority of his scripture, he did not assume he had the right to change it.* One is forced to choose: *either* Marcion more or less preserved the prototype gospel he inherited, *or* he felt at liberty to cut out or change what he did not like. There is no satisfying compromise.

Let's pursue this logic to the end: if Marcion's Gospel already had authoritative status for him, he would not have deliberately emended it to fit his theology. Tertullian observes that Marcion did not even emend his Gospel's original (utterly bland) *title*—"Gospel." Marcion could have easily changed the epigraph to read: "Gospel of (or according to) Paul" or "Gospel of Christ"—but he did not. Marcion considered himself to be a disciple of Paul, but a mere disciple of Paul did not have the authority to correct Paul's Gospel according to his own lights. Marcion did not consider himself to be an inspired prophet or an apostle. Assuming he inherited (and did not write) his Gospel, the Pontian knew that he lacked the personal or institutional authority to emend a written revelation from Christ.[62]

---

59. Wilson, *Marcion*, 97.

60. The idea that he purified a falsified edition is an entirely modern idea, as Klinghardt observes (*Oldest Gospel* 1.137).

61. Norelli, *Markion und der biblischen Kanon* (Berlin: de Gruyter, 2016), 16 (*Nur die Schrift erlaubte Markion so vorzugehen, wie er es für angemessen hielt: er behielt den herkömmlichen Text so getreu wie möglich bei, hier und dort etwas streichend, manchmal nur ein Wort oder einen Teil eines Wortes ändernd; soweit er konnte, gewann er nur durch Auslegung den für ihn richtigen Sinn*).

62. *Pace* Wilson, *Marcion*, 137; Barton, "Marcion Revisited," 345. Cf. the attitude of the anonymous anti-Montanist writer cited by Eusebius *Hist. eccl.* 5.16.3. See further van Unnik, "De la regle Μήτε προσθεῖναι μήτε ἀφελεῖν dans l'histoire du canon" *VC* 3 (1949): 1–36.

Marcion the Text Critic?

To be sure, it is more charitable to "emend" the portrait of "Marcion the mutilator" into "Marcion the text critic" who used the philological tools of his time.[63] Nonetheless, this theory amounts to little more than a redescription of the heresiological theory. It puts a positive spin on a faulty, illogical theory—that Marcion was a theological editor, just a terribly inconsistent one. Marcion the text critic still assumes that Marcion's "philology is only a weapon for his theology."[64] Finally, it runs into the obvious and insurmountable problem: there is no surviving evidence that Marcion ever claimed to be a text critic.[65]

Nevertheless, some scholars have even developed "rules" that supposedly explain why Marcion omitted passages from his scriptures.[66] But these rules are almost all based on a heresiological construal of Marcion's theology—that he omitted references to the Old Testament, or passages favoring Jews, or verses concerning judgment and resurrection, or indications of Jesus's humanity. These rules are manifestly flawed, because they are riddled with exceptions—exceptions that are so numerous they can no longer be called exceptions. As the chapters of this book will prove, Marcion's Gospel *does* attest to Hebrew Bible quotations, passages putting ancient Jews in a favorable light, verses on judgment and resurrection, and the solid nature of Jesus's flesh.

The attempt to explain why the differences in Marcion's Gospel reflect his theological editing is an old heresiological exercise in *post hoc* reasoning. The heresiologists were the first to imagine the "likely story" why Marcion "had to" remove certain passages based on *their* understanding of his theology. But this exercise in reading Marcion's mind impedes responsible inquiry. The fact remains, *there is no convincing reason* why Marcion would remove the parables of the Prodigal Son or the Good Samaritan from his Gospel. These are parables

63. Robert Grant, *Heresy and Criticism: The Search for Authenticity in Early Christian Literature* (Louisville: Westminster John Knox, 1993); Christoph Markschies, *Christian Theology and Its Institutions in the Early Roman Empire: Prolegomena to a History of Early Christian Theology*, trans. Wayne Coppins (Waco: Baylor University Press, 2015), 224.

64. Robert Grant, *The Letter and the Spirit* (London: SPCK, 1957), 115.

65. Grant admitted that there is "no record" of Marcion using a literary critical method (*Heresy and Criticism*, 44).

66. Grant, *Letter and Spirit*, 115–119; Moll, *Arch-heretic*, 92–98.

that strongly accord with Marcion's God of grace and love. To omit them, Marcion would have sawed the branch on which he sat.

The appeal to Marcionite allegory does not convince. According to one theory, Marcion would have interpreted the father to whom the prodigal son returns as "a trope for the God of the Old Testament."[67] It's more likely, however, that Marcion would have viewed the father as representing the *true* God, whom he already called Father. One cannot assume, moreover, that for Marcion the older son represented "Judaism" or that Marcion was offended that the two sons had the same father.[68] Marcion's interpretation of the parable is unknown, but its illustration of the Father's love and grace does not require allegory.

The whole question stands or falls with the issue of priority. The view that Marcion was a theological editor only works if one takes up the heresiological assumption that Marcion used canonical Luke. But such heresiological hindsight has no foresight if Marcion did *not* in fact use canonical Luke. Any argument that the differences in Marcion's text prove that he was an editor are unconvincing if Marcion inherited his Gospel which already contained most of the differences.[69]

Marcion the Evangelist?

No ancient source ever claims that Marcion wrote his Gospel outright. Tertullian says that Marcion used a knife—not a pen—to produce the Evangelion.[70] If the heresiologists knew that Marcion wrote his Gospel, they would have shouted it from the rooftops, because to them it would be the ultimate proof that Marcion's Gospel was false and that he himself was a fraud. Only one current scholar proposes that Marcion was "the first Gospel writer."[71] He was "author" of his Gospel in the sense that he devised, ordered, and compiled it.[72]

---

67. Hays, "Marcion vs. Luke," 220–221.

68. Grant, *Letter and Spirit*, 116, citing Irenaeus, *Haer.* 4.36.7; Tertullian, *Cast.* 8.

69. Grant, *Heresy and Criticism*, 43, citing his own *Letter and the Spirit*, 115–119.

70. Tertullian, *Praescr.* 38.9. Cf. Vinzent, *Marcion and the Dating of the Synoptic Gospels*, 278.

71. Vinzent, *Marcion and the Dating of the Synoptic Gospels*, 157.

72. Vinzent, *Marcion and the Dating of the Synoptic Gospels*, 157.

According to this theory, Marcion produced two drafts of his Gospel. He first produced a "school-text" version, a "first draft of the Gospel, probably for his classroom."[73] This first draft was pirated, and from it were created the four Gospels now considered canonical.[74] Sometime later, Marcion found out about these "re-writings of his own text" and in response "published his (revised?) version of his Gospel, together with his Antitheses and Paul's letters."[75] In short, the theory is that what became the four canonical Gospels are plagiarized versions of a corrupted Marcionite school text. Canonical Luke looks most like Marcion's Gospel because "Luke" adhered more closely to it than the authors of Matthew, Mark, and John.[76]

The theory appeals to a passage in Tertullian's *Against Marcion* (4.4.2):

> As a general rule, how absurd it would be, if we have proved ours the older and that Marcion's [Gospel] emerged later, ours should seem false before it took material from truth, and Marcion's be believed to have been emulated by ours before it was even published?

The theory must assume that the passage represents Marcion's point of view. Marcion had a prepublished Gospel that was falsified and made into what are now the canonical Gospels.[77]

But in interpreting this passage, philology reigns as queen. What Tertullian says is part of a conditional sentence (beginning with "if"). Moreover, it is only from *Tertullian's* point of view that Marcion's Gospel was not published before Luke. This is not actually an expression of Marcion's point of view. Tertullian never says that he is representing Marcion's point of view. Rather, Tertullian thinks he has already proved that Marcion's Gospel came later, and then infers the following: Marcion's Gospel could not have been emulated by the canonical gospels (which all date to the first century, from Tertullian's point of view) if it was not yet published (Marcion only

73. Vinzent, *Marcion and the Dating of the Synoptic Gospels*, 100.

74. Vinzent, *Marcion and the Dating of the Synoptic Gospels*, 99.

75. Vinzent, *Marcion and the Dating of the Synoptic Gospels*, 188.

76. Vinzent, *Marcion and the Dating of the Synoptic Gospels*, 138–39.

77. Vinzent, *Tertullian's Preface*, 305.

arose in the reign of Antoninus). It was not yet published, Tertullian thought, because the canonical Gospels came first. The circularity of the argument is exquisite, and it tells us more about Tertullian's rhetoric than about the history of Marcion's text.[78]

Appeal has been made to a peculiar interpretation of Marcion the *evangelizator*, as recorded by Tertullian.[79] This Latin term, which can be rendered "evangelizer," might suggest that Marcion composed his gospel. Modern translators have opted for "gospel-maker," and even "gospel writer."[80]

According to Tertullian, however, Marcion is an *evangelizator* because he "tells the Gospel in a different way," not because he writes a gospel.[81] When Tertullian calls Paul an *evangelizator*, he means that Paul is a "preacher of good things."[82] The plural *evangelizatores* means "preachers of the gospel."[83] There are also "Judaic preachers of the gospel."[84] None of these other preachers are gospel writers. Thus the argument that Marcion was a "gospel writer" is unconvincing.[85]

There is also the strange claim that Marcion "created the new literary genre of the 'Gospel'" and that he "had no historical precedent in the combination of Christ's sayings and narratives."[86] To be sure, Tertullian speaks of a "new form of talking in Christ" exemplified in the Gospels. But Tertullian actually denies that there was a new gospel form of speaking. Both Jesus's parables and his expositions had precedents in the Psalms (e.g., Ps 78:2).[87]

---

78. *Pace* Vinzent, *Tertullian's Preface*, 262–266.

79. Tertullian, *AM* 4.4.5.

80. Vinzent, *Marcion and the Dating of the Synoptic Gospels*, 92 (quoting E. Evans and V. Luker); cf. Vinzent, *Christ's Resurrection*, 87–88.

81. Tertullian, *AM* 4.4.5 (*quia aliter evangelizavit*).

82. Tertullian, *AM* 5.5.2 (trans. Evans).

83. Tertullian, *AM* 5.7.11.

84. Tertullian, *AM* 5.19.6 (*Iudaici evangelizatores*).

85. Roth, "Link Between Luke and Marcion's Gospel," 70.

86. Vinzent, *Marcion and the Dating of the Synoptic Gospels*, 71.

87. Tertullian, *AM* 4.11–12 (*nec forma sermonis in Christo nova*). Roth, "Link Between Luke and Marcion's Gospel," 70–71; Roth, "Marcion's Gospel and the Synoptic Problem," in *Gospel Interpretation and the Q Hypothesis*, 272.

Finally, one should investigate the so-called anti-Marcionite prologue to John.[88] Normally this prologue is understood to mean that Papias, an early second-century Christian writer, wrote down John's Gospel when John dictated it. Yet according to a newly proposed punctuation, Marcion wrote down a gospel, and John dictated another (true) gospel: "The *Gospel of John* was published and distributed to the churches by John while he was still alive, as the Hieropolitan, called Papias, the beloved disciple of John, has reported in his explications (?), namely the last (?) five books. Marcion, the heretic, however (*verum*), wrote down a Gospel/described the Gospel [as a false one], while John dictated correctly the true one."[89]

A shift in topic is signaled by the Latin word *verum*—"*but* Marcion the heretic, when he was disapproved by him, because he believed opposite things, was expelled."[90] The one who wrote the Gospel—meaning the Gospel of John—at John's dictation was, reportedly, Papias. The text therefore says nothing about Marcion writing a gospel. Even if one assumed that Marcion wrote his Gospel, one cannot grant that this (probably fifth-century) prologue, seething with anachronism, represents anything remotely historical.

In sum, it is not likely that Marcion authored his Gospel. First of all, there is no surviving evidence that Marcion ever *claimed* to have written it, or even to have edited it. Marcion evidently believed that he inherited the authentic and original Gospel of Paul. It is thus misleading to portray Marcion as an "author of an apocryphal Gospel."[91] Marcion did not consider himself to be an author, and he hardly thought of his Gospel as apocryphal. For him, it was the only true Gospel. If Marcion himself composed this Gospel, he could no longer claim that it was original or Paul's. No opponent of Marcion even said

---

88. Vinzent, *Marcion and the Dating of the Synoptic Gospels*, 17–18.

89. Vinzent, *Marcion and the Dating of the Synoptic Gospels*, 16. The Latin text (from Zwierlein, *Die antihäretischen Evangelienprologe* 24) reads: *Hoc igitur evangelium post apocalypsin scriptum manifestatum et datum est ecclesiis in Asia a Iohanne adhuc in corpore constituto, sicut Papias nomine Hierapolitanus episcopus, discipulus Iohannis et carus, in ἐξηγήσεως suae V libro retulit; qui hoc evangelium Iohanne sibi dictante conscripsit. Verum Marcion hereticus, cum ab eo fuisset reprobatus eo quod contraria sentiret, proiectus est.*

90. Carlson, *Papias*, 75–77.

91. Simon Gathercole, *The Apocryphal Gospels: Translated with an Introduction* (London: Penguin, 2021), 85.

that the Pontian composed his Gospel. If they knew that he had composed it, they would have ridiculed him as a non-apostolic innovator.

Marcion's Edition

If Marcion did not write his Gospel, he did transcribe it. That is to say, he released his own edition of the familiar prototype for use in his own church.[92] The Pontian evidently copied out his Gospel and Pauline letter collection onto a single codex so that they would be read together. In the process of copying, he probably made several transcriptional changes—perhaps a few to his advantage—but he was not a conscious theological editor of his text. Transcriptional changes were part of the ordinary process of scribal copying, not part of a deliberate and consistent decision to omit or change the gospel to conform with one's theology. Scribes sometimes (inconsistently and even accidentally) changed the scriptures they wrote, often by making small changes—sometimes significant ones.[93] Thus, Marcion's Gospel was probably different from the prototype Gospel he had inherited, but mostly in small ways that did not radically change its overall meaning.

After inscribing his Gospel and Apostolikon in a codex, Marcion probably paid good money for copies of his edition to be made and disseminated. In the early third century, Tertullian obtained an edition of Marcion's Gospel and Apostolikon, as did Epiphanius in the mid fourth. Its availability suggests that it was still being copied out as a discrete version of Christian scripture, which—certainly by the fourth century—was a conscious alternative to other versions.

Of course Marcion's edition underwent further changes between the second and fourth centuries. Every hand-copied text undergoes changes. There is no compelling evidence, however, that the changes were radical—at least not any more radical than the kinds of changes made in early catholic editions. Tertullian claims that Marcionites reshape their gospel every day, but he never

---

92. *Pace* Barton: "There was no sense that he had established a kind of 'scripture' in editing Luke, and in that sense Marcion's rival to the gospels was not 'canonical,' any more than the gospels then were for the larger church ("Marcion Revisited," 347).

93. See further Bart Ehrman, *The Orthodox Corruption of Scripture: The Effect of Early Christological Controversies on the Text of the New Testament* (New York: Oxford University Press, 1993).

cites a single example.[94] He simply assumes that "heresy" in general always emends and corrupts the Gospels.[95] But that is an unfair and overgeneralizing assumption. Besides, if Marcionites *did* daily change their text, it would undermine Tertullian's entire polemical strategy—namely, to use Marcion's text to combat Marcion's views. Marcionites could have simply said, "that's not our text (anymore)"; but they did not. Accordingly, the objection that Marcion's text is unrecoverable because the version Tertullian had in the third century is different than the version Epiphanius had in the fourth is unconvincing. There was variation; but if scholars can make a critical edition of the catholic New Testament, then they can do the same for Marcion's scriptures.

* * *

The evidence suggests that Marcion's Gospel was probably prior to canonical Luke. It was a pre-Lukan Gospel that Marcion likely used in Pontus, and brought with him to Rome.[96] It had already accrued considerable authority by Marcion's time, and Marcion did not feel at liberty to edit it according to his theology.

Marcion was not a theological editor or a trained text critic; if anything, he was conservative in the transmission of his scriptures. They were his *scriptures* after all, thought to be divinely inspired. Marcion treated his scriptures as sacred. He did not feel at liberty to alter his sacred text at will. According to present evidence, the Pontian never claimed that he had a higher revelation, or that he was inspired by a superior spirit. Marcion may have assumed that he had the holy Spirit by virtue of his baptism, but that was the same Spirit possessed by every Christian. Marcion did not consider himself to be the medium of God's revelation—that was Paul's remit. God's revelation had already occurred, and it was written down in the Gospel and Apostolikon—texts that Marcion did not create but conserved. Marcion never once claimed to be an editor or to change a single jot or tittle of his Gospel. The changes he did make to the prototype were the kinds of small-scale changes all gospels went through in the process of copying and transmission. It is high time to lay to rest the heresiological slander of Marcion the scriptural mutilator.

---

94. Tertullian, *AM* 4.5.7.

95. Tertullian, *AM* 4.4.5.

96. Gregory, *Reception of Luke and Acts*, 295.

CHAPTER FOUR

The Shape of Marcion's Canon

None of the letters are lacking there.
Thus the truth written in the holy Gospel
With the letters of the alphabet
Is a perfect measure which admits of neither less nor more.

—Ephrem of Nisibis, *Hymns against Heresies* 22.1

MOST PEOPLE WHO did creative work in antiquity did not want to be known as innovators. Marcion was one of them. His innovation is not that he wrote one gospel out of many, but that, when he encountered many gospels, he held so doggedly to his own. The Pontian is the first person to deliberately and consistently claim that there was only one authoritative written account about Jesus—one single Gospel.[1] Accordingly, Marcion was motivated to be textually conservative, even radically so. He tried to oppose the proliferation of gospels by valorizing and delimiting his single Gospel along with a limited set of Pauline letters.

Marcion and the development of a Christian "canon" is a well-worn subject. However, continued disagreement shows that more can be clarified. First of all, canonical texts are not the same as authoritative texts. One can have many authoritative texts, but if one has a canon, then one takes the additional step of deliberately *excluding* other documents as scripture. Marcion was not the decisive factor in the canonization of early *catholic* scriptures. After all, early catholics did not come up with definitive canon lists until the mid-fourth century.[2] Well into the late fourth century, catholics disagreed on what

1. Gregory, *Reception of Luke and Acts*, 196; cf. 210.

2. The thirty-ninth Festal Letter of Athanasius (367 CE) was a watershed because it listed for the first time what are today considered to be the twenty-seven books of the New Testament.

should belong to their New Testament. (One could even argue that "orthodox" Christians never really came to an agreement, since different communions today still uphold different canons.)[3]

What is clear is that early catholics came to add substantially to Marcion's more limited collection: three other gospels ("according to 'Matthew,' 'Mark,' and 'John'") and at least four other "Pauline" letters (the Pastorals plus Hebrews), not to mention the catholic Epistles (letters attributed to James, Jude, John, and Peter) and a final Apocalypse. The leap from eleven to twenty-seven New Testament books was large—and some ancient manuscripts indicate that even more authoritative books were included (such as the Shepherd of Hermas, the Letter of Barnabas, 1–2 Clement, and 3 Corinthians, for instance).

The Pontian was not simply a catalyst in the making of his New Testament.[4] Insofar as the New Testament is a closed and authoritative collection of books uniting Gospel literature and Pauline Epistles, then Marcion arguably invented it.[5] The exact content of Marcion's canon did not prevail, but the basic shape of it did. In short, Marcion was the first known person to combine a biography of Jesus (a Gospel) with a Pauline letter collection (his Apostolos, aka Apostolikon). This structure for the New Testament has perdured in every single later instantiation of it, despite many modifications, expansions, and changes in the order of the books.[6]

---

3. On canon in general, see Lee Martin McDonald and James A. Sanders, ed., *The Canon Debate* (Peabody: Hendrickson, 2002); Brakke, "Scriptural Practices in Early Christianity: Towards a New History of the New Testament Canon," in *Invention, Rewriting, Usurpation: Discursive Fights Over Religious Tradition in Antiquity*, ed. Jörg Ulrich, David Brakke and Anders-Christian Jacobsen (Frankfurt am Main: Peter Lang, 2012), 263–280.

4. *Pace* Gamble, "Marcion and the 'Canon,'" in *The Cambridge History of Christianity*, ed. Margaret M. Mitchell and Frances Young (Cambridge: Cambridge University Press, 2006), 192–213 at 211; Lieu, *Marcion*, 432.

5. Cf. von Campenhausen, *Formation of the Christian Bible*, trans. J. A. Baker (Philadelphia: Fortress, 1972), 163, 203; Hoffmann, "How Then Know," 180; May, "Markion in seiner Zeit," 6–7; Norelli, "Marcione lettore dell'epistola ai Romani," *Cristianesimo nella storia* 15 (1994): 635–675 at 674; Jason D. BeDuhn, *The First New Testament: Marcion's Scriptural Canon* (Salem: Polebridge, 2013), 26, 29, 60. Barton agrees that "the question of canon became *overt* for the first time through Marcion" (*Holy Writings*, 36, emphasis original).

6. Knox, *Marcion*, 31.

The view that Marcion edited a stable, preexisting Gospel plus Pauline collection cannot stand.[7] True, Christians before Marcion were aware of gospels and apostolic letters as the twofold fount of Christian teaching. Nonetheless, they never limited themselves to one *particular* gospel and to one *particular* collection of Pauline writings.[8] Churches before Marcion emphasized gospel plus apostle(s) as a common structure of authority, but in most cases they were referring to *persons* (Jesus, Peter, Paul, Andrew, and so on), not to texts.[9] It was Marcion who firmly and unambiguously textualized gospel and apostle. In the course of limiting the gospel to a single *written* Gospel, and the apostle to a single *written* collection, Marcion excluded other gospels and apostolic letters. It was this act of exclusion that made Marcion a canon-maker, and—among Christians—apparently the first of his kind.

Generally speaking, Marcion's church upheld his canon in the course of its history. One can see this point of view advanced in the early fourth-century *Adamantius* dialogue, where the Marcionite speakers (Megethius and Markus) insist that evidence be drawn solely from their canon. "Do you obey the apostle?" an early catholic asks. Markus responds, "I obey my Apostolikon."[10] And when the early catholic cites the story of Lazarus raised from the dead, Megethius answers: "That's not written in our Gospel."[11] In the end, Markus and Megethius are not entirely consistent in their citations, but this inconsistency may be laid at the feet of the catholic writer who wrote up the debate.

Even if Marcionites came to quote passages from Matthew or the Pastorals, these texts were not thereby new members of Marcion's canon. In the fourth century, John Chrysostom commented on 2 Timothy 1:18 ("may the lord give him mercy from the lord"), by pointing out that

---

7. *Pace* Andreas Lindemann, "Die Sammlung der Paulusbriefe 1. und 2. Jahrhundert," in *The Biblical Canons*, ed. J.-M. Auwers and H. J. De Jonge (Leuven: Peeters, 2003), 321–352 at 343–344.

8. Barton, "Marcion Revisited," 352; Gamble, "Marcion and the 'Canon,'" 211. See, e.g., 1 Clem 42:1–3; Ignatius, *Magn.* 13.1; *Phil.* 5.1.

9. *Pace* François Bovon, "The Canonical Structure of Gospel and Apostle," in *The Canon Debate*, ed. Lee Martin McDonald and James A. Sanders (Peabody: Hendrickson, 2002), 516–527.

10. *Adamantius* 2.5 (824.8–9).

11. *Adamantius* 1.17 (815d).

Marcionites see two different lords.[12] In context, however, it is not clear that the Marcionites actually refer to 2 Timothy as opposed to Psalm 110:1 ("the lord said to my lord") and Gen 19:24 ("the lord rained down from the lord"). Even if they did refer to 2 Timothy 1:18, they did not thereby understand 2 Timothy as scriptural, any more than they understood Psalms or Genesis as Scripture.

Later Marcionites did not feel free to amplify Marcion's canon.[13] The addition of the Pastorals among the Marcionite prologues does not mean that later Marcionites added them.[14] It was early catholics who expanded the prologues, sometimes using surprisingly Marcionite language. The supposed "new book of psalms for Marcion" does not refer to a canonical text, but comes from a confused passage in the Muratorian fragment (lines 81–83), a fragment that is probably a forgery, and thus not a reliable witness to the Marcionite use of texts.[15]

Marcion did not merely publish a separate edition of Christian books; he made a canon for his church.[16] His interest was not primarily philological. The Pontian had no advanced training in Alexandrian or any other kind of text criticism. Neither Marcion nor his followers ever presented him as a text critic. They could not, because Marcion the shipmaster probably did not advance beyond grammar school. Marcion's primary motivations were religious. He was a church organizer more than a man of letters. He created a canon to solidify the identity of his Christian group, which read distinctly Christian scriptures.

---

12. Harnack, *Marcion*, 129–133*, 170–72*. John Chrysostom, *Hom* 10.2 on 2 Tim. 1:18 (PG 62.615).

13. *Pace* Barton, *Holy Writings*, 38; Alain Le Boulluec, "The Bible in Use among the Marginally Orthodox in the Second and Third Centuries," in *The Bible in Greek Christian Antiquity*, ed. and trans. Paul M. Blowers (Notre Dame: University of Notre Dame Press, 1997), 197–216 at 201; Enrico Norelli, *Markion und der biblischen Kanon* (Berlin: de Gruyter, 2016), 11, 22; Tomas Bokedal, *The Formation and Significance of the Christian Biblical Canon: A Study in Text, Ritual and Interpretation* (London: Bloomsbury, 2014), 188.

14. Harnack, *Marcion*, 129–133*, 170–172*.

15. Claire Rothschild, *The Muratorian Fragment: Text, Translation, and Commentary* (Tübingen: Mohr Siebeck, 2022).

16. Here agreeing with Knox, *Marcion*, 19–21.

Marcion did not merely present his canon as a set of "reliable ancient documents."[17] Insofar as he effectively replaced the "Old" Testament with his Gospel and Apostolikon, these two scriptural parts functioned as Scripture for his group. The Gospel, for the Pontian, was not merely a historical record of Jesus, a kind of "memory jogger" to learn Jesus's sayings.[18] No, by canonizing Gospel and Apostolikon, Marcion was upholding scriptural truth, a rock on which he built his church. The "living voice" of oral tradition about Jesus was no longer "lasting," and Marcion knew it. He thus became a voice urging the transition of Christian authority from oral to written tradition. By fixing scriptural tradition in writing, Marcion worked to solidify a distinctive and coherent Christian identity based on a discrete set of texts and not on others.

Naming the "New Testament"

Presumably, the Pontian was familiar with Paul's use of "new testament (*or* covenant)" to designate the new agreement God made with humanity (2 Cor 3:6). But the apostle did not use "new testament" to refer to a discrete collection of texts.

Marcion pioneered the concept of the New Testament, but he probably did not invent its name. In his *Prescription against Heretics* (written before *Against Marcion*), Tertullian says that, "Marcion separated the New Testament from the Old."[19] It's unclear whether this language is Marcion's or Tertullian's. Tertullian observes in *Against Marcion* that it "is more usual" to refer to the scriptures with the word "testament," instead of "instrument," but it is not necessary to conclude that it is *Marcion* who called his scriptures "[New] Testament."[20] The titles "New" and "Old Testament" were not common among elite writers, but they came to be favored "among simple believers."[21]

17. Barton, *Holy Writings*, 40.

18. *Pace* John Barton, "Marcion Revisited," in *The Canon Debate,* 345.

19. Tertullian, *Praescr.* 30. For dating Tertullian's works, see Timothy David Barnes, *Tertullian: A Historical and Literary Study* (Oxford: Clarendon, 1971), 55.

20. *Pace* Wolfram Kinzig, "Καινὴ διαθήκη: The Title of New Testament in the Second and Third Centuries," *JTS* 45.2 (1994): 519–544 at 540; DeConick, *Comparing Christianities,* 43, 46.

21. Kinzig, "Καινὴ διαθήκη," 534.

Marcion was mainly concerned to distinguish two different beings: the true God from the Judean lord. This task involved him in distinguishing two different sets of scripture, but it's not known whether he referred to them with the adjectives "New" and "Old" Testaments.[22] Since Marcion did not recognize an "Old Testament" *as scripture*, however, he had no compelling reason to call *his* scriptures "New Testament." His name for them, apparently, was "Gospel and Apostolos, aka Apostolikon."[23]

The Pontian was the first to *consistently* refer to his biography of Jesus as "Gospel," rather than by using other circumlocutions (such as "the sayings of the Lord" or "the memoirs of the apostles)."[24] By calling his Gospel "*the* Gospel," Marcion excluded competing gospels.[25] For him, "the Gospel" was incomparable. There were many biographies of Jesus, but his "Gospel" was one of a kind.

Marcion was also the first known user of a Pauline letter collection.[26] The corpus consisted of ten Pauline letters to seven churches. The Pontian need not have created the collection himself.[27] It was a collection he probably found circulating in Asia Minor, where the Pauline letters already had a measure of authority.

---

22. *Pace* Vinzent, *Christ's Resurrection*, 150.

23. Epiphanius, *Pan.* 42.10.2.

24. James A. Kelhoffer, "'How Soon a Book' Revisited: ΕΥΑΓΓΕΛΙΟΝ as a Reference to 'Gospel' Materials in the First Half of the Second Century," *ZNW* 95 (2004): 1–34. Cf. Helmut Koester, "From the Kerygma-gospel to Written Gospels," *New Testament Studies* 35 (1989): 361–381 at 381.

25. Kelhoffer, "How Soon a Book," 34.

26. Judith M. Lieu, "Marcion and the Canonical Paul," in *Receptions of Paul in Early Christianity: The Person of Paul and His Writings Through the Eyes of his Early Interpreters*, ed. Jens Schröter, Simon Butticaz and Andreas Dettwiler (Berlin: de Gruyter, 2018), 779–797 at 783.

27. John J. Clabeaux, *A Lost Edition of the Letters of Paul: A Reassessment of the Text of the Pauline Corpus Attested by Marcion* (Washington, Catholic Biblical Association of America, 1989), 4; Harry Y. Gamble, *Books and Readers: A History of Early Christian Texts* (New Haven: Yale University Press, 1995), 58–63, 100; Schmid, *Marcion*, 284–298; Benjamin P. Laird, *The Pauline Corpus in Early Christianity: Its Formation, Publication, and Circulation* (Peabody: Hendrickson, 2022), 154.

The Order of the Books

The order of Marcion's canon was as follows:

1. Gospel
2. Galatians
3. 1 Corinthians
4. 2 Corinthians
5. Romans
6. 1 Thessalonians
7. 2 Thessalonians
8. Laodiceans (Marcion's name for Ephesians)
9. Colossians
10. Philemon
11. Philippians

According to Marcion's order, Philemon was probably thought of as part of the correspondence to Colossae. Thus it makes sense that Philemon would follow Colossians. This order is attested by Epiphanius.[28] Tertullian, however, mentions Philemon after Philippians, which might indicate that in his version of the Apostolikon, Philemon was placed last.[29]

The letters are generally ordered from longest to shortest (with 1–2 Corinthians taken as one letter, and likewise 1–2 Thessalonians). This means that Galatians, a shorter letter, was moved to the head of the collection for other reasons. This may have been Marcion's deliberate adjustment, designed to highlight the priority of Galatians. Scholars often note that a small minority of ancient Pauline collections began with Galatians too.[30] Yet when one looks at them, they diverged in other ways from Marcion's order.[31]

---

28. Epiphanius, *Pan.* 42.9.4; 42.11.8, 12.

29. Tertullian, *AM* 5.21.1.

30. A Syriac canon list and the old Latin prologues to the Pauline letters are mentioned for instance, by Gamble, "Marcion and the 'Canon,'" 209.

31. Lieu, *Marcion*, 239–240, with the important caveats of Dirk Jongkind, "On the Marcionite Prologues to the Letters of Paul," in *Studies on the Text of the New Testament and*

For Marcion, there was something special about Galatians. He did not place it first because he thought it was chronologically prior. The Pontian shows no independent interest in chronology or insistence on chronological ordering. Most likely, Galatians was first because it was theologically and hermeneutically central.[32] Even if Marcion adapted an Apostolikon with Galatians already in first place, he had his own reasons for prioritizing the letter. Galatians spelled the "destruction of the old Law"—one of the central thrusts of Paul's—and Marcion's—Gospel.[33]

The Coherence of Marcion's Edition

The Gospels "according to 'Matthew,' 'Mark,' 'Luke,' and 'John'" do not agree in what they say about Jesus. They are different in detail and design, and deliberately so. Marcion's New Testament manifests less tension for the simple reason that it contains less material. There is one single Gospel—considered to be Paul's, combined with a ten-letter collection of Paul's writings, addressed to exactly seven churches (a number indicating universality, as seen in Revelation 2–3).

Marcion seems to have believed that Paul's Gospel was already written during Paul's lifetime. Paul referred to "my gospel" in the singular (Rom 2:16). Most modern readers take Paul's "gospel" here and elsewhere to refer to an oral proclamation, but Marcion apparently imagined that Paul could pull his Gospel out from his knapsack. Paul's was the only Gospel revealed by a direct revelation of Jesus Christ (Gal 1:12), and the Pontian had it in his possession.[34]

According to surviving evidence, Marcion did not claim that Paul wrote his Gospel. The Gospel was anonymous, and Marcion left it so, perhaps to

---

Early Christianity: Essays in Honour of Michael W. Holmes on the Occasion of his 65th Birthday (Leiden: Brill, 2015) 389–407. Older sources in Gamble, *Books and Readers*, 272n80.

32. *Pace* May, "Der Streit zwischen Petrus und Paulus," 40–41. Gamble posits a seven-churches edition that had been revised to offer a chronological sequence ("Marcion and the 'Canon,'" 210), but the early church's concern for chronological sequence is undemonstrated. See further Eric W. Scherbenske, "Marcionite Paratexts, Pretexts, and Edition of the Corpus Paulinum," in *Canonizing Paul: Ancient Editorial Practice and the Corpus Paulinum* (Oxford: Oxford University Press, 2013), 84, 92–93.

33. Tertullian, *AM* 5.2.1.

34. Eusebius also understood Rom 2:16 to refer to a written text, in this case Luke (*Hist. eccl.* 3.4.7).

emphasize its ultimate divine authorship and origins. Later Marcionites claimed that Jesus wrote the Evangelion and that Paul added the stories of Christ's death and resurrection.[35] Marcion likely thought that Christ, or the Spirit of Christ, inspired it. Just like Paul himself, the Gospel was not from human beings but through Jesus Christ (Gal 1:1).

The Pauline Gospel fit perfectly with the Pauline letters because Paul's gospel, preached in the letters, confirms the one Gospel. Marcion excluded other Gospels because he thought that Paul did: "There is no other [Gospel] in accord with my Gospel" (Gal 1:7).[36] According to Marcion, Paul's (written) Gospel was complete and sufficient. There was no other Gospel given by any other being, whether angelic or apostolic (Gal 1:8). Once Marcion had made the identification of his Gospel with Paul's Gospel, then it was inevitable that he would identify all other competing Gospels as corrupt. From surviving evidence, it is not clear that Marcion's Apostolikon was ranked lower than the Evangelion.[37] The very act of their being bound together in the same codex suggests their equal status.

* * *

When it came to Paul's Gospel, Marcion's influence was pivotal. Elite writers in Rome such as Justin Martyr and the author of the Shepherd of Hermas do not mention Paul, even if they were influenced by him. Marcion's highly Pauline canon forced Roman Christians either to reject Paul or receive him with open arms.[38] Although Tertullian called Paul the "Apostle of the heretics," early catholics generally chose to embrace him.[39] They never systematically ignored or repudiated Paul. At the same time, Marcion incited catholics to make Paul a major part of their scriptures. Paul became, to put it cheekily,

35. *Adamantius* 1.808d.3–8.

36. BeDuhn, *First New Testament*, 229, citing Tertullian, *AM* 5.2.5–6, 4.3.2; *Adamantius* 1.6 ("The Apostle says that there is only one Gospel . . . he did not say 'according to my Gospels,' but 'according to my Gospel." Then the verse is quoted: "There is no other in accord with my Gospel (κατὰ τὸ εὐαγγέλιον μοῦ, cf. Rom 2:16).

37. *Pace* May, "In welchem Sinn kann Markion als der Begründer des neutestamentlichen Kanons angesehen werden?" in *Gesammelte Aufsätze*, 85–91 at 87. May suggests a triple ranking: first Gospel, then Apostolikon, then *Antitheses* (88).

38. Knox, *Marcion*, 36.

39. Tertullian, *AM* 3.5.4.

"Mr. I wrote half the New Testament books"—in fact, slightly over half, if the letter to the Hebrews is considered Pauline (as it typically was in antiquity). And so Paul attained a position out of proportion to his subordinate place in the apostolic college ("least of the apostles").[40] To be sure, Marcion did not raise Paul out of oblivion.[41] The Pontian ensured, however, that what became the New Testament, from the very beginning, was a richly Pauline product. It became Petrine and Johannine with time and to varying degrees. But the Pauline voice always sounded above the choir.

40. Knox, *Marcion*, 159.

41. Andreas Lindemann, *Paulus im ältesten Christentum: Das Bild des Apostels und die Rezeption der paulinischen Theologie in der frühchristlichen Literatur bis Marcion* (Tübingen: Mohr Siebeck, 1979), 36–395; Ernst Dassmann, *Der Stachel im Fleisch. Paulus in der frühchristlichen Literatur bis Irenäus* (Münster: Aschendorff, 1979), 176–192.

CHAPTER FIVE

Reconstructing Marcion's Scriptures

> "Every biblical story reflects something that mattered to its author. Whenever we figure out what it was and why it mattered, we move a step closer to knowing who wrote a part of the Bible."
>
> —Richard Elliott Friedman, *Who Wrote the Bible?* (1987)

MARCION'S GOSPEL IS not like Q. Q is a purely hypothetical text. It has never been found; it has no manuscript attestation. By contrast, Marcion's Gospel is attested over 700 times by over fifteen witnesses.[1] These witnesses—all of them hostile—sometimes quote the exact words of his text and point out key differences from "according to Luke."

It is often said that everything known about Marcion proceeds from the lips of his enemies.[2] But Marcion's Gospel and Apostolikon are something of an exception. Of course, these scriptures must be reconstructed from the church fathers. There is no unmediated Marcion. But once the reconstruction of Marcion's scriptures has reliably occurred, it is a testament not only to the thought of hostile witnesses, but to the thought of *Marcion*, since Marcion's Gospel preexisted the heresiologists, and shaped their response, not the other way around.

There are rules for reliably reconstructing Marcion's Gospel and Apostolikon. It is important for readers to understand them, since, with one possible exception (Papyrus 69) not a single manuscript of Marcion's Bible survives, even if Marcionite readings percolate other biblical manuscripts.[3] The

1. Bilby, *The First Gospel*, 31.

2. For example, Lieu, *Marcion*, 9.

3. BeDuhn (*First New Testament*, 41–42) argues that P69 (P. Oxy 2383) is a fragment of Marcion's Gospel.

reason for this is that Marcion's text represents a particular textual cluster that was popular in the second century, both in the East and West. This cluster or type was then folded, or recycled, into the later copies of the New Testament, far into late antiquity and beyond. Generally speaking, however, it is not safe to use variant readings from catholic scriptures to reconstruct Marcion's text. Catholic versions of the New Testament, even the distinctive witness of Codex Bezae, are not witnesses to Marcion's text. At best, they can only serve to corroborate the primary witnesses to Marcion's Gospel and Apostolikon.

Primary Witnesses

Marcion's primary witnesses are Tertullian (from early third-century North Africa) and Epiphanius (from late fourth-century Cyprus). They were not neutral scholars trying to reconstruct Marcion's text. They were avid polemicists on the hunt for ways that they could use Marcion's Bible against him. They collected passages that they thought either agreed with their own theology or opposed what they thought was Marcion's theology. Tertullian commented on Marcion's text systematically but not exhaustively. Epiphanius, for his part, wrote out a set of passages from Marcion's Bible. Later he attached explanatory notes to them in order to refute Marcion, requoting the passages he had earlier collected.

Epiphanius was writing in Greek, Tertullian in Latin. Probably Tertullian had a Greek copy of Marcion's Gospel and Apostolikon, making his own translations as he went along.[4] Tertullian was more thorough in picking out passages for comment. Yet he also left sizeable gaps, and—due to writer's fatigue and the desire to avoid repetition—he became less and less thorough as he progressed. Many times he would simply skip over a passage that either did not differ from his version of the New Testament, or which he felt did not suit his argument against Marcion. In the end, then, there are many passages in Marcion's text that must be marked "unattested." These are passages that Tertullian, Epiphanius—and others—skipped over, without informing us

4. Tertullian even quotes the Gospel in Greek at *AM* 4.23.1. See further Clabeaux, *Lost Edition*, 52–54; Schmid, *Marcion*, 40–59; Dieter Roth, "Did Tertullian Possess a Greek Copy or Latin Translation of Marcion's Gospel?" *Vigiliae Christianae* 63 (2009): 429–467; T. J. Lang, "Did Tertullian Read Marcion in Latin? Grammatical Evidence from the Greek of Ephesians 3:9 in Marcion's Apostolikon as Presented in the Latin of Tertullian's *Adversus Marcionem*," *Journal of Ancient Christianity*, 21 (2017): 63–72; Klinghardt, *Oldest Gospel* 72.

whether they were there in Marcion's text or not. They are not evidence that Marcion omitted these passages.

It is often the case, moreover, that Tertullian paraphrased Marcion's text, deleted words, or changed word order and conjunctions to suit his own writing context and style. Tertullian had his own citation habit—his own peculiar way of quoting biblical texts, clear from his other writings.[5] Just as today some English speakers revert to the language of the King James Version (KJV), Tertullian reverted to the Latin text that was familiar to him, and to the Gospel that was most favored by him, namely Matthew. Occasionally, Tertullian even rebuked Marcion for not citing passages in Matthew, when Marcion never set out to do so.[6] All this data indicates that, from Tertullian—although one cannot reconstruct the exact wording of a particular Greek text—one can often get a good sense for the *gist* of Marcion's text. (It is modern scholars, to be clear, who have *retranslated* Tertullian's Latin into Greek).

The God of This Aeon

Let's take an example of how someone might go about reconstructing a particular verse, in this case 2 Corinthians 4:4. One cannot start with the verse as it survives in extant manuscripts. Instead, one turns first to Tertullian and Epiphanius to see if they quoted 2 Corinthians 4:4 from Marcion's text. Thankfully, the verse drew the attention of Tertullian, who mentions it in his *Against Marcion (AM)*:

> *AM* 5.11.9: **'In whom the god of this aeon'**—so that, by indicating the creator as the god of this aeon, he [Marcion] can suggest a god of another aeon. We, by contrast, say what needs to be distinguished: 'In whom God,' *then* 'in this aeon he **blinded the minds of the faithless.**'[7]

5. Clabeaux, *Lost Edition*, 40; Roth, *Text of Marcion's Gospel*, 46–409.

6. Tertullian, *AM* 3.13.6 (Matt 2:11); 4.7.4; 4.9.15; 4.12.14; 5.14.14 (Matt 5:17); 4.7.5 (Matt 15:24 and 26). Tertullian knew that Marcion rejected Matthew (*AM* 4.34.2). See further Dieter Roth, "Matthean Texts and Tertullian's Accusations in *Adversus Marcionem*," *Journal of Theological Studies* 59, no. 2 (2008): 580–97.

7. *In quibus deus aevi huius, ut creatorem ostendens deum huius aevi alium suggerat deum alterius aevi. Nos contra sic distinguendum diciumus: In quibus deus, dehnic: aevi huius excaecavit mentes infidelium.*

AM 5.11.12: The whole chain [of clauses] . . . belongs to the creator, **the god of this aeon.**[8]

AM 5.17.9: He will be the devil, whom in another passage (as they yet want the apostle to be read) we recognize **the god of this aeon.**[9]

Here quotations in bold represent Marcion's presumed text. Tertullian never claimed to be giving an exact quote, and he did not regularly signal a quote with the words "here Marcion has" or "in these words" or the like. Nevertheless, one can get a sense of what Marcion's text read. Tertullian began to quote the initial phrase of 2 Corinthians 4:4, "In whom the God of this aeon." He then made an immediate aside about how Marcionites read the passage: a god of this aeon suggests a God of another aeon. Tertullian then gave his own understanding of where to read "of this aeon." He then returned to quoting Marcion's text: "blinded the minds of the faithless." In the two other instances, Tertullian gives the Marcionite reading of a single clause: "the god of this aeon." He thus ignores the final half of 2 Corinthians 4:4, which must be left unattested. Scholars may presume that it was there, but there is no reliable evidence of its wording, so it is best to leave it blank. This is the basic process of reconstruction. It involves close and discerning reading, but it is not rocket science.

Why So Many Reconstructions?

For almost a hundred years, Harnack's edition of Marcion's Gospel and Apostolikon reigned supreme.[10] Now it has been replaced by other reconstructions—and more reconstructions continue to appear.[11] The beginner rightly asks, Why are there so many (recent) reconstructions of Marcion's scriptures?

This is an important question because the diversity of scholarly reconstructions might give an excuse to those who would rather not engage with

8. *tota series . . . creatoris est, dei huius aevi.*

9. *Hic erit diabolus, quem et alibi (si tamen ita et apostolum legi volunt) deum aevi huius agnoscemus.*

10. Harnack, *Marcion*, 183*–240*.

11. Schmid; Roth; Klinghardt; BeDuhn-Bilby.

Marcion's text for theological or other reasons. Even among experts, the uncertainty of reconstruction might induce one to think that a reconstruction is not possible. Recent reconstructions of Marcion's text are different, to be sure, but largely because they work with different sources and methods. Readers can understand those sources and methods, and so make judgments as to which reconstruction is best.

Tertullian and Epiphanius are our main sources, with Tertullian generally seen as more reliable (since he had Marcion's text directly in front of him while writing *Against Marcion*, whereas Epiphanius only had his notes). Most scholars also allow readings from the *Adamantius*. This is an early fourth-century dialogue, written by an early catholic, that initially features a debate with two Marcionite speakers (Megethius and Markus). Scholars have cast doubt on the *Adamantius* because the Greek version is attested only by medieval manuscripts, which may have corrupt quotations. If the dialogue depends on an earlier anti-Marcionite source (as some have argued), then it probably had no direct access to Marcion's scriptures. The *Adamantius* is also frequently loose in its biblical citations, inconsistent with itself, and it shows a bias for a Matthean rendering of verses.[12] Thus while some scholars allow the *Adamantius* as a witness to Marcion's Gospel, they do not think it attests its exact wording.[13] Others only use the *Adamantius* as a check on Tertullian and Epiphanius. When the *Adamantius* stands alone, it can offer at best a reading with "slight probability."[14]

In the example above (2 Cor 4:4), the *Adamantius* offers a direct quotation: "For thus it says, 'among whom the god of this aeon blinded the minds of the faithless so that they do not perceive their enlightenment.'"[15] From this text, one can fill in some of the latter half of 2 Corinthians 4:4 in Marcion's version. It ends up being different from the modern critical edition, which says that the faithless do not "behold the enlightenment of the gospel of the

---

12. Clabeaux, *Lost Edition*, 58, 62; Tsutsui, *Die Auseinandersetzung mit dem Markioniten im Adamantios Dialog: Ein Kommentar zu den Büchern I-II* (Berlin: de Gruyter, 2004) 22–43, 78–110 (esp. 92); Roth, 352–358.

13. BeDuhn, *First New Testament*, 40.

14. Roth, *Text*, 358.

15. *Adamantius* 2.21 (832c): οὕτω γὰρ λέγει ἐν οἷς, φησίν, ὁ θεὸς τοῦ αἰῶνος τούτου ἐτύφλωσε τὰ νοήματα τῶν ἀπίστων . . . πρὸς τὸ μὴ διαυγάσαι αὐτῶν τὸν φωτισμόν.

glory of the Christ, who is the image of God." Even if the Marcionite speaker chose not to quote the entire verse, his version is different, causing editors to decide whether the differences are due to a citation from memory or because Marcion's text was in fact shorter. At any rate, what one can reconstruct of the first half of 2 Corinthians 4:4 in Marcion's text has more certainty than what one can glean about its second half.

Other sources for reconstructing Marcion's Gospel include Irenaeus, Clement of Alexandria, Origen, the Refutator, Pseudo-Tertullian, Ephrem, (Pseudo-)Ephrem, Jerome, Filaster, Eznik of Kolb, and Jacob of Serugh.[16] All these witnesses, however, do not systematically attest Marcion's Gospel. Some of them are quite late (fifth or sixth century), they often make only a passing reference to Marcion, and it is difficult to know if they had direct access to Marcion's scriptures. Different scholars will use them in different ways, creating minor—though occasionally significant—differences in their reconstructions.

Reconstructions that try to fill in material from texts that are actually—or not explicitly—sources for Marcion's texts, are methodologically questionable.[17] Texts like Codex Bezae, manuscripts of the later Gospels, and Pseudo-Ephrem's *Exposition of the Gospel* ("Pseudo-Ephrem A") are not explicit sources for Marcion's Gospel.[18] One might use these texts as supporting evidence, but they can never stand alone, and they should not trump the main witnesses (Tertullian and Epiphanius). It is the duty of the reader to check the footnotes of a scholar's reconstruction.

Methods

In reconstructions prior to the mid-1990s, editorial decisions about what to print were still often based on a presumed knowledge of what Marcion *would* have added to, changed, or deleted from canonical Luke due to his supposedly theological editing. Regardless of one's position on the priority of Marcion's

16. For discussion, see BeDuhn, *First New Testament*, 40–45; Roth, *Text*, 396–409.

17. For example, Klinghardt; Bilby.

18. Dieter Roth, "The Link Between Luke and Marcion's Gospel: Prolegomena and Initial Considerations," in *Luke on Jesus, Paul and Christianity: What Did He Really Know?*, ed. Joseph Verheyden and John S. Kloppenborg (Leuven: Peeters, 2017), 59–82 at 64–67. One should add here the text quoted by Jacob of Serugh, as analyzed by Forness, "Anonymous Source," 541–559.

Gospel, it is now widely agreed that one should *not* reconstruct a text based on presumed knowledge of Marcion's ideological tendencies. Scholars are not mind readers, and heresiologists are often misleading. Accordingly, one must first reconstruct a text on the basis of empirical evidence—actual attestations in patristic sources. This methodological advance means that Harnack's reconstruction—and any earlier ones—are unreliable and should be avoided.

Furthermore, reconstructions that do not take systematic account of the citation habits of patristic authors (how they normally cite a verse) are inferior to reconstructions that do. This is because when patristic authors quote or paraphrase Marcion's text, they often let their own favored way to cite a verse in turn shape what they write. What they quote, in other words, is based on their memory, a memory that is contaminated by the biblical version they prefer. It is like a conservative Christian who, having been taught the KJV on their mother's knee, easily slides into the cadence and vocabulary of the KJV even when claiming to cite another version of the Bible. If Tertullian "cites" Marcion in a way that conforms exactly to his other citations in his other works, then he is probably misrepresenting Marcion's text.

Knowing an author's citation habits provides an important check, but it is not foolproof. Sometimes there are no other examples of a heresiologist citing a particular verse. Tertullian and Epiphanius wrote a lot, and so they sometimes preserved multiple citations of a verse. In other cases, however, multiple citations are lacking. They are generally lacking in the *Adamantius*, for example, because it is a singular text with an unknown author. Accordingly, although paying attention to citation habit is important, it is not always possible.

Compounding the problem is that our sources, for instance Tertullian, know the text of Matthew's Gospel best. This makes it hard to determine whether the Matthean readings in Marcion's text are original or later imported by the heresiologists. At the very least, each Matthean reading should be weighed with care before it is printed in reconstructions of Marcion's Gospel.

Cases of Conflict

Matters become more complex when the heresiologists conflict with each other. When heresiologists disagree on a reading of Marcion's text, they do so about 63 percent of the time.[19] Many of these disagreements are not

19. Klinghardt, *Oldest Gospel*, 59, 81, 415.

semantically earthshaking. They differ regarding the word order of a sentence, the use of conjunctions, the tense of verbs, and so on. Occasionally, however, their wording is significantly different, and the editorial decision about what to print becomes momentous.

This is when attention to method becomes doubly important. Sometimes, citation habit can solve the problem. Tertullian might have gotten a verse of the Evangelion wrong because he cited it in his own peculiar way. Sometimes multiple attestations can help—for example, when Tertullian and *Adamantius* agree against Epiphanius, or when Epiphanius and *Adamantius* agree against Tertullian. At other times, one can turn to the manuscript tradition to help make the decision. Occasionally a second-century reading agreeing with Marcion's text is preserved in the manuscripts of canonical Luke, especially in so-called Western witnesses like Old Latin manuscripts and Codex Bezae.

The goal of scholarly reconstruction is not to fill in all possible gaps in Marcion's scriptures, but to produce a reconstruction out of actually attested material. Aesthetically, of course, people would like to read a text of Marcion's scriptures without gaps. It is natural to prefer a continuous narrative with complete sentences and paragraph divisions. But that is simply not possible in all cases, given the nature of our sources. Accordingly, in careful scholarship, reliability trumps aesthetics, and the only reliable text is one attested in a patristic source.

If scholars print an unattested text because they judge that the logic of the passage demands it, or because they assume that the heresiologists simply skipped over it, that unattested text should never stand alone as evidence. One should not make an argument about what Marcion thought based on an unattested text. One should base one's conclusions only on what exists, not on what might have existed, however logical or probable. This means that there will inevitably be gaps in good reconstructions of Marcion's text, but it is better to eat Swiss cheese than a solid hunk of moldy Gouda.

A final point: a translation of Marcion's scriptures is often beguiling because it suggests that there is an exact and stable text "underneath" it. In the Greek, however, the exact sequence of verbs, their tenses, and the choice of conjunction are often unclear, and scholars simply have to guess. The basic rule to keep in mind is this: there will always be some degree of fluidity and uncertainty in any reconstruction of Marcion's text. Patristic authors paraphrased, condensed, translated, and reworded their sources, making the exact wording of the text obscure.[20]

Given this situation, it is probably best to look at multiple scholarly reconstructions (made after 1995). Conservative reconstructions (such as the Gospel reconstruction published by Dieter Roth), often serve as a check against more liberal reconstructions of "the oldest Gospel" (such as that published by Matthias Klinghardt).[21] English speakers are well served by Jason BeDuhn's translation of both Marcion's Gospel and Apostolikon in 2013 (with an update expected). BeDuhn has now published a corresponding Greek text of Marcion's scriptures. The present book employs the reconstructions of Klinghardt, Roth, and BeDuhn on the Evangelion, and Ulrich Schmid and BeDuhn on the Apostolikon. In cases of conflict, this volume prefers BeDuhn's Greek edition as a moderate and balanced reconstruction.[22]

20. See further Williams, "Reconsidering Marcion's Gospel," 477–496; Roth, *Text*, 83–409.

21. As Dieter Roth points out, the text which Klinghardt reconstructs is not Marcion's Gospel as attested in its explicit sources, but "a text sometimes attested by heresiological sources for Marcion's Gospel and sometimes in the broader Lukan MS [manuscript] tradition" ("Review Article," *TC: A Journal of Biblical Textual Criticism* 27 [2022]: 93–103 at 95).

22. BeDuhn-Bilby.

CHAPTER SIX

Marcion's *Antitheses*, with a Hypothetical Reconstruction

> Whenever we read the obscene stories, the voluptuous debaucheries, the cruel and torturous executions, the unrelenting vindictiveness, with which more than half the Bible is filled, it would be more consistent that we call it the word of a demon rather than the word of God.
>
> —Thomas Paine, *The Age of Reason*

MARCION'S SPECIAL TALENT was contrasting information gleaned from the Hebrew Bible with knowledge gained from his scriptures. He collected his contrasts into a work entitled *Antitheses* (or *Oppositions*); though its full title could have been *The Antitheses of Good and Evil*.[1] This work Marcion apparently attached as a kind of preface to his Bible.[2] It was not itself scriptural, but served as a kind of introduction. These kinds of introductions are familiar in modern study Bibles. If it is too impertinent to say that Marcion gave the

1. *Ref.* 7.30.1–2.

2. For the *Antitheses*, see Lampe, *From Valentinus*, 253; Eric W. Scherbenske, "Marcion's *Antitheses* and the Isagogic Genre," *Vigiliae Christianae* 64, no. 3 (2010): 255–279—somewhat revised in his "Marcionite Paratexts," 73–85; Winrich Löhr, "Editors and Commentators: Some Observations on the Craft of Second Century Theologians," in *Pascha Nostrum Christus: Essays in Honour of Raniero Cantalamessa*, ed. Pier Franco Beatrice and Bernard Pouderon (Paris: Beauchesne, 2016), 65–84 at 73–80. The '*Antitheses*' stood *in summo instrumento* as an introduction to the Gospel. Lieu, *Marcion*, 209. *In summo* can indicate position ("first") or evaluation ("most important"). Marcion set up his *Antitheses* beforehand (*praestruendo*) (Tertullian, *AM* 4.6.1); and Marcionites "display" Marcion's *Antitheses* (*praeferunt*), a verb that can also mean "place before" (*AM* 4.4.4). See further Scherbenske, "Marcionite Paratexts," 77–78, 82; Lieu, *Marcion*, 273, 284.

world its first study Bible, he is still the first known author to attach a sort of "reader's guide" or key to the scriptures.

Despite what may be read out of Tertullian, the primary purpose of the *Antitheses* was not to show the separation of Law (Jewish scriptures) and Gospel (Christian scriptures).[3] Proving the fundamental difference between these "testaments" was only instrumental. The chief end was to prove that these two anthologies described the character of two different *beings*: the true God revealed by Jesus, and the local Judean lord.[4] In brief, Marcion's *Antitheses* contrasted the character, legislation, and miracles of two different superhuman entities by describing their recorded practices, or those of their human representatives.[5]

Harnack thought that the opening line of the *Antitheses* read: "O wonder beyond wonders, rapture, power, and amazement is it, that one can say nothing at all about it [the Gospel], or even conceive of it, or compare it with anything."[6] The problem is that the text that quotes this line, says that it comes from a work of Marcion called *Proevangelium* (or *Pre-Gospel*). Since Tertullian says that Marcion set his *Antitheses* before his Gospel, one can connect the dots and identify the *Antitheses* with this *Proevangelium*. The doxology stood

3. Cf. Tertullian, *AM* 1.19.4; 4.6.1; 4.9.3.

4. Tertullian, *AM* 4.1.1. Cf. Lieu, *Marcion*, 285.

5. Tertullian, *AM* 1.19.4; 2.29.1. Tertullian understood that Marcionites "prove the difference between the gods by the difference of the two documents' propositions" (*ex diversitate sententiarum utriusque instrumenti diversitatem quoque argumententur deorum*). Tertullian indicates that the focus of Marcion's attention in his *Antitheses* was the *ingenium* (character) of the two gods as revealed by their laws (*leges*) and miracles (*virtutes*) (*AM* 2.29.1). See further Winrich Löhr, "Did Marcion Distinguish between a Just God and a Good God?" in *Marcion und seine kirchengeschichtliche Wirkung*, ed. Gerhard May and Katharina Greschat (Berlin: De Gruyter, 2002), 145.

6. Harnack, *Marcion*, 59. The text (*O Wunder über Wunder, Verzückung, Macht, und Staunen ist das, dass man gar nichts über es sagen, noch über es denken, noch es mit irgend etwas vergleichen kann*) is translated from Joseph Schäfers, *Eine altsyrische antimarkionitischen Erklärung von Parabeln des Herrn und zwei andere altsyrische Abhandlungen zu Texten des Evangeliums. Mit Beiträgen zu Tatians Diatessaron und Markions Neuem Testament* (Münster: Aschendorff, 1917), 4–5. Cf. the translation of George A. Egan: "O the exceeding greatness, the folly, the [wisdom of the] power, and the wonders, for there is nothing to say about it, nor to think concerning it, and there is nothing to render like unto it" (*Saint Ephrem: An Exposition of the Gospel* [Leuven: Secretariat of the Corpus SCO, 1968], 1). Words in square brackets indicate the alternative reading of another manuscript.

"at the beginning" of the *Proevangelium*.[7] Arguments that the *Proevangelium* refers to Marcion's Gospel itself or to some other Marcionite work are not convincing.[8]

Harnack proposed that the *Antitheses* went on to discuss Paul's relation to the apostles as well as to false brothers. He believed that Marcion here explicitly rejected the four Gospels and their titles, perhaps also the book of Acts and Revelation.[9] One cannot absolutely deny these hypotheses. Tertullian mentions these points but never attributes them directly to the *Antitheses*. The Carthaginian does say, however, that in his *Antitheses*, Marcion criticized certain "defenders of Judaism" as interpolators of the Gospel, who tried to unite it to the Law and Prophets.[10] From the fusion of Law and Gospel, they created a fictional Christ.[11]

The *Antitheses* as Literature

Although the *Antitheses* does not survive today, reports and reminiscences of it indicate that it belonged to a genre in the ancient world called the introductory text (*eisagōgē*). These kinds of texts were designed to initiate new trainees into a discipline and to reinforce the essentials for those already familiar with the topic.[12] The *Antitheses* was a "preliminary prospectus"; one might even say "primer."[13]

---

7. Schäfers, *Eine altsyrische antimarkionitischen Erklärung*, 5 (*im Anfänge jener Schrift*).

8. Scherbenske, *Canonizing Paul* 279n56, *contra* Moll, *Arch-heretic*, 119–120.

9. Harnack, *Marcion*, 256*–57*.

10. Christopher M. Hays claims that *interpolare* generally means "falsify," "alter," or "give a new form," though he acknowledges that the meaning "to insert, interpolate" is possible, citing Cicero, *Verr.* 2.1.61 §168 (Hays, "Marcion vs. Luke," 218).

11. Tertullian, *AM* 4.4.3–4 (*Marcion per Antithesis suas arguit ut interpolatum a protectoribus Iudaismi ad concorporationem legis et prophetarum, quo etiam Christum inde confingerent, utique non potuisset arguere nisi quod invenerat*).

12. Tertullian observed that Marcionites are "initiated and reinforced" (*initiantur et indurantur*) into Marcion's thought by the *Antitheses* (*AM* 1.19.4). See further Scherbenske, "Marcion's *Antitheses*," 258.

13. Lieu, *Marcion*, 275.

As a primer, the *Antitheses* was probably not a full-scale commentary, a passage by passage explanation of the Gospel and Apostolikon.[14] Nor was it a "doctrinal handbook, containing a short creedal section followed by an exegetical guide."[15] It could have contained commentary on Gospel passages. Primarily, it was a set of oppositions showing the difference between the true God and the Judean lord. Reading these oppositions, however, had the effect of shaping the minds of Marcion's readers to interpret the Scriptures in a particular way.[16] The *Antitheses* allowed readers to immediately grasp the broader history of the creator, and how his system of worship differed from the revelation in Christ, as revealed in the Gospel and Apostolikon.

Of course, the *Antitheses* was also a polemical tract using well-known rhetorical devices and selective quoting to drive home a point. In this respect, it resembled works like Tatian's *Oration against the Greeks*, which roasted Greek poets for exhibiting contradictory opinions about the gods.[17]

The structure of the *Antitheses* likely assumes that Marcion knew the antitheses in Matthew (5:21–48).[18] Irenaeus indicates that Marcionites read and approved of some Matthean antitheses.[19] In fact, the Marcionite Megethius approvingly cites the Matthean form of an antithesis: "The lord in the Law says, 'You will love the one who loves you and you will hate your enemy.' But our Lord, who is good, says, 'Love your enemies and pray for your persecutors'" (Matt 5:43–44).[20] Matthew's attempt to transcend the "eye for eye" principle (5:38) was also adapted by Marcion. In essence, Matthew contrasted the ordinances of Moses with those of Jesus. Marcion went a step

---

14. Barton, "Marcion Revisited," 353, who follows Harnack, *Marcion*, 54, 56.

15. Barton, "Marcion Revisited," 353.

16. See further Scherbenske, "Marcionite Paratexts," 71–115; Moll, *Arch-heretic* 107–114; Lieu, *Marcion*, 272–289; Markus Vinzent, *Tertullian's Preface*, 267–292; Dieter Roth, "Evil in Marcion's Concept of the Old Testament God" in *Evil in Second Temple Judaism and Early Christianity*, ed. Christ Keith and Loren T. Stuckenbruck (Tübingen: Mohr Siebeck, 2016), 340–356 at 352–353; Tsutsui, *Auseinandersetzung*, 148–152.

17. Tatian, *Or.* 8. See further Dungan, "Reactionary Trends," 189, 195 (where Dungan points out that Tatian tried to undermine the practice of allegorizing Greek poetry in *Or.* 21).

18. Harnack, *Marcion*, 154, n.29.

19. Irenaeus, *Haer.* 4.13.1.

20. *Adamantius* 1.12 (812d18–21).

further by contrasting the character of the being who gave Torah with the God who gave the Gospel.

Apparently the *Antitheses* was addressed to a man whom Marcion called a "fellow wretch" (*suntalaipōros*), a man hated together (*summisoumenos*) with Marcion himself.[21] The haters were perhaps incipient catholics, hostile Hellenes, or both. Evidently Marcion was riffing on Paul, who also called himself a "wretch" (*talaipōros*) since he was trapped in a "body of this death" (Rom 7:24). There may also be an allusion to Evangelion 21:17, where Christ predicts that the disciples will be hated (*misoumenoi*) because of his name.

Ordering the Oppositions

Marcion's *Antitheses* itself is lost, but its poignant contrasts are reflected in later literature. In the latter half of *Against Marcion*, book 2, Tertullian attempts what he calls a "destruction" of Marcion's *Antitheses*.[22] He admits that he only attacked them in summary fashion, but his summary indicates the original order of at least some of the individual antitheses. When the Carthaginian treated Marcion's scriptures (in *Against Marcion*, 4–5), he proceeded according to the order of the passage as found in Marcion's text. Likely, Tertullian proceeded similarly when he critiqued Marcion's *Antitheses*.

Tertullian begins with a brief summary of the antitheses illustrating the creator's cruelty: the sending of the great flood, the hardening of Pharoah's heart, and the unleashing of she-bears against children.[23] Next he attacks Marcion's objections against the Torah's injustices: the law of retaliation (or *lex talionis*), the fact that the creator pronounces certain animals unclean—the animals he elsewhere blessed (Gen 1:22, 25), the creator's detailed commands to sacrifice while claiming "What use to me is the multitude of your sacrifices?" (Isa 1:11 LXX),[24] and finally the command to despoil Egypt of gold, silver, and other articles.[25]

21. Tertullian, *AM* 4.9.3, which opens with a reference to the *antithesis*.

22. Tertullian, *AM* 2.29.1.

23. Tertullian, *AM* 2.14.4.

24. Tertullian, *AM* 2.18.1–3.

25. Tertullian, *AM* 2.20.1–2.

Subsequently Tertullian describes acts indicating the creator's inconsistency and self-contradiction. The creator demands strict Sabbath observance but tells Joshua to carry the ark around Jericho on the Sabbath.[26] He forbids carved images (Exod 20:9), but tells Moses to make the bronze serpent (Num 21:8–9).[27] He commands sacrifices while claiming, "I will not drink the blood of bulls" (Ps 50:13).[28]

Next Tertullian copies out contentions regarding the creator's caprice—that he disapproved of men whom he previously approved, lacked foresight into their failures, and reversed his previous judgments. The key example is Saul, whom Samuel anointed according to the creator's command. But later that same creator said, "I regret that I have made Saul king" (1 Kgdms 15:11), and he gave the kingship to David (15:28).[29] The creator also admitted error with respect to the Ninevites, whom he intended to punish, but in the end repented (Jonah 4:2).[30]

Finally, Tertullian came to instances of the creator's pettiness, weakness, and ignorance. The maker apparently did not know Adam's location in the garden of Eden (Gen 3:9).[31] He also did not know the extent of Sodom and Gomorrah's sin, forcing him to come down and investigate (Gen 18:21).[32] He swore by himself, showing his ignorance of the God superior to him.[33] He chose the nation of Israel but, in the golden calf episode, said to Moses that he would replace Israel (Exod 32:10).[34] At this point, Tertullian signals that he omitted further instances of the creator's pettiness and weakness.[35]

26. Tertullian, *AM* 2.21.1.

27. Tertullian, *AM* 2.22.1–2.

28. Tertullian, *AM* 2.22.2–4.

29. Tertullian, *AM* 2.23–24.1.

30. Tertullian, *AM* 2.24.2–3.

31. Tertullian, *AM* 2.25.1.

32. Tertullian, *AM* 2.25.6.

33. Tertullian, *AM* 2.26.1–2.

34. Tertullian, *AM* 2.26.3–4.

35. Tertullian, *AM* 2.27.1.

Despite this premature ending, one can reconstruct the order of at least a section of Marcion's *Antitheses*, under four major headings:

1. **The creator's malice**
   1.1 Great Flood
   1.2 Hardening Pharoah's heart
   1.3 She-bears devour children
2. **Injustices in the Law**
   2.1 The *lex talionis*
   2.2 Food laws
   2.3 Sacrificial system
   2.4 Despoliation of Egypt
   2.5 Sabbath breach at Jericho
   2.6 Bronze serpent
3. **The creator's caprice and inconsistency**
   3.1 Rejection of Saul to favor David
   3.2 Ninevites unpunished
4. **The creator's pettiness, weakness, and ignorance**
   4.1 Can't find Adam
   4.2 Self-swearing
   4.3 Threatened destruction of Israel

If it is true that Tertullian preserved the order of some *Antitheses*, one can give their fuller forms in the same sequence. These fuller forms are preserved elsewhere by Tertullian and the *Adamantius*.

The antitheses in the *Adamantius* are later, but they are not necessarily secondary or unreliable.[36] The *Adamantius* and Tertullian overlap in at least two antitheses: the despoliation of Egypt and the she-bears. Tertullian and "Adamantius" were evidently using similar material. Furthermore, if it is conceded that the *Adamantius* preserves quotations of Marcion's Gospel and Apostolikon, then there is no reason to deny that it could preserve quotations or paraphrases of Marcion's *Antitheses*. To be sure, much of this material could be secondhand, but this is not necessarily an objection against its authenticity. Moreover, when one examines the individual antitheses in *Adamantius*, they

36. *Pace* Lieu, *Marcion*, 289.

are often longer and contain direct scriptural quotes rather than paraphrases. This indicates that *Adamantius* not only preserves some of Marcion's antitheses, but preserves them in a more original form, since these same antitheses, when they were quoted and requoted, it seems, were increasingly shortened, paraphrased, and streamlined. Let's comment on some examples.[37]

Unleashing She-bears

> See, Christ loves the little ones, and teaches that all who ever wish to be the greater must be like them (G 9:46–48). The creator, however, unleashed bears against boys to avenge Elisha the prophet for the mockery he had suffered from them (4 Kgdms 2:23–25).[38]

This is Tertullian's version. The antithesis appears with a Gospel quote in the *Adamantius*:

> The prophet of the god of generation told a bear to come out of a thicket and devour the children who met him, but the good Lord says, "Let the children come to me, for of such is the kingdom of heaven!" (G 18:16).[39]

This is manifestly the same antithesis, but the language is different and the order is reversed. This is a reminder that one cannot reconstruct the exact wording of the *Antitheses*, though one can ascertain its gist.

To understand the full impact of this particular opposition, the scriptural stories should be read in context. While the prophet Elisha was traveling to the city of Bethel, he was met by young children who mocked his baldness. The prophet responded by cursing the children in the name of the creator. The creator immediately fulfilled the curse by sending two bears against the children who mauled them (4 Kgdms 2:23–25).

37. The following commentary adapts Litwa, *Evil Creator: Origins of An Early Christian Idea* (New York: Oxford, 2021), 69–88.

38. Tertullian, *AM* 4.23.4.

39. *Adamantius* 1.16 (814c.24–27). Cf. Matt 19:14; Mark 10:14.

It is tempting to soft-peddle the brutality of this story. According to the Septuagint, Elisha cursed not teenage toughs, but "small children" (*paidaria mikra*). He cursed not just two or three of these children but "forty-two" of them. He cursed them not for a repeated offense, but for a single occurrence of jesting, and for a relatively minor infraction—for exposing the prophet's lack of hair. Consequently, Elisha's cursing of the children indicates moral flaws in both his character and the character of the being he represented—the Judean lord.

The prophet's action was not the main problem. To Marcion, the cursing prophet represented the character of the one he represented—the creator. In the bear attack episode, it was the creator who actually perpetrated the crime, for it is he who sent the bears against the children. These bears quite literally tore the children apart. The Greek verb at play (*anerrēxan*) expresses incredible violence. It can be used to describe breaking through a wall, or a lion ripping open a carcass. Etymologically, the verb means "break up" and one can almost hear the sound of the children's bones cracked by the bears' teeth—though their screams go unmentioned. Far from showing any compassion, the cursing prophet continued his journey as if nothing had ever happened.[40]

Marcion opposed Elisha's curse against the children to what occurs in his Gospel. Votaries of Jesus brought infants and small children to him so that he could bless them. When his disciples tried to prevent this, Jesus invited the children to approach, saying, "Let the little children come to me . . . for the kingdom of the heavens is made up of their kind" (G 18:16). In short, Jesus transmitted the blessings of the true God to the children, whereas Elisha destroyed children by the curse of the creator.

One can argue that the two scenes are fundamentally different. The children of the Gospel, after all, do not mock Jesus. If they did, perhaps his response would have been different. But there is little reason to think so, for when Jesus was rejected and refused hospitality by the (adult) Samarians, he did not curse them. The disciples suggest that they call down fire from heaven like Elijah of old (4 Kgdms 1:9–13). According to this story, Elijah's lord killed a hundred men by unleashing a fireball against them. Jesus, who obviously knew the story, rebuked his disciples as if they were stark raving mad

40. See further David Penchansky, *What Rough Beast? Images of God in the Hebrew Bible* (Louisville: Westminster John Knox, 1999), 81–90; Brian P. Irwin, "The Curious Incident of the Boys and the Bears: 2 Kings 2 and the Prophetic Authority of Elisha," *Tyndale Bulletin* 67:1 (2016): 23–35.

(G 9:54–55).[41] According to Marcion, Jesus was on a different wavelength than the prophets of the creator. He did not represent their character. He certainly did not replicate the creator's cruelty.

Lex talionis

> It says in the Law, "An eye for an eye and a tooth for a tooth," but the Lord, because he is good, says in the Gospel, "If anyone slaps you on the cheek, turn the other one to him" (G 6:29).[42]

The creator commanded the Israelites: "Show no pity: eye for eye, tooth for tooth, foot for foot" (Deut 19:21; cf. Exod 21:24; Lev 24:20). The order "show no pity" indicates that the Judean lord was not speaking metaphorically. He actually demanded that, if someone knocked out a person's eye or tooth, that same act had to be performed on the perpetrator. It was a brutal logic in which punishment literally fit the crime.

By the second century CE, this law of retaliation was not assumed to be just, especially by Christians familiar with Jesus's sayings. Perhaps the most poignant and memorable of these sayings is "turn the other cheek" (6:29). Marcion understood Christ's command to engage in self-sacrificial submission as a rejection of retaliation. He apparently assumed a proposition articulated by Justin: "a law placed against another law abrogates the earlier one."[43] Even Tertullian agreed that the eye-for-eye principle "has been cancelled" and "abolished." "For the old Law used to . . . gouge out eye for eye and would pay back injury with revenge. However, the new Law [of Christ] ordained clemency."[44]

41. Tertullian, *AM* 4.23.8. Dale C. Allison, no Marcionite, makes a significant comment on Luke 9:52–56: "There is at this point no harmony between old and new. Jesus' unelaborated rebuke seemingly implies that violent vengeance is wrong at all times and places . . . the pericope . . . belongs to a tradition that rejects human vengeance on the ground of God's nature" ("Rejecting Violent Judgment: Luke 9:52–56 and Its Relatives," *Journal of Biblical Literature* 121, no. 3 [2002]: 459–478 at 476). See further Lieu, *Marcion* 280.

42. *Adamantius* 1.15 (814a.3–6). Cf. Tertullian, *AM* 2.18.1; 4.16.4–6; Origen, *Cels.* 7.25; *Acts of Archelaus* 44.9; Augustine, *Against Adimantus* 8.

43. Justin, *Dialogue with Trypho* 11.2 (νόμος δὲ κατὰ νόμου τεθεὶς τὸν πρὸ αὐτοῦ ἔπαυσε).

44. Tertullian, *Adv. Jud.* 3.10. Geoffrey D. Dunn, who dates this work to 195–196 CE, considers the work to be authentic and to be addressed to a primarily Christian audience

Marcion rejected the creator's law of retaliation not only because it was unkind, but because it was unjust. This was not simply a disagreement of law but of principle. Christ forbade retaliation, while the creator enforced it. The moral character of the Christ who rejected retaliation was different from the creator who commanded it.

Despoiling Egypt

> The creator led out the departing convoy of the children of Israel from Egypt loaded down with those famous spoils of gold and silver vessels, clothes, as well as with the burdens of their dough (Exod 12:34–36). Christ, however, ordered his disciples not even to take a staff for the journey (G 10:4; 9:3).[45]

So Tertullian. This antithesis appears (again with quotations) in *Adamantius*:

> The god of generation ordered Moses as he left the land of Egypt, saying, "Be prepared! Have your loins girded, your sandals tied, your staffs in your hands and your wallets attached. Cart off from the Egyptians gold, silver and everything else." But our Lord, the good, when he sent out his disciples into the world, says, "Don't have shoes on your feet, nor wallets, nor two shirts, nor small change in your belts" (G 9:1–3)[46]

In short, Marcion(ites) contrasted the creator's demand to despoil with Christ's command to his disciples not to carry extra supplies with them on their missionary journey. Although the contexts of the commands are different, Marcion thought them worthy of contrast. He assumed, like other Christians, that if both "testaments" came from a single deity, there should be a theological continuity between them. If Jesus was the Christ of the creator, their instructions for advancing the kingdom should have aligned.

(*Tertullian's Adversus Iudaeos: A Rhetorical Analysis* [Washington, DC: Catholic University of America Press, 2003], 173–182).

45. Tertullian, *AM* 4.24.2.

46. *Adamantius* 1.10. Cf. Tertullian, *AM* 4.24.1–2.

Yet this is not the case. In the one passage, Jesus invited his disciples to accept voluntary poverty and full dependence upon God as they preached the gospel. In Exodus, by contrast, the creator ordered the Hebrews to weigh themselves down with gold, silver, and clothing so they could decorate his tabernacle in the desert (Exod 26).[47] In short, the creator commanded his people to get rich off the spoils of their enemies—many of whom had perished in the preceding plagues. Taking such spoils, even if they were given on the spur of the moment, was a form of robbery.[48]

Marcion's chief criticism was that the creator commanded theft.[49] This command contradicted one of the Ten Commandments ("do not steal," Exod 20:15), widely taken to exemplify baseline morality. Far from upholding this morality, the creator ordered his servants to engage in serious robbery—what amounted to pillage. These were immoral acts, not fully explained by the objection that the Israelites were only claiming compensation. If the Judean lord sought compensation, he should have said so.

The following antitheses are attested in the *Adamantius*, but unaccounted for in Tertullian.

Healing Lepers

Christ and Elisha both healed lepers, but in different ways. This opposition is interesting, because it is directly built into Marcion's Gospel, in the scene when Jesus heals the ten lepers (G 17:12–14). The ten lepers beg Jesus to heal them as he passes through Samaria. Jesus concedes, and they are healed as they go to present themselves to the priests. One former leper, a Samarian "foreigner" returns to thank Jesus.

As Jesus points out, Elisha healed no lepers in Israel, only the Syrian "foreigner" Naaman. To heal Naaman, Elisha set up an elaborate ritual of seven dips into the river Jordan. Christ could heal by a simple command.[50] The fact that he healed *ten* lepers—both Israelite and foreign—indicates a

47. Irenaeus, *Haer.* 4.30.1.

48. See further J. Allen, "Ezekiel the Tragedian and the Despoliation of Egypt," *Journal for the Study of the Pseudepigrapha* 17, no. 1 (2007): 3–19.

49. Tertullian, *AM* 2.28.2; cf. 5.13.6.

50. Tertullian, *AM* 4.9.8.

generosity and grace that was apparently unavailable from Elisha, prophet of the creator. Tertullian seems to summarize Marcion's point: "whereas Elisha needed a material help, and made use of water, seven times at that, Christ by the act of his word alone, without repeating it, immediately put the healing into effect."[51]

Making the Blind See

> The god of generation did not restore the sight of Isaac suffering from cataracts (Gen 27:1), but our Lord, because he is good, opened the eyes of many blind people (G 7:22).[52]

Christ's healing of the blind was one of his signature miracles. It is striking that the creator would not even heal the eyes of one of Israel's most famous patriarchs. According to Marcion, not only does the creator not restore sight, he actively blinds people so that they do not behold the enlightenment of the Gospel of Christ (2 Cor 4:4).[53]

A paradigm prooftext for the god who blinds was Isaiah 6:9–10 (LXX). Here the heart of the Israelites "became stupid; they heard poorly with their ears and they closed their eyes so that they do not see with their eyes." The word "stupid" represents a passive verb, often taken to be a divine passive. The creator, in this interpretation, is the one who incites the stupidity, an interpretation in accord with the previous verse, where the creator orders Isaiah: "Go and say to this people, 'With hearing you will hear and certainly not understand; seeing you will see and certainly not perceive" (Isa 6:9).[54] The statement is worded like a prediction. But the certainty of the speaker indicates that he played a role in its fulfillment. As is learned from the context (6:11),

51. Tertullian, *AM* 4.9.7 (trans. Evans)

52. *Adamantius* 1.20 (816c.1–3). Harnack attributed this line to the *Antitheses* (*Marcion*, 89–92; further sources in his appendix to the German edition, *Marcion*, 266*–296*).

53. Tertullian, *AM* 5.11.9–11. See further Litwa, *Evil Creator*, 90–108.

54. Joseph Ziegler, ed., *Isaias*, 3rd ed., Septuaginta 14 (Göttingen: Vandenhoeck & Ruprecht, 1983), 143–144. See further Heikki Räisänen, *The Idea of Divine Hardening: A Comparative Study of the Notion of Divine Hardening, Leading Astray and Inciting to Evil in the Bible and the Quran* (Helsinki: Finnish Exegetical Society, 1976), 60–66, 88–93.

the lord had already stated Israel's fate: the people would be exiled and their country destroyed.[55]

In all likelihood, Marcion cited Isaiah 6:9 somewhere in his *Antitheses*. Tertullian remarks: "that pronouncement of the creator to the people, 'with the ear you shall hear, and shall not hear,' has frequently given Christ occasion to insist, 'he that has ears, let him hear' (e.g., G 8:8)."[56] It is Marcion who, in context, probably suggested that "Christ was giving back the hearing which the creator had taken away from them."[57] In short, Christ opened up the ears of the heart (the minds) of his disciples so that they could understand spiritual mysteries. The creator, by contrast, mentally incapacitated people so that they would not understand the Gospel. The contrast in character is clear.

Tertullian cites a similar antithesis. He recalls the blind men of ancient Jerusalem who tried to prevent David's capture of their city. In the end, David violently took over the city and ordered the blind to be struck with daggers (2 Kgdms 5:6–8). Contrast this with Christ, who went out of his way to call the blind man who called him "son of David" on the road to Jericho (G 18:35–43). In this scene, Christ proved that he was far different from David by healing this man and by entering peacefully into Jerusalem.[58]

Violent in War

Three other antitheses in the *Adamantius* deal with war:

> The prophet of the god of generation says, "My bows are taut and my arrows are sharpened" (Isa 5:28; Deut 32:23), but the apostle says,

55. C. A. Evans shows that later versions of Isa 6:10 (LXX, Targums, and Peshitta) soften the theme of divinely-inflicted obduracy (*To See and Not Perceive: Isa 6.9–10 in Early Jewish and Christian Interpretation* [London: Bloomsbury, 2009], 61–80, 164.

56. Tertullian, *AM* 4.19.2 (trans. Evans).

57. Tertullian, *AM* 4.19.2 (trans. Evans). The Marcionite use of Isa 6:9–10 can be gleaned from Irenaeus, *Haer.* 4.29.1 (which seems to follow the Hebrew text); cf. Tertullian, *AM* 3.6.5; 5.11.9. Cf. Harnack, *Marcion* 61.

58. Tertullian, *AM* 4.36.13.

"Put on the full armor of God, that you may be able to quench the fiery arrows of the evil one" (Laod 6:11, 16).[59]

The prophet of the god of generation, in order to kill as many as possible in battle, had the sun stand still that it might not go down until the adversaries of the people were utterly annihilated (Josh 10); but the Lord, since he is good, says, "Let not the sun set on your rage" (Laod 4:26).[60]

The prophet of the god of generation, when a battle commenced against his people, climbed to the top of a mountain and extended his hands to his god in order to slaughter masses of people in the battle (Exod. 17:8–9). But our Lord, since he is good, stretched out his hands [on the cross] not to slaughter humans but to save them.[61]

To understand these oppositions, one must examine their backstories. In an apparent attempt to protect their borders, the Amalekite nation drew up its battle lines against Israel (Exodus 17:8–15).[62] According to Exodus, over half a million armed Israelite men had recently marched from Egypt and were moving up toward the southern deserts of Israel. This was the homeland of the Amalekites, a people stemming from the grandson of Israel's brother Esau (Gen 36:12). According to this family tree, Amalekites and Israelites were cousins. Yet family ties could not prevent the clash of war.

Moses ordered his military lieutenant Joshua to choose his best troops to array themselves against the Amalekites. For his part, Moses climbed a nearby hill to oversee the battle. Whenever Moses lifted his hands, the Israelite

---

59. *Adamantius* 1.19 (816b.11–19)

60. *Adamantius* 1.13 (813a20–23):

61. *Adamantius* 1.11 (811b.24–29).

62. Philo wrote that the king of Amalek feared being pillaged by the incoming Israelites (πόρθησιν εὐλαβηθείς, *Life of Moses* 1.215).

troops savaged their enemies. But when his arms lowered in exhaustion, the Amalekites rallied. Realizing this, Moses's companions sat him down and supported each of his arms until the Israelites completely slaughtered, not just the Amalekite army, but also its civilian population with the edge of the sword.[63] The creator then sent Moses a dispatch that he would "utterly wipe out the memory of Amalek from under heaven."[64]

Yet it was the Israelites themselves who did the dirty work, for Moses later commanded them to "wipe out the name of Amalek from under heaven" with the heated warning, "Do not forget!" (Deut 25:19). This command," in the words of a modern interpreter, was meant "to return Amalek to a state of non-existence, i.e., Amalek is to be drummed out of the world order."[65]

What interested Marcion in this story was the contrast in divine character, a contrast he illustrated by a posture dear to Christians—the outstretched hands. In Marcion's day, Christian writers interpreted Moses's outstretched hands as a foreshadowing of Christ's arms extended on the cross.[66] For Christians, the open arms were a sign of sacrificial love and forgiveness. For Marcion, however, Moses's outstretched hands signaled the opposite—war, bloodlust, the slashing of swords, and the (attempted) annihilation of an entire people.

Such was the character of the creator, who held a grudge against Amalek not simply for four generations—but for centuries—secretly warring against them (Exod 17:16) until he could annihilate every man, woman, child—and animal. There was simply no similarity, for Marcionites, between the outstretched hands of Moses and Christ. "What is the likeness here?" cried the Marcionite in the *Adamantius*. "The one by stretching out his hands slaughters, while the other saves!"[67]

---

63. ἐτρέψατο Ἰησοῦς τὸν Αμαληκ *καὶ πάντα τὸν λαὸν αὐτοῦ ἐν φόνῳ μαχαίρας* (Exod 17:13, emphasis added) in John William Wevers, ed., *Exodus* (Göttingen: Vandenhoeck & Ruprecht, 1991), 220–222.

64. Ἀλοιφῇ ἐξαλείψω τὸ μνημόσυνον Ἀμαλῆκ ἐκ τῆς ὑπὸ τὸν οὐρανόν (Exod 17:14). See further Avi Sagi, "The Punishment of Amalek in Jewish Tradition: Coping with the Moral Problem," *Harvard Theological Review* 87, no. 3 (1994): 323–346; Louis H. Feldman, *"Remember Amalek!" Vengeance, Zealotry, and Group Destruction in the Bible according to Philo, Pseudo-Philo, and Josephus* (Cincinnati: Hebrew Union College Press, 2004), 19–21, 29–37.

65. Feldman, *"Remember Amalek!"* 10.

66. *Barn.* 12.2; Justin, *Dial.* 90.4; Irenaeus, *Haer.* 4.21.1; *Sib. Or.* 8.251–52.

67. *Adamantius* 1.11 (812b). See further Tsutsui, *Auseinandersetzung*, 161–162; Lieu, *Marcion*, 288–289.

Another antithesis refers to Joshua 10:1–15. In this scene, Moses had recently died. The Israelites invaded Canaan under Joshua's command. Their armies annihilated several towns west of the Jordan River, but one of the cities guilefully signed a peace treaty with Israel. A coalition of Canaanite kings then attacked that city. When Joshua's army came to its defense, his soldiers proceeded to slaughter their opponents to a man. Realizing that there was not enough time in the day to kill them all, Joshua commanded the sun to stand still to provide sufficient light to cut them down.

Marcion contrasted this halting of the sun—caused by none other than the creator—with the biblical saying not to let the sun set on one's rage. This particular directive comes from "the Lord" in a broad sense, since it is found in a Pauline letter (Laod 4:26). But Marcionites understood the Pauline Epistles as inspired by the true deity. The contrast highlighted a difference in character. The creator interfered with the physical laws of the universe to make time for Joshua to finish spilling human blood in the Judean hills. By contrast, the Lord known to Paul was not willing for his servants to stay angry overnight before reconciling. The creator, in support of a bloody battle, cut short the night; the true God commanded that anger cease before nightfall.

The final contrast quotes the book of Isaiah. In context, the prophet had just finished an oracle condemning Israelites for buying up too many properties, for being excessively drunk at parties, and for acquitting people who accepted bribes (Isa 5:8–23). He then launched this speech:

> The Lord of armies was enraged with wrath against his people; he pressed his hand against them and struck them. The mountains shuddered; their bodies became like dung on the street. Yet with all this, his anger did not abate, his hand remained high. And so, he will raise a signal to the nations far away and will whistle for them from the height of earth—swiftly they will come. They will not labor nor tire; they will not doze nor sleep; they will not loose their belts or untie their sandals—their arrows are sharp and their bows are taut. (Isa 5:25–28)

The *Antitheses* reads as if the creator spoke it in the first person: "*My* bows are taut and *my* arrows are sharpened." This may be a simple deduction: since it is the creator who organized the attack on his people, effectively he is the one who bent the bows and launched the arrows.

Yet Marcion may have blended in his memory of Deuteronomy 32:23, 42 where the creator said against his people, "I will gather evils against them and expend all my arrows against them . . . I will make my arrows drunk with blood." Whatever the case may be, the creator was ultimately responsible for declaring war against his own people. To Marcion, the creator seemed hostile, warlike, and unstable—traits indicating a malign character.

The contrast Marcion drew in this instance is unlike anything yet observed. It comes from a Pauline letter that invites Christians to don the armor of God. The armor is spiritual because, as the author points out, "our battle is not against flesh and blood but . . . against the spiritual forces of evil" (Laod 6:12). Thus the call to arms is not a call to literal war. It is a call for defense against spirit beings, and specifically against "all the fiery arrows of the evil one" (6:16). But the only arrows of which Isaiah 5:28 and Deuteronomy 32:23 speak are the arrows of the creator. The "arrows of the evil one" are in fact arrows of the creator. The creator, for Marcion, was evil.

This interpretation is daring, but not arbitrary. Even apart from the intertextual connections, the evil of the creator had already been established elsewhere in the "Old" Testament. Marcionites knew that the creator was a being who—using human armies to be sure—fought and killed his own people, leaving their bodies like dung on the streets. This is not the action of a good lord. The creator's abandonment and killing of his own people—though it might be "just" from the perspective of the scriptural author—is yet another example of his desire for vengeance and jealous hostility when his people fail. In Marcion's view, one could hardly force oneself to love this being. The only appropriate action was to take defensive measures against him in an attempt to quench the flames of his demon-like attack.

A Reconstruction of the Antitheses

Harnack wrote that Marcion's *Antitheses* could not be reconstructed because its arrangement is unknown.[68] Nevertheless, Tertullian gives a clue as to the structure of at least fourteen antitheses. What survives of the others can be placed after this material—though in no particular sequence. The introductory material—such as Marcion's hymnic opening and his reference to the corruption of his Gospel—logically occurred before the antitheses sketched by

68. Harnack, *Marcion*, 57. So also von Campenhausen, *Formation of the Christian Bible*, 161.

Tertullian. It also makes sense for Marcion to have begun his *Antitheses* with a critique of the initial chapters of Genesis. Tertullian began his sequenced critique of the *Antitheses* with the great flood, but Marcion also addressed what commonly goes under the name of the "fall narrative" (Gen 3).

The following reconstruction makes no claim to represent anything like Marcion's exact wording. It merely tries to remain faithful to the Marcionite critiques found in Tertullian and *Adamantius*. The reconstruction is presented less as a stable text than as a thought experiment, a way to exercise the imagination to give it a sense for the gist of Marcion's critiques. In the end, the sequencing and language of the material is the result of educated guesswork, and scholars will doubtless refine these results.[69]

Introduction

O wonder beyond wonders, rapture, power, and amazement, that one can say nothing at all about the Gospel, or even conceive of it, or compare it with anything!

But the defenders of Judaism have snuck in to corrupt the one Gospel, trying to unite it with the Law and Prophets to make a single body. From this union of Law and Gospel, they invent a fictional Christ.[70] Peter and the others from James did not walk uprightly according to the truth of the Gospel (Gal 2:14).[71] In their wake, certain false apostles perverted the Gospel of Christ, and these perverted Gospels are accredited with apostolic names.[72]

But we know that our Lord said, "A good tree cannot bear bad fruit, nor can a rotten tree bear healthy fruit" (G 6:43). The good Lord said, "One is

69. For a previous reconstruction of the *Antitheses*, see Augustus Hahn, *Antitheses Marcionis Gnostici* (Hartung: Regiomonti Boruss, 1823). Both Harnack and Hahn were agreed that the *Antitheses* was a long text filled with scholia-like comments on biblical passages. My reconstruction is much shorter than Hahn's, and focuses only on actual antitheses cited in Tertullian and *Adamantius*. Tsutsui (*Auseinandersetzung*, 148) finds seventeen antitheses in the *Adamantius*, but seven of these (40.12–16; 42.28–44.2; 46.1–11; 48.1–9; 50.9–14; 52.10–14; 64.28–66.2) are not true antitheses and thus I do not include them. Watson collected passages in Tertullian's *AM* that mention the *Antitheses* (*What is a Gospel?*, 205–213).

70. Tertullian, *AM* 4.4.3–4.

71. Tertullian, *AM* 1.20.3.

72. Tertullian, *AM* 4.3.2.

good, God, the Father" (G 18:19).[73] Yet the creator affirmed, "I am he who creates evils" (Isa 45:7) and "behold, I send evils against you" (Jer 18:11).

The Fall

The creator made the tree of the knowledge of good and evil and commanded Adam not to eat from it (Gen 2:17). The creator, well aware that the first humans were going to fall headlong, put them on the edge of a precipice.[74] And when humanity sinned, the creator became a judge, stern and savage. The female (Eve) is immediately condemned to bear children in sorrow and to be in service to her husband (Gen 3:16). Previously she had heard of the increase of humankind without sadness, in the words of the blessing, "Increase and multiply" (Gen 1:28). She had been intended to help the man (Gen 2:18), not for servitude.

Straightaway the earth also is cursed (Gen 3:17–18), which had previously been blessed; straightaway there are thorns and thistles where before there had been grass, when it was fertile with herbs and trees. Immediately there is sweat and toil for bread (Gen 3:19), though before, from every tree there was livelihood without stint and food in sure supply. From that point on, humanity is bent down toward the earth, who before was taken from earth (Gen 2:7). From that point on, humanity is turned toward death, though previously toward life. From that point, they are in coats of skin, who before were naked and unashamed (Gen 2:25).

Flood, Fire, Plague

The wickedness of the old world was unjustly smitten by a flood and afterwards by fire (Gen 6, 18). It was unjust that Egypt should be struck with tenfold chastisement, since the creator hardened Pharoah's heart (Exod 10:1).[75]

She-bears

The creator unleashed bears from the thicket to devour little children and avenge Elisha the prophet for the mockery he had suffered from them

73. Tertullian, *AM* 1.17.4; 1.27.5; 2.12.3.

74. Tertullian, *AM* 4.38.1.

75. Tertullian, *AM* 2.14.4.

(2 Kgdms 2:23–25), but the good Lord says, "Let the little children come to me, for of such is the kingdom of heaven!" (G 18:16), and he teaches that all who ever wish to be greater must be like children (G 9:46–48).

Lex talionis

Moses says in the Law, "An eye for an eye, a tooth for a tooth" (Deut 19:21), but the Lord, because he is good, says in the Gospel, "If anyone slaps you on the cheek, turn the other one to him" (G 6:29).[76] In the Law it says, "garment for garment," but the good Lord says, "If someone takes your garment, given to him your undershirt as well" (G 6:29).[77] The one in the Law ordered love for the friend and hatred for the enemy, while the Good bids us to love even enemies.[78]

Food Laws

The creator takes away foods and pronounces animals unclean, the very animals he elsewhere blessed (Gen 1:22, 25).[79]

Sacrificial System

The creator commanded burdensome sacrifices, annoying, meticulous procedures and oblations as though he personally desired such things for himself. At the same time, he claimed, "What use to me is the multitude of your sacrifices . . . Who required these from your hands?" (Isa 1:11–12).[80] The Law has made all manner of regulations up to and including the care of cups and plates, so that men faced at every point with these legal teachings might never

---

76. *Adamantius* 1.15 (814a.3–6). Cf. Tertullian, *AM* 2.18.1; 4.16.4–6; Origen, *Cels.* 7.25.

77. *Adamantius* 1.18 (815e.1–3). The Law never says, "garment for garment." Perhaps this is a later expansion of the antithesis by someone who understood "garment for garment" as part of the creator's general principle of retaliation. Cf. Origen, *Cels.* 7.25; Tertullian, *AM* 2.18; 4.16.6; Theodoret, *Fab.* 1.22.1.

78. Theodoret, *Fab.* 1.22.1.

79. Tertullian, *AM* 2.18.2.

80. Tertullian, *AM* 2.18.3.

for an instant be occupied with the thought of God.[81] But God said, "I will not drink the blood of bulls" (Ps 50:13) and "the eternal God neither hungers nor thirsts" (Isa 40:28). Yet the creator inclined to the sacrifices of Abel and greedily smelled Noah's whole burnt offering (Gen 4:4; 8:20–21). What pleasure is there either in sheep intestines or the stench of burning victims? "To what purpose is the multitude of your services to me? I am weary of . . . your solemnities, festal days, and sabbaths" (Isa 1:11, 14).[82]

Despoliation of Egypt

The creator ordered Moses as he left the land of Egypt, saying, "Be prepared! Have your loins girded, your sandals tied, your staffs in your hands and your wallets attached. Cart off from the Egyptians gold and silver vessels and clothes" (Exod 12:34–36). But our Lord, who is good, when he sent out his disciples into the world, says, "Don't have shoes on your feet, nor wallets, nor staffs, nor two shirts, nor cheap coins in your belts" (G 9:1–3).[83]

Sabbath Breach at Jericho

The creator forbids labor on Sabbath days and yet at the storming of the city of Jericho he commands the ark to be carried round during eight days which includes the Sabbath.[84]

Bronze Serpent

The creator forbids the making of the likeness of anything in heaven and on earth and in the waters, saying, "You shall not worship nor serve them" (Exod 20:5). But the image of the bronze serpent that this lord afterwards commanded Moses to make (Num 21:8–9), was an instance of idolatry.[85]

81. Tertullian, *AM* 2.19.1.

82. Tertullian, *AM* 2.22.2–4.

83. *Adamantius* 1.10. Cf. Tertullian, *AM* 4.24.2.

84. Tertullian, *AM* 2.21.1.

85. Tertullian, *AM* 2.22.1.

"I will smite, he says, and I will heal; I will slay, he says, and also make alive, by establishing evil things and making peace" (Deut 32:39; Isa 45:7). He is fickle and inconstant, in forbidding what he commands and commanding what he forbids.[86]

Rejection of Saul

The creator is capricious concerning persons as well as institutions, when he expresses disapproval of men previously approved of, or when he lacks foresight in approving men who afterward meet with his disapproval. Here he either reverses his previous judgments or is ignorant of those he will afterward make. Saul, for instance, is promoted, but the creator says, "I regret that I have made Saul king" (1 Kgdms 15:11). Solomon is rejected when he is in bondage to foreign wives and in subjection to the idols of the Moabites and Sidonians.[87] And the creator admits error in respect of the Ninevites, for Jonah says, "God repented of the evil which he said he would do to them, and he did not do it" (Jonah 3:10).[88]

Adam Unfound

The creator did not know the location of Adam, saying, "Where are you?" (Gen 3:9). And when Adam says he hid out of shame for his nakedness, the creator asks whether it was because he had eaten from the tree—as though he had doubt about it.[89] By contrast, Christ knew the inner thoughts of human beings (G 6:8).[90]

The creator demands of Cain where his brother is, as though he had not already heard the voice of Abel's blood crying from the ground (Gen 4:10).

86. Tertullian, *AM* 4.1.10. In context, Tertullian twice uses the term *antithesis*, disclosing his source.

87. Tertullian, *AM* 2.23.1–2.

88. Tertullian, *AM* 2.24.1–2.

89. Tertullian, *AM* 2.25.1.

90. *Adamantius* 1.17 (815c.13–14); cf. Tertullian, *AM* 4.20.8.

The creator cursed Cain; and even though Cain wanted to cleanse his sin by death, for a time the creator refused to let him die (Gen 4:11–15).[91]

Descending to Sodom

The creator descended to Sodom and Gomorrah, saying, "I will see if they are performing in accordance with the outcry reaching me, and if not, I will know" (Gen 18:21). Do you see how from ignorance he is in doubt and wanting to know?[92] Do you see how the god of the Law did not know what happened in Sodom unless he descended to see and sent those to learn?[93]

Self-swearing

The creator pointlessly and falsely swears by himself (Isa 45:23). What else could he imagine doing, when he was unaware of the existence of any other God, and in fact was then and there taking a lying oath that besides him there is no other God at all?[94]

Threatened Destruction of Israel

This "god" proved quite petty in his fierce anger when in his wrath against Israel because of the consecration of the calf, he demanded of his slave Moses, "Leave me alone, and I, with extreme rage, will destroy them and make you into a great nation" (Exod 32:10). Here Moses was a better person than his own "god"—praying to soothe and even forbid his wrath, for he says, "Do not do this, or else, destroy me with them" (Exod 32:32).[95]

Healing Lepers

Out of all the many lepers in Israel, Elisha, prophet of the creator, cleansed only one, Naaman the Syrian. Christ, by contrast, healed an Israelite (G 5:13)

91. Tertullian, *AM* 2.25.3, 5.

92. Tertullian, *AM* 2.25.6.

93. Origen, *Hom* 4.6 on Genesis 18:21 (*ecce nesciebat deus legis, quid ageretur in Sodomis, nisi descendisset, ut videret, et misisset, qui discerent*).

94. Tertullian, *AM* 2.26.1.

95. Tertullian, *AM* 2.27.3. The sequence of the following antitheses is uncertain.

whom the creator had not been willing to heal. Elisha needed to use material water for healing, and it had to be applied seven times (4 Kgdms 5:10). Christ, however, healed by means of a single, simple word, and it was done at once. Elisha healed only one leper, but Christ healed ten by means of his silent power, by word alone (G 17:14).[96]

Healing the Blind and Deaf

The creator did not restore the sight of Isaac suffering from cataracts (Gen 27:1), but our Lord, because he is good, opened the eyes of many blind people (G 7:22).[97] David struck the blind and the lame with daggers when he attacked Jerusalem (2 Kgdms 5:6–8), but Christ healed the blind man who called him "son of David" (G 18:35–43).[98]

The creator said, "with the ear you shall hear, and shall not hear" (Isa 6:9), but Christ insisted, "the one who has ears, hear!" (e.g., G 8:8). Christ was giving back the hearing that the creator had taken away.[99]

Fire Sent Down

At the request of Elijah, the creator sent a burst of fire to destroy one hundred men (4 Kgdms 1:9–13), but Christ rebuked his disciples for even requesting to send down fire upon the Samarians (G 9:54–55). Note the judge's sternness, and contrast Christ's gentleness when reproving the disciples as they call for the same punishment.[100]

Tax Collectors

The creator rejects tax collectors as outside the Law and unclean; but Christ, as one hostile to the Law, chose a tax collector to be his disciple (G 5:27).[101]

96. Here adapting language from Harnack, *Marcion*, 61.

97. *Adamantius* 1.20 (816c.1–3). Harnack attributed this line to the *Antitheses* (*Marcion*, 89–92; further sources in *Marcion* 266*–296*).

98. Tertullian, *AM* 4.36.13.

99. Tertullian, *AM* 4.19.2.

100. Tertullian, *AM* 4.23.8.

101. Tertullian, *AM* 4.11.1.

The Hemorrhaging Woman

The Law forbids touching a woman who has an issue of blood (Lev 15:19); Christ not only permitted himself to be touched by such a woman, but healed her as well (G 8:43–48).[102]

Ruler and Judge

Moses intervened in the dispute of the brothers without being invited and rebuked the offender: "Why are you striking your neighbor?" This man castigated Moses, "Who made you master or judge over us?" (Exod 2:14). Christ, however, when a man demanded that he arbitrate a dispute with his brother over an inheritance, refused to take part, saying, "Who made me a judge over you?" (G 12:13).[103]

Divorce

Christ forbids divorce: "The man divorcing his wife and marrying another commits adultery, and likewise the one who marries the divorced woman is an adulterer" (G 16:18). Moses, however, permits divorce: "If any man takes a wife and lives with her and it happens that she finds no favor with him because something inappropriate has been found in her, he will write a bill of divorce, give it into her hand and send her away from his house" (Deut 24:1). Notice the contrast between Law and Gospel, between Moses and Christ.[104]

Stopping the Sun

The prophet of the creator, in order to kill as many as possible in battle, had the sun stand still that it might not go down until the adversaries of the people were utterly annihilated (Josh 10); but the Lord, since he is good, says, "Let not the sun set on your rage" (Laod 4:26).[105]

---

102. Tertullian, *AM* 4.20.9.

103. Here I take language from Harnack, *Marcion*, 60.

104. Tertullian, *AM* 4.34.1–2. cf. 5.7.6: *Christus vetat divortium, Moyses vero permittet.*

105. *Adamantius* 1.13 (813a20–23).

Sharpened Arrows

The prophet of the creator says, "My bows are taut and my arrows are sharpened" (Isa 5:28; Deut 32:23), but the apostle says, "Put on the full armor of God, that you may be able to quench the fiery arrows of the evil one" (Laod 6:11, 16).[106]

Extended hands

The prophet of the creator, when a battle commenced against his people, climbed to the top of a mountain and extended his hands to his god in order to slaughter masses of people in the battle (Exod. 17:8–9). But our Lord, since he is good, stretched out his hands [on the cross] not to slaughter human beings but to save.[107]

Peroration

Oh worthless lord, unstable, unfaithful, withdrawing that which he established![108] His old and decrepit deeds are accounted as foolishness, weakness, dishonor, pettiness, and contempt. What is more foolish, what more weak, than the creator's demand of bloody sacrifices and the stench of whole burnt offerings? What is weaker than the cleansing of dishes and beds? What more ignoble than the further dishonor of the flesh that is already ashamed?[109] What more pathetic than the demand of eye for eye? What more contemptible than the excluding of foods?[110]

This being is not the Father of Jesus Christ.

---

106. *Adamantius* 1.19 (816b.11–19).

107. *Adamantius* 1.11 (811b.24–29).

108. Tertullian, *AM* 2.7.3.

109. Here an apparent reference to circumcision.

110. Tertullian, *AM* 5.5.9–10.

CHAPTER SEVEN

Marcion, Judaism, and Jewish Scripture

Marcion shared the Jewish view that Old Testament texts belonged to Judaism, not to Christianity.

—John Barton, "Marcion Revisited"

AFTER READING THE *Antitheses*, one might get the impression that Marcion's hostility toward the Judean lord meant enmity toward the Jewish people. But such is not necessarily the case. In fact, Marcion's enemy Tertullian accused the Pontian of aligning himself with Jewish thought and interpretation since Marcion believed in the coming of a Jewish political messiah and interpreted Jewish prophecies in a literal way.[1] Indeed, it was because of this accusation that Harnack proposed that Marcion was himself born Jewish or had at one time become a Jewish proselyte.[2]

Marcion the Jew?

Marcion's interpretation of the Jewish messiah may indeed have been influenced by Jewish interpretations. His approach is significant, because no other Christian of the time was willing to concede that the Jewish concept of their own messiah was even remotely correct. Christian writers typically claimed that the Jews were wrong about how they envisioned their messiah, and thus they failed to recognize Jesus. At the same time, Marcion's acceptance of an

1. Tertullian, *AM* 3.7.1; 3.6.1–4; 3.8.1.

2. Harnack, *Marcion*, 15; cf. Hoffmann, *Marcion*, 29; Hoffmann, "How Then Know," 181; Markus Vinzent "Marcion the Jew," *Judaïsme ancien* 1 (2013): 186, 190. Earlier Vinzent wrote that Marcion "was already so far removed from Jews and Jewish Christians that he did not notice how many Rabbinic ideas he absorbed by reading Paul" (*Christ's Resurrection*, 180).

independent Jewish messiah is not a strong reason for thinking that Marcion was himself Jewish or a one-time convert to Judaism.

Nor is it safe to say that Marcion had a "double Christology": two Christ's affording two paths of salvation for Jews and gentiles.[3] The separate Jewish messiah, according to Marcion, will come, and he will regather the Jews from their dispersion and bestow on them the promised kingdom—but this is not equivalent to salvation.[4] The Jewish kingdom is earthly and temporary, as is the coming Jewish messiah. Marcion evidently called this figure a messiah, but he was not the true Christ who brings permanent, celestial salvation to all who believe.

As is evident from the *Antitheses*, Marcion knew the Hebrew scriptures well. He read a range of Jewish sacred literature, and he had an eye for detail. In itself, this is not evidence that Marcion was raised a Jew, or that he turned against his pious "Jewish" way of reading scripture when he became a Christian. Marcion's way of reading the Jewish Bible was not against Jews per se, but against their lord.

The Pontian was not the creator of a new religion called Christianity, a system separate from the practices and institutions of Judaism. The distinct religious movement called "Christianity" already existed and is attested in early second-century documents like the Ignatian epistles, the apologist Aristides, the *Preaching of Peter*, and the *Epistle to Diognetus*. Marcion lived in an era and in an area in which many devotees of Jesus already felt that they needed to disassociate from the practice of Judaism for both theological and political reasons.

In the early 130s CE, Jewish radicals tried to free Palestine from Roman domination. Rome lost many soldiers and expended great resources to put down the Bar Kokhba revolt.[5] In the 140s and 150s, the Jewish people were still recovering their reputation in the eyes of Rome. Judaism may have been seen as an old and venerable religion at the time, but these sentiments were mitigated by the persistent view that Jews were impious and rebellious.[6]

3. *Pace* John W. Marshall, "Misunderstanding the New Paul: Marcion's Transformation of the *Sonderzeit* Paul," *Journal of Early Christian Studies* 20, no. 1 (2012): 28–29.

4. Tertullian, *AM* 3.21.1; 4.6.3.

5. Martin Goodman, *Rome and Jerusalem: The Clash of Ancient Civilizations* (New York: Vintage, 2008), 465

6. Origen, *Cels.* 8.69. See further Goodman, *Rome and Jerusalem*, 469–477.

During this time, it was still felt to be socially advantageous for Christians to disassociate themselves from Jewish synagogues, Jewish rites like Sabbath and circumcision, and distinctively Jewish scriptures.[7] Of course, gentile Christians never managed to completely divorce themselves from Jewish traditions—and practically, they *could* not. Their religion had grown out of a larger Jewish matrix, and both Jesus and Paul were Jewish. Christians, whether or not they were aware of it, continued in the traditions of Jewish theology, liturgy, and scriptural interpretation even if they renounced Judaism and "Judaizing" movements.

Marcion was one of these Christians. He was not, it seems, anti-Jewish—at least not any more than other gentile Christians of his time. He did not remove all things Jewish from his Bible (chapter 3). At the same time, he understood that his mode of worship, the "new covenant" based on trust and love, had moved away from the practice and traditions of Torah, and that anyone trying to tie salvation to the practice of Judaism was misled.

In this regard, Marcion probably viewed himself as continuing the mission of Paul, and specifically his legacy of opposing "false brethren," namely false "Judaic" (but mostly gentile) leaders who were bent on making Christianity a sort of second ("true") phase of Judaism overly dependent on Jewish cultural traditions and texts.

Marcion and the Hebrew Scriptures

Marcion considered his canon to be the new bottle for the new wine of Christ's truth. One does not use old bottles (the books of the "Old" Testament) for the sweet wine of Christ's new revelation. Accordingly, in Marcion's liturgy, the Law and Prophets were not read. The Pontian replaced the liturgical reading of Jewish scripture with the reading of his own distinctly Christian scriptures (Gospel and Apostolikon). This was a daring step. Even if before Marcion a number of gentile Christians disregarded certain precepts from Jewish Law, no Christian had replaced Christian scriptures with distinctly Christian books as the only normative documents of Christianity, the sole basis for doctrine and preaching.[8]

---

7. Goodman, *Rome and Jerusalem*, 505–506.

8. Here I adapt the language of Vinzent, *Christ's Resurrection*, 81.

Marcion did not reject Jewish scripture as such.[9] He rejected it *as Christian scripture*. As it stood, however, the Jewish Bible had much to reveal about the Judean lord, the history of Israel, and, to a certain extent, the history of humankind. Far from showing a "lack of interest in the Jewish Scriptures,"[10] Marcion made full use of them as historical and theological documents.

One should thus question Tertullian's gloss on Evangelion 9:35. In this scene, Jesus is transfigured and speaks with Moses and Elijah in glory. Peter suggests the construction of three tents, but he is humbled by a booming voice. Tertullian writes, "Evidently that voice from heaven wanted this to be understood, 'This is my beloved son, listen to him'—that is, not any longer to Moses and Elijah."[11] Tertullian's comment is not necessarily a quotation from Marcion, representing "Marcion's interpretation" of Evangelion 9:35.[12] The interpretation is entangled and possibly even confused with Tertullian's own views. It is actually Tertullian who affirms that Christians need not listen to Moses and Elijah.[13] By contrast, Marcion's Evangelion 16:29 recommends (in the voice of Abraham) that people listen to Moses and the prophets.[14] Moreover, Jesus in Gospel 18:20 quotes commands written by Moses—which assumes that, to some extent, even Jesus continued to listen to Moses. Accordingly, Marcion did not necessarily reject or denigrate Moses and Elijah.[15] If Marcion thought that Jesus superseded Moses and Elijah, he did not deem them "irrelevant."[16]

---

9. *Pace* Barton, *Holy Writings*, 42 ("Marcion of course rejected the Old Testament"). Barton (*Holy Writings*, 40) refers to "the wholesale deletion of the Old Testament." Heikki Räisänen writes, "Marcion completely rejected the Old Testament" ("Marcion" in *A Companion to Second-century Christian "Heretics"*, ed. Antti Marjanen and Petri Luomanen, VCSup 76 [Leiden: Brill, 2005], 100–124 at 113).

10. Gerard Luttikhuizen, *Gnostic Revisions of Genesis Stories and Early Jesus Traditions* (Leiden: Brill, 2006), 24.

11. Tertullian, *AM* 4.22.1.

12. *Pace* Dieter Roth, "Transfiguring the Transfiguration: Reading Luke 9:35 *Adversus Marcionem*," *Catholic Biblical Quarterly* 85, no. 4 (2023): 722–736 at 724.

13. Roth, "Transfiguring the Transfiguration," 726–727.

14. Roth, "Transfiguring the Transfiguration," 725.

15. *Pace* Roth, "Transfiguring the Transfiguration," 727, 732.

16. Roth, "Transfiguring the Transfiguration," 734.

Marcion's intense usage of the Jewish Bible and his reuse of prophetic characters belies the claim that he "obviously hated the Old Testament."[17] The Pontian could not have hated the Old Testament if his Bible said, "the Law is holy and the commandment holy, just, and good" (Rom 7:12). He may have despised the creator, but the creator's scriptures were both profitable and useful for his enterprise. Marcion used Jewish scripture to show how it contradicted the revelation in Christ.[18] Only by contrasting the God revealed in Christ did the evil of the creator become manifest.[19]

If Marcion used Jewish scriptures as evidentiary authority, he must have considered them accurate on some level. He treated them as useful and relevant for Christian faith.[20] They were still relevant because they helped Marcion negatively define Christian faith, to show what it was not. It was not reverence for the Judean lord, the acceptance of violence, or the practice of Jewish rites. The Hebrew scriptures were important as a counterpoint, a foil to Christian faith.[21] In contrast with the lower creator, Marcion revealed a God who was truly good. By contrast with the Jewish messiah, Marcion sketched the contours of his Christ, a heavenly prince of peace.

Marcion's Bible was not meant to supplement the Jewish Bible, but to replace it as Christian scripture. One could say that Marcion's canon helped to create the "Old" Testament as a Christian concept: a discrete set of Jewish books that speak of the creator, which are chronologically older than the distinctly Christian revelation. But using the phrase "Old" Testament, already takes an early catholic perspective, for it was early catholics who wanted to preserve the Hebrew scriptures as part of their two-part Bible: an "Old" Testament foreshadowing a "New" one.

Marcion probably did not refer to an "Old" Testament. He had no reason to deny that the creator had made a covenant with the Jews and had inspired some of their writings. But since the creator was not the true God, this covenant or testament was not binding or authoritative for Christians. The inspired

17. Dungan, "Reactionary Trends," 186.

18. Lieu, *Marcion*, 357; Litwa, *Evil Creator*, 67–89.

19. *Pace* Moll, *Arch-heretic*, 58, cf. 82, 106.

20. Joseph B. Tyson, "Anti-Judaism in Marcion and His Opponents," *Studies in Christian-Jewish Relations* 1 (2005–2006), 196–208 at 202, 207.

21. Gerhard May, "Marcions Genesisauslegung," *Vigiliae Christianae* 24 (1970): 89–98.

writings of the Jews were important and influential. They did not, however, have authority for Christians, because their inspiration was not from God.

Revising Misconceptions

It is mistaken to think that Marcion's "primary concern was to eliminate Jewish influences in the churches, including their first scriptures and references to the God of the Jews."[22] In his *Antitheses*, Marcion highlighted Jewish scripture and the character of the creator in order to contrast his own views and to shape his particular brand of Christian faith. Without Jewish scripture, there would have been no Marcionite difference.

It has been argued that "Marcion's primary aim was the separation of Christian tradition from its Jewish heritage and its origin in Judaism."[23] There is a half-truth lurking here, but one must search for a fairer formulation. It is an important question whether Marcion himself considered Judaism to be the "heritage" of Christianity. Modern people see clearly that the earliest Christian leaders, including Jesus and Paul, were all Jewish and practiced Judaism to varying degrees. Practically, then, the Pontian *could* not have entirely separated Christian tradition from its origin in Judaism. Nor did he aim to do so in any systematic sense; hence the fact that so many Jewish characters, quotations, and stories appear in his scriptures (chapter 3).

Harnack called Marcion, "the great enemy of the Jews."[24] Nevertheless, the Pontian's rejection of the Jewish Bible as Christian scripture did not mean that he hated "Jews and everything Jewish"; nor did he establish "an anti-Jewish religion."[25] Even more extreme—and false—are claims that "Marcion removed all Jewish elements from the Christian religion," that he preached a "hate-filled message," and that he had an "anti-Jewish agenda."[26] Such views,

22. McDonald, *Before There Was a Bible*, 49.

23. McDonald, *Before There Was a Bible*, 50.

24. Harnack, "Die Neuheit des Evangeliums nach Marcion," *Aus der Werkstatt des Vollendeten*, ed. Axel von Harnack (Giessen: Topelmann, 1930), 136 (*Marcion, der große Feind der Juden*).

25. Ehrman, *Lost Christianities*, 111.

26. Dungan, *History of the Synoptic Problem*, 48, 56–57.

in addition to being wrong, attribute too much power to Marcion by making him the founder of an alternative religion.

Marcion did not actively strive against the Jewish people. His battle was against Judaizing Christians, most of whom were ethnically gentile.[27] The Pontian did not attack the Jews in any surviving report; rather, he attacked their lord. One could infer that an attack on the Judean lord was an attack on the Jews themselves. But this would be a poor inference. A better one might be that Marcion's attack on the Judean lord implied an attack on Judaism. That may well be; but being anti-Judaism—as virtually all early catholic writers were—was not the same as being anti-Jewish.[28] Given surviving evidence, one cannot determine Marcion's attitude toward flesh-and-blood Jews. Recall that Tertullian considered Marcion to be allied with Jews and Jewish interpretation. If Tertullian knew that Marcion actually hated Jews, he would not have been able to make this argument.

If Marcion was not anti-Jewish, he was not pro-Jewish either. His Bible contained comments that the Law and the Prophets had ceased (G 16:16), and that the Jews had killed "the lord" (1 Thess 2:15), meaning Jesus. Marcion's own interpretation of Jesus's death blamed the creator more than the Jews.[29] At the same time, he probably did not intend entirely to exculpate the Jews. He simply did not focus the blame on them (contrast Matt 27:25: "His blood be on us and on our children").

Thus to try and distinguish between Marcion's "alter-Judaism" and broader catholic "anti-Judaism" may not, in the end, satisfy.[30] Marcion adopted the supercessionism of his Christian colleagues: the worship of Christ was better than the piety practiced in the synagogues. Gentiles, if they wished to be saved, ought not to practice Jewish rites. In these respects, Marcion was in full agreement with early catholics.

---

27. S. G. Wilson "Marcion and the Jews," in *Anti-Judaism in Early Christianity*, vol. 2, *Separation and Polemic* (Waterloo, ON: Wilfrid Laurier University Press, 1986), 45–46.

28. Wilson, "Marcion and the Jews," 52–53. Ulrike Margarethe Salome Röhl writes that to Marcion "both the Old Testament and also the Jews appeared as evil" (*erscheinen ihm sowohl das Alte Testament als auch die Juden als böse*) (*Der Paulusschüler Markion: Eine kritische Untersuchung zum Antijudaismus im 2.Jahrhundert* [Marburg: Tectum, 2014]), 421).

29. Litwa, *Evil Creator*, 122–156.

30. *Pace* Vinzent, "Marcion the Jew," 189.

In other respects, the Pontian diverged from catholic anti-Judaism. Tertullian, for instance, understands Galatians as the primary epistle against Judaism, but that's not Marcion's view.[31] Marcion was evidently happy to let Jews practice their religion. They were apparently right to await their own messiah because it was to their own political advantage. Tertullian assumes that Marcion's Paul was the "destroyer of Judaism."[32] But this is wrong. Marcion's Paul went beyond Judaism, with no need to destroy it. Paul could still be a Jew to Jews, and Jesus could still conceivably be a good Jew even if he violated Torah. It is thus incorrect to state that Marcion's theology rejects "Israel's covenantal relationship with the God of Abraham." The covenant of the creator with the Jews is not undermined by Marcion's theology, at least not explicitly.[33]

Marcion's position on Jewish scripture is arguably less anti-Jewish than the developing catholic position of his time. Addressing a Jew in his *Dialogue with Trypho*, Justin wrote that "your [Jewish] scriptures are rather not yours, but ours. For we believe and obey them, whereas you, though you read them, do not grasp their spirit."[34] Marcion, by contrast, did not try to wrest the Jewish scriptures away from the Jews or to deny all aspects of Jewish interpretation. He felt no need to engage in open conflict or hermeneutical wrangling with the Jews. His work, the *Antitheses*, was directed at Christians. Marcion let Jews interpret their own scriptures, and he may well have adopted their perspective and employed their interpretive techniques. By contrast, Justin's typological—or broadly allegorical—style of reading was weaponized against Jews, and implicitly against Marcion himself.[35]

Early catholic typological reading is not innocent. In terms of its sociopolitical effect, it is a form of cultural appropriation. It adapted the laws and stories of Judaism and made them into signs and symbols of Christianity and

---

31. Tertullian, *AM* 5.2.1.

32. Tertullian, *AM* 5.5.1.

33. Richard Hays, *Echoes of Scripture in the Gospels* (Waco: Baylor Univeristy Press, 2016), 362.

34. Justin, *Dial.* 29.2.

35. Charles H. Cosgrove, "Justin Martyr and the Emerging Christian Canon: Observations on the Purpose and destination of the Dialogue with Trypho," *Vigiliae Christianae* 36, no. 3 (1982): 220. Matthijs den Dulk, *Between Jews and Heretics: Refiguring Justin Martyr's Dialogue with Trypho* (London: Routledge, 2018), 52–144.

the catholic messiah. In Marcion's day, early catholic allegorical reading was just beginning to flex its muscles. Eventually, however, it would become the dominant, "Christian" way of reading Jewish scripture, with some frankly troubling consequences.

In sum, Marcion allowed the Jews the keep their god, their scriptures, their messiah, and their Law. Like many Christians, he considered these beings and benefits to be superseded by the gospel. Yet early catholics said, "We'll take your God, your messiah, your Scriptures, and some of your law; as for you, you are disinherited, cast into a limbo, and your survival serves only as a warning of the consequences of obdurate wickedness."[36] If Marcionites were supersessionists, early catholics were super-supersessionists because they also avidly appropriated the Jewish religious heritage. A key tool of appropriation was allegory.

Marcion on Allegory

The word "allegory" comes from a combination of Greek words that literally mean "to speak something else." To read a text allegorically means to read a text as saying something different from what is usually taken to be its plain or historical meaning. In antiquity, allegorical reading was often a subset of apologetical reading. Hellenic scholars allegorized the poets Homer and Hesiod, for instance, to defend Homer against literal readings of his poetry, which shamed the gods or supported immoral actions. The options were stark: either the poets spoke allegorically, or they were blasphemers against the gods, involving them in adultery, bloodlust, greed, spite, and other vices.[37]

Harnack believed that Marcion rejected the allegorical method as such.[38] But this view is unlikely, because Paul himself used allegory in Galatians 4:21–31 (Hagar and Sarah as representing two covenants and two Jerusalems) and in 1 Corinthians 9:9–10 (treating oxen as symbols of human laborers deserving a wage). Marcion also used a form of allegory, likening the creator

36. Wilson, "Marcion and the Jews," 58. See further Wolfgang A. Bienert, "Marcion und der Antijudaismus," in May and Greschat, *Marcion und seine kirchengeschichtliche Wirkung*, 191–206.

37. Heraclitus, *Homeric Problems*, trans. D. A. Russell and David Konstan (Atlanta: SBL Press, 2005), 3 (§1.1).

38. Harnack, *Marcion*, 59, cf. 154n26; cf. Barton, *Holy Writings*, 41, 53.

to a bad tree (G 6:43) and the Gospel to new wine (G 5:36).[39] The Pontian was probably like most ancient interpreters in that he was prepared to use allegory to defend his own views, but renounced allegory when criticizing the views of others.[40] In his *Antitheses*, Marcion used literal readings of Jewish scriptures as the tool of choice, fit for a critique. But literal interpretation was not his only principle of interpretation fit for all situations.[41]

* * *

In sum, Marcion was an enemy to the Judean lord, but not of the Jews themselves. Marcion's views imply anti-Judaism, but in this respect he was no different from early catholics, who were arguably more anti-Jewish than Marcion, since they felt the need to claim ownership of the Jewish scriptures. Marcion's own stance toward Jewish scripture may have been informed by Jewish interpretations. He felt no need to appropriate Jewish signs and symbols for Christianity. By rejecting the Jewish Bible as Christian scripture, the Pontian helped Christians, at least in his group, take one more step in the long and tangled process of separating Jewish and Christian theology and modes of worship. But Marcion never explicitly aimed to reject Christianity's Jewish heritage, nor did he have the power to deny it. His own Bible disproves it.

If Marcionite Christianity had triumphed, Christian history might well have been considerably less violent against Jews. There's something called "the narcissism of small differences": religious people who quarrel the most are the ones most like each other.[42] If Christians had given up the idea of appropriating the Jewish religious heritage (embodied in the Jewish scriptures), they would have probably felt less threatened by Jews themselves and the continuing practice of Judaism in Europe and elsewhere. In the end, one will never know how history might have been, even if it is useful to imagine it.

39. Dungan, "Reactionary Trends," 187.

40. Cf. Origen, *Cels.* 4.48; 6.29.

41. Dungan, "Reactionary Trends," 198; cf. Gager, "Marcion and Philosophy," 58; Schmid, 255–260.

42. J. Z. Smith, "What a Difference a Difference Makes," in *Relating Religion: Essays in the Study of Religion* (Chicago: Chicago University Press, 2004), 251–302.

CHAPTER EIGHT

Marcion's View of Church History

> From the time of Constantine church discipline declines; the whole Roman world having become nominally Christian, and the host of hypocritical professors multiplying beyond all control.
>
> —Philip Schaff, *History of the Christian Church*, vol. 3

MARCION BELIEVED THAT the church had fallen. Later Christians would date the church's fall to the reign of Constantine or to the time of the medieval popes. Marcion dated the church's fall to the time of the apostles. The Pontian probably had no other source for his fall narrative than his Gospel and Apostolikon. He shows no knowledge of Acts; and even if he knew it, he would not have believed it. Paul's ten authentic letters were enough for him to tell a convincing story.

Marcion's Apostolikon spoke of false brothers and false apostles, wolves in sheep's clothing devouring the sheep. "There are certain people who are disturbing you and wishing to change" the Gospel "into a different Gospel of Christ" (Gal 1:7). In a meeting at Jerusalem, "false brothers" crept in "to spy upon our freedom which we have in Christ" (2:4). In another letter, Paul refers to "false apostles," and "deceitful workers" who infiltrated the assembly (2 Cor 11:13).[1] These false brothers or apostles were apparently widespread, and Paul confronted them, clarifying that, "even if we or an angel from heaven were to proclaim to you (something) else than what we have proclaimed to you, may that one be damned!" (Gal 1:8).

According to Galatians 2:12–14, some of Jesus's original apostles themselves did not "walk correctly in the truth of the Gospel." Peter, who used to eat with non-Jews, withdrew to eat kosher meals with Jews "in fear of those

1. Lieu, *Marcion*, 245.

from the circumcision party." This was not just a matter of misguided practice; the misguided practice arose out of a more fundamental misunderstanding of Gospel "truth."[2] And Peter was not the only one to blame; the other apostolic "pillars"—James and John—were implicated in Peter's error.[3]

At the same time, Paul did not accuse the pillars of distorting his *written* Gospel, and neither, on present evidence, did Marcion. Tertullian put it this way: Marcion "castigates even the apostles themselves . . . and simultaneously (*simul et*) accuses certain false apostles." The *simul et* is easily missed, but it indicates two distinct groups: apostles and false apostles.[4] It may be true that the original apostles (the Eleven) did not understand Jesus's message until he clarified it after the resurrection (G 24:25–26).[5] It would go beyond the evidence to claim that they *never* came to understand it. Presumably Jesus would not have told the apostles to preach the gospel to the world if he knew they still misunderstood it and always would (24:47).

When reading the heresiologists, one could easily get the impression that Marcion attacked Peter, James, and John as false apostles who distorted the Scriptures. Irenaeus, for instance, claims that Marcionites maintain "that the apostles intermingled the things of the Law with the words of the Savior."[6] But he never names *these* apostles as Matthew or John, for instance. It is thus precipitous to claim that Marcion considered Peter and the (reconstituted) Twelve to be "false apostles" if by that one supposes that they corrupted scripture.[7]

Marcion did not accuse James and Peter of perverting his (written) Gospel.[8] He accused them of not living up to it. Misleadingly, they followed the Jewish food laws, and they exerted social pressure on gentiles that they be

2. Gerhard May, "Der Streit zwischen Petrus und Paulus in Antiochien bei Markion," in *Gesammelte Aufsätze* 35–43 at 38–39. Enrico Norelli calls Tertullian's separation of "practice" and "doctrine" "diametrically opposed to the spirit of Gal 2" ("La funzione di Paolo nel pensiero di Marcione," *Rivista Biblica* 34 (1986): 543–97 at 563.

3. Norelli, "La funzione di Paolo," 550–558.

4. Tertullian, *AM* 4.3.2.

5. Enrico Norelli, "Marcion et les disciples de Jésus," *Apocrypha* 19 (2008): 9–42.

6. Irenaeus, *Haer.* 3.2.2.

7. Hays, "Marcion vs. Luke," 216.

8. See also Harnack, *Marcion*, 258*; BeDuhn, "Myth of Marcion," 39.

circumcised. In Marcion's Apostolikon, the false brothers (Gal 2:4) or false apostles (2 Cor 11:13) are not identified with members of the Twelve (such as Peter and John) or with members of Jesus's family (like James). In fact, Marcion's scriptures recorded that the church was "built upon the foundation of the apostles"—note the plural; it cannot just refer to Paul (Laod. 2:20; cf. 1 Cor 12:28). Paul acknowledges that there were "apostles" before him, and he does not call them false (Gal 1:17). Colossians also refers positively to "subapostolic" men like Mark, cousin of Barnabas, and Luke, a man evidently well known to Paul (Col 4:10, 14).

True, Tertullian remarks, "If Marcion's complaint is that the apostles are held suspect of crookedness or pretense, even to the debasing of the Gospel."[9] But note the *if.* Tertullian does not know Marcion's precise complaint. In surviving evidence, Marcion never accused Peter or John themselves of debasing the Gospel in the sense of rewriting or interpolating it. On the basis of Galatians 2:12–14, however, Marcion, following Paul, could well accuse Peter of dissimulation. If debasing the Gospel means that Peter did not live up to it, this is something different from corrupting its text.

In sum, Marcion probably accused false apostles—not the Twelve specifically—of creating other, false Gospels associated with apostolic or subapostolic names.[10] Marcion's ecclesial "fall narrative" is thus not as severe as some have taken it. He probably believed that apostles and apostolic men existed (actual men called Matthew, Mark, Luke, and John). In their names, other *un*named false brothers (or false apostles) produced false Gospels.[11]

Marcion and Other Gospels

In Paul's day, there were no written gospels. Paul's "false brothers" and "false apostles" were *preaching* a different gospel, not writing gospels or corrupting gospels already written. Written gospels were, however, in existence by the early second century, and both Marcion's Gospel and what became canonical Luke were probably dependent on a common prototype (chapter 3).

9. Tertullian, *AM* 4.3.4 (*usque ad evangelii depravationem*).

10. Tertullian, *AM* 4.3.4; 4.4.1–5.

11. Tertullian, *AM* 4.3.2. Cf. Norelli, "La funzione di Paolo" 555, 588.

Perhaps there were already two editions of the prototype in existence during Marcion's lifetime: one for "the Jewish Christian mission" heavily laced with Jewish scriptural traditions, and one for "The Gentile Christian mission" without such intertextuality.[12] According to this reconstruction, Marcion was familiar with the prototype of the gentile Christian mission. But when he came to Rome, he found a Gospel according to Luke expanded according to the needs of the "Jewish Christian mission." The Pontian assumed, at any rate, that his gospel message had been corrupted.[13]

This reconstruction could be right, but the idea of a distinct "Jewish Christian" and a "gentile" Christian mission seems to be an oversimplification. The actual targets of the "Jewish Christian" mission are unclear. The very category of "Jewish Christian" has come under fire.[14] It seems that virtually everywhere, gentiles were the prime focus of recruiting by the second century, and the written gospels were aimed at them. Marcion's battle, it seems, was largely with gentile Christian writers intent on scripturalizing Jewish texts and traditions. These "Judaic" (yet ethnically gentile) Christians were increasingly and apologetically trying to fuse the story of Jesus to Jewish prophecy and history. Witness Justin Martyr's *Dialogue with Trypho.*

It seems reasonable that Marcion, at least by the 150s CE, was familiar with other gospels—such as Mark—and that, given his conservative state of mind, he rejected them as false. He probably viewed the competition between his Gospel and the other gospels as a zero-sum game. The age of the fourfold Gospel had not arrived. Marcion encountered other gospels as individual texts that were on their way to gaining authority, without being scripturalized everywhere. Attacking these other gospels, Marcion likely believed, shored up the authority of his own, Pauline Gospel.[15] In short, the Pontian affirmed that there was one true Pauline Gospel inspired by direct revelation of Jesus; all other gospels were apocryphal, supposedly corrupted by false apostles.

---

12. BeDuhn, "Myth of Marcion" 40.

13. BeDuhn, "Myth of Marcion" 37.

14. Matt Jackson-McCabe, *Jewish Christianity Reconsidered: Rethinking Ancient Groups and Texts* (Minneapolis: Fortress, 2007), 7–38; Jackson-McCabe, *Jewish Christianity: The Making of the Christianity-Judaism Divide* (New Haven: Yale University Press, 2020).

15. Tertullian, *AM* 4.3.4–5.

When canonical Luke appeared—probably around the year 150 CE—Marcion thought that it was a distortion of his Gospel. Tertullian framed the dispute: "I affirm that Marcion's Gospel is adulterated, Marcion, that mine is."[16] Tertullian's "Gospel" here may specifically refer to Luke or to an abstract fourfold Gospel of which Luke was a part. Marcion argued that his Gospel was "falsified" or "interpolated" (*interpolatum*) by the "defenders of Judaism."[17] Tertullian assumed that the falsified gospel is canonical Luke. Here Marcion may have referred more broadly to the corruption of his message, "the good news" by an (oral) counter proclamation.[18] But given Marcion's own fixation on texts, it's probably better to think of the corruption as textual—his text was corrupted by a competing Gospel text, whether or not that was specifically canonical Luke.[19]

The Pontian probably did not view the "defenders of Judaism" as Jews; they were, rather, the incipient catholic leaders of his own day. They were well-connected gentiles, much like Marcion himself. Many of these "Judaic" Christian leaders were in Rome (for instance, Justin), others in Asia Minor (like Polycarp), and others were scattered throughout the empire. To Marcion, they were the heirs of the false teaching propounded by the "false apostles" and "false brothers" against whom Paul struggled a century before.

Marcionite Prologues

The so-called Marcionite prologues are fascinating because they all exist in catholic editions of the New Testament, but some of them seem to have originally been written by Marcionites. Although some have argued that there is nothing distinctly Marcionite about the Marcionite prologues, at least one remark in them is based on Marcionite assumptions.[20] The

16. Tertullian, *AM* 4.4.1.

17. Tertullian, *AM* 4.3.4.

18. BeDuhn, "Myth of Marcion," 38.

19. Klinghardt 1.181.

20. Nils A. Dahl, "Origin of the Earliest Prologues to the Pauline Letters," *Semeia* 12 (1978): 233–277. The Marcionite origin of the prologues is also indicated by the original order of the letters (Galatians, Corinthians, Romans, Thessalonians, Laodiceans, Colossians, and Philippians). Although other editions of Paul's letters did begin with Galatians, none of

prologue to Romans states that "false apostles" preceded Paul in Rome and led (or possibly seduced) people "into the Law and Prophets."[21] Early catholic Christians would have no problem with the Romans being led into "the Law and Prophets"—the writings of the Jewish Bible—since they scripturalized these texts.

Yet Marcion and his followers disagreed. It was a major problem that the Romans were led into the Law and Prophets, as opposed to Paul's Gospel of grace and love.[22] From Marcion's point of view, it seems, the work of the false apostles continued to have major—and negative—repercussions in Rome, where the Hebrew prophets, at least, were read in church liturgies.[23] The poison of the false apostles had not been completely counteracted by Paul, which means that the Roman church had, since Paul's time, remained at least partially "fallen" and unfaithful to Paul's Gospel.

All this would imply that, when Marcion settled in Rome, he did not think that he was coming to a church pure and rooted in the apostolic faith. He believed, rather, that he came to a church that had been corrupted and poisoned at the root. That corruption had evidently been allowed to fester because, when Marcion arrived, Roman Christians were still honoring the Jewish Bible as their scripture (witness *1 Clement* and Justin's *Dialogue with Trypho*). Perhaps Marcion, in his own mind, came to Rome to finish what Paul started—to call the Romans back to true evangelical faith.[24]

One Body with Law and Prophets

According to Tertullian, Marcion believed that the corruption of his Gospel consisted of its being "made into a single unit (or body) with the Law and

---

them follows the Marcionite order exactly. The prologues also ignore or discount the book of Acts when it comes to determining Paul's movements. See further Scherbenske, "Marcionite Paratexts," 85–93.

21. *Hi praeventi sunt a falsis apostolis, et sub nomine domini nostri Jesu Christi in legem et prophetas errant inducti* (text in Jongkind, "On the Marcionite Prologues," 393).

22. *Adamantius* 2.10, 12. Cf. BeDuhn, *First New Testament*, 43.

23. Justin, *1 Apol.* 67.3.

24. Cf. Ambrosiaster, *Comm. Rom.*, pref. in Gerald L. Bray, ed., *Ambrosiaster: Commentaries on Romans and 1–2 Corinthians* (Downers Grove: IVP Academic, 2009), 1–2.

Prophets."[25] In part, this statement probably means that the author of canonical Luke added—much like Matthew did to Mark—explicit quotes and traditions from the Law and Prophets in order to systematically connect his Gospel to Jewish scriptural traditions.[26]

Probably more is implied, however. After all, several Jewish Bible quotations were already embedded in Marcion's Gospel. What Marcion may have envisioned by the "con-corporation of the Law and Prophets" is a Christian Bible that unites the writings of Paul and the Prophets under a single umbrella, so that they form a single scriptural "body."[27] Fusing "Old" and "New" Testaments would ensure that, for all future time, the Gospel would be read in terms of and in light of what were taken to be prophecies and types of the messiah in the Jewish scriptures. This is how Justin Martyr read the Jewish scriptures. In Justin's church, one either read from the "memoirs of the apostles" (the Gospels) or from the prophets. Apparently, both were considered equally scriptural.[28]

Marcion represented a different point of view, insisting that one single and putatively pure Gospel alone was scripture. It was acceptable to read the Law and Prophets for information and intellectual preparation (chapter 7), but these documents, he thought, ought not to be read in the liturgy as part of the same scriptural body of texts. The point of learning the Hebrew Bible was to reject it as scripture. The "old things" had passed away (2 Cor 5:17)—including the "Old" Testament. Therefore, it ought not to control the reading of what is distinctly Christian scripture.

Gospel Origins

In antiquity, Marcionites claimed that their gospel represented the oldest written Gospel, the Gospel represented by Paul. By affirming that their Gospel was corrupted, they implicitly affirmed that the Marcionite Gospel was Luke's source. Some Marcionites even implied that the Evangelion was the source for

---

25. Tertullian, *AM* 4.3.4 (*ad concorporationem legis et prophetarum*).

26. Zwierlein, *antihäretischen Evangelienprologe*, 77–83.

27. Klinghardt, 1.139–40 (who answers his critics).

28. Justin, *1 Apol.* 67.3.

all Gospels, since any corruption of *the* Pauline Gospel assumes the priority of Paul's Gospel—represented by Marcion's text.

One gathers these points from Celsus, who—as Origen observes—made use of Marcionite arguments. At some point in the later second century CE, Celsus accused some Christians of taking it upon themselves "to debase the Gospel from its first composition into a threefold, fourfold, and manifold (composition) and to counterfeit material so that they have the means to deny the refutations (of critics)." Origen comments: "I don't know of any debasers of the gospel other than the followers of Marcion and Valentinus. I suspect also Lucanus' followers"—Lucanus being another Marcionite (chapter 14).[29]

Origen knew that Celsus was informed by Marcionite arguments.[30] It is reasonable to hypothesize, then, that Celsus's critique of Gospel corruption adapts another Marcionite charge. The metaphor of corruption employed presumes that the Marcionite Gospel was the "original coin," stamped with the true image of Christ, as it were. The other "three" gospels would evidently refer to the Gospels "according to 'Matthew,' 'Mark,' and 'John.'" The "four" gospels would apparently be these plus the one "according to Luke." (By the 160s, Marcionites were aware of still more gospels, so they logically included a reference to more.) Celsus's Marcionites apparently assumed that *all* other gospels were created on the basis of their Gospel. The four Gospels in particular were like coins with the original image defaced and replaced with a false one, like Irenaeus's example of a mosaic designed to represent a king but rearranged to depict a fox.[31]

Marcion and his followers proposed that these other Gospels had been created or edited for apologetic reasons—to deal with objections that cropped up over the years. But they also included some purely invented material, for an "invented" Christ is specifically mentioned. For Marcion and Marcionites, any material not in their original Gospel was probably seen as invented or fictional to some degree.

---

29. Celsus in Origen, *Cels* 2.27 (Μετὰ ταῦτά τινας τῶν πιστευόντων, φησὶν, ὡς ἐκ μέθης ἥκοντας εἰς τὸ ἐφεστάναι αὑτοῖς μεταχαράττειν ἐκ τῆς πρώτης γραφῆς τὸ εὐαγγέλιον τριχῇ καὶ τετραχῇ καὶ πολλαχῇ καὶ μεταπλάττειν, ἵν' ἔχοιεν πρὸς τοὺς ἐλέγχους ἀρνεῖσθαι).

30. Origen, *Cels.* 5.54.

31. Irenaeus, *Haer.* 1.8.1. See further Coogan, "Meddling with the Gospel," 400–422.

Regarding the apologetic aims of the four Gospels (to deflect external criticism), the Marcionite theory is not far off from modern notions. In a recent book, a Jesuit professor emeritus of the Biblical Institute of Rome, concludes that Luke's abundant repetition of biblical phraseology and models is the means by which he shows that Jesus's message is in complete continuity with the holy books of Israel, and that by affirming that Jesus has fulfilled the biblical books, he indirectly responds to outsiders who accused the Jesus movement of being a newfangled cult.[32]

The critics of Christianity (like Celsus) could easily attack Christians by saying, in a nutshell, that the cult of Christ appeared out of nowhere. Accordingly, later Gospel revisions (including canonical Luke) took greater care to root Christianity more deeply in the long and respected Jewish tradition. According to Marcion and Marcionites, Luke is demonstrably later because it is more apologetically oriented in this respect. It was born out of a desire to answer second-century objections stemming from critics like Celsus.

To be sure, Celsus's Marcionites were not necessarily right about their Gospel being chronologically first. Marcion's Gospel did probably precede "according to Luke" (chapter 3); but the Marcionites were mistaken if they believed that their Gospel preceded (at least the initial versions of) Mark and Matthew. One has to reckon with serious textual fluidity during this period.[33] The original scripts of Markan and Matthean tradition may have appeared in the late first century, but they underwent revision during and after Marcion's lifetime (which explains features like the longer and shorter endings of Mark, the woman caught in adultery added to John 8, and so on).[34]

At the same time, Celsus's curt rehash of a Marcionite argument is important, because it indicates that Marcionites themselves believed that Matthew, Mark, and John were somehow generated *out of their* Gospel. How

---

32. Jean-Noël Aletti, *Without Typology—No Gospels: A Suffering Messiah. A Challenge for Matthew, Mark and Luke* (Rome: Pontifical Biblical Institute, 2022), 177.

33. Judith Lieu, "Marcion and the Synoptic Problem," in *New Studies in the Synoptic Problem. Oxford Conference, April 2008: Essays in Honour of Christopher M. Tuckett*, ed. P. Foster et al. (Leuven: Peeters, 2011), 731–751; cf. Lieu, *Marcion*, 208–209.

34. Knust and Wasserman, *To Cast the First Stone*; James A. Kelhoffer, *Miracle and Mission: The Authentication of Missionaries and Their Message in the Longer Ending of Mark*, WUNT II/112 (Tübingen: Mohr Siebeck, 2005); Matthew Larsen, *Gospels Before the Book* (New York: Oxford Univeristy Press, 2018).

exactly Marcionites came to this theory is unknown. Presumably Marcionites could see the many linguistic overlaps and parallels between their Gospel and the others (especially the Synoptics). It is fair to say that Matthew is a Judaizing redaction of Mark.[35] Marcionites apparently concluded that all four Gospels were Judaizing corruptions of their Evangelion.[36]

Fascinatingly, some modern scholars have recapitulated the view of Celsus's Marcionites. They think that Marcion's Gospel was the source for what became "according to 'Matthew,' 'Mark,' 'Luke,' and 'John.'" From this point of view, Marcion's Gospel becomes the key for explaining Gospel origins.[37] These theories boldly reverse the modern consensus concerning Markan priority (the notion that Mark came first and was adapted by both Matthew and Luke).

In terms of historical method, it is questionable to adopt (or adapt) either the perspective of the heresiologists (that Marcion's Gospel is a mutilation of Luke) or the Marcionites (that the four Gospels are a corruption of Marcion's Gospel). The truth lies somewhere in between. Canonical Luke *does* have a literary connection to Marcion's Gospel, probably through a common ancestor (or prototype). How Marcion's Gospel actually relates to Mark, Matthew, and John, however, is another matter altogether. All one can safely say is that Marcion's Gospel does not solve the Synoptic problem, it complicates it.

* * *

According to Marcion, there was no apostolic golden age. The era of the apostles is also the time of the church's fall. Just as it began life, "the" church was poisoned at the roots. Paul alone knew the truth, and that truth was corrupted during his lifetime. Marcion's communion alone preserved the pristine Pauline Gospel. Other churches were fooled into accepting corrupted versions of this Gospel. These other texts were leagued with the Law and Prophets, and read in Roman catholic rites. Marcion would have none of it. Whether or not he viewed himself as a reformer, he was at least a preserver of the Gospel, a light shining in the darkness, a purist preserving the original Pauline coin, the unfallen form of Christian faith.

---

35. Anne M. O'Leary, *Matthew's Judaization of Mark: Examined in the Context of the Use of Sources in Graeco-Roman Antiquity* (London: T&T Clark, 2006).

36. Tertullian, *AM* 4.3.4: "false apostles" falsifying "the truth of their gospels, and from them our copies are derived."

37. Vinzent, *Marcion and the Dating of the Synoptic Gospels*; Klinghardt.

Part III

Beginning with the Gospel—What Did Marcion Believe?

CHAPTER NINE

The Good God

> [W]e should not mistake the accusations of Marcion's opponents for the substance of his opinions.
>
> —R. Joseph Hoffman, "How Then Know," 179.

God is Good

THE FUNDAMENTAL POINT about God, for Marcion, is that God is good. In fact, God is "*the* Good." As Marcion's scriptures affirmed, "one is good—the Father" (G 18:19).[1] God is the "father of mercies" (2 Cor 1:3). God is kind even to those who are ungrateful, even to those who are outright evil (G 6:35). Tertullian called the goodness of Marcion's God irrational, and perhaps by worldly standards, it is.[2] But Marcion, did not himself speak in terms of what is rational or irrational in God. Whether rational or not, God's radical goodness was for him the quintessential doctrine of scripture.[3]

Yet more than scripture was needed for Marcion to arrive at his theology. After all, all Christians accepted the idea that God was good. The Marcionite distinction was that God was *solely* good.[4] If God was solely good, then God could not be jealous, warlike, judgmental, wrathful, or tribalistic. God could not do violence or any kind of evil, even if it was strategic, disciplinary, or

1. The importance of this verse for Marcionites is underscored by Origen, *Princ.* 2.5.1.

2. Tertullian, *AM* 2.6.

3. See further Enrico Norelli, "Marcion: ein christlicher Philosoph oder ein Christ gegen die Philosophie?" in May and Greschat, *Marcion und seine kirchengeschichtliche Wirkung*, 113–130.

4. Tertullian, *AM* 2.12.3.

limited.[5] Indeed, it was sacrilegious to say that God caused anything wicked or harmful.[6] Thus whatever entity causes evil in the world must not be God.[7]

Trickled down Platonism almost certainly played a role in Marcion's thought. He was not a card-carrying Platonist, but he still followed Platonic ideas, whether consciously or not. Plato's *Republic* presents two guidelines that determine what is fitting for God. First of all, God must be viewed as the cause of goods only, and not of evils like flood, fire, war, disease, and so on. Second, since God is perfect and most beautiful; God never changes into another form, including a human one.[8] Christians who affirmed the incarnation could not accept the second guideline, but they could accept the first; and Marcion was among them.

God Creates

Marcion's God of radical goodness is largely conceded; whether this God *creates* is the bone of contention. Even today, it is common coin that Marcion's Good God did not create anything—despite the fact that this assertion is in tension both with Marcion's scriptures and our earliest patristic evidence.[9]

According to Marcion's Apostolikon, there is "one God, the Father, *from whom come all things*" (1 Cor 8:5–6). If all things come from the Father, that includes this world. If so, then in some sense Marcion's Father is also a creator or at least originator of—not just something—but everything. Moreover, Marcion's letter to the Laodiceans refers to "the mystery that has been hidden from the aeons by God, who created everything" (3:9). If this reading is correct, it states that God—evidently the true one—created everything.

This reading, however, is disputed. Tertullian accuses Marcion of removing a word from the verse (the Greek preposition *en*).[10] With the preposition

5. Plato, *Republic* 379b-c; cf. 509b.

6. Plato, *Timaeus* 29e.

7. Plato, *Republic* 379b-c; 380b-c; 391e1–2; cf. Plato's *Laws* 672b; 899b; 900d; 941b; Philo, *Decalogue* 176; cf. *Confusion of Tongues* 180; *On the Creation* 74–75; Plutarch, *Obsolescence of Oracles* 423d; *Epicurus Makes a Pleasant Life Impossible* 1102d; Alcinous, *Handbook* 10.3; Numenius frags. 2, 16, 19 (des Places).

8. Plato, *Republic* 380c, 381b.

9. *Ref.* 10.19.2.

10. The preposition is not missing in *Adamantius* 2.20 (Greek).

removed, Tertullian understands the mystery to be hidden "*from* God, who created everything."[11] In this reading, "God"—or rather "god"—refers to the creator, who was ignorant of the true God's mystery.

Nonetheless, Tertullian was probably not reporting a distinctly Marcionite reading, but what he *thought* Marcion must have believed.[12] Several early manuscripts, none of them Marcionite, lack the preposition *en* in this verse.[13] Even without it, the use of "God" in the dative case (*tōi theōi*) does not readily express the idea of separation "from God" but agency, "by God." Accordingly, Marcion probably did understand God, the true God, to be a creator. This reading is confirmed by Jerome (or perhaps Origen, whom Jerome followed). He assumes that Marcion read the preposition *en* in Laodiceans 3:8, and that Marcion's God is specifically the "maker of the invisible world."[14]

Heresiologists touted the idea that Marcion's Good was divorced from creation, a true alien to all. But if God created everything, according to Marcion's scripture, their heresiological dogma must be revised.

Our earliest patristic evidence attests that Marcion's God creates. Justin Martyr states that Marcion causes many people "to deny the maker god of this universe here, and to confess a certain other, as if superior, to having created superior things than this one."[15] Two editors of this text, change the reading of the manuscript to reflect, as they admit, the heresiological dogma that Marcion's God did not create anything. According to them, Marcion made people "deny God the Maker of this universe and confess some other

11. Tertullian, *AM* 5.18.2.

12. BeDuhn, *First New Testament* 312; T. J. Lang, "Did Tertullian Read Marcion in Latin," 69–70.

13. Clabeaux (*Lost Edition* 33, 121) lists codex Sinaiticus (original hand), 614, and 2412.

14. Jerome, *Comm. Eph* 3.8 (*Origen and Jerome on St Paul's Epistle to the Ephesians*, trans. Ronald E. Heine [Oxford: Oxford University Press, 2002], 149).

15. Justin, *1 Apol.* 26.5, my emphasis, and without emending Parasinus supplement grec 450 (ἀρνεῖσθαι τὸν ποιητὴν τοῦδε τοῦ παντὸς θεόν, ἄλλον δέ τινα, ὡς ὄντα μείζονα τὰ μείζονα παρὰ τοῦτον ὁμολογεῖν πεποιηκέναι), as printed by Charles Munier, ed., *Justin: Apologie pour les Chrétiens*, SC 507 (Paris: Cerf, 2006), 200. Trobisch (*Origin of Christian Scripture: The Evolution of the New Testament Canon in the Second Century CE* [Minneapolis: Fortress, 2023], 13) understands τὸν ποιητὴν as a predicate ("teaching men to deny that God is the maker of all things"), but that translation would better reflect a different word order, such as ἀρνεῖσθαι τὸν θεόν τοῦδε τοῦ παντὸς ποιητήν.

who is greater, beyond him."[16] But heresiological dogma should not overturn the manuscript reading.

According to Justin, Marcion's God *made greater things* than the creator. Properly speaking, the latter being should be called the *lower* creator, for the supreme Father is also a creator—simply a higher one. It is Justin who calls the lower creator "maker of all"—but this being, according to Marcion, evidently did *not* make *everything*, only things inferior to what the true God made.

Perhaps, however, one should adopt the translation that Marcion's God "did" greater things than the Judean lord. This is a possible translation of the Greek verb (a form of *poieō*, that can mean "to make" or "to do").[17] It seems tendentious, however, to restrict the meaning of this verb only to "doing" without reckoning with its other meanings, for the creative power of Marcion's God is acknowledged, as already seen, in Marcion's scriptures.

If there is any doubt that Marcion's God creates, Tertullian resolves it. Despite some inconsistency, the Carthaginian clearly conceives of Marcion's God as a creator. He rhetorically addresses Marcion: "Your God no less has his own creation, his own world, and his own heaven."[18] The Father's world is the world of invisible, not visible realities.[19] It is the world, and the heaven, from which Christ descended.[20]

In the *Adamantius*, the Marcionite Megethius denies—not that his God is a creator (*demiourgos*)—but that he is creator "*of evils*." Megethius does

---

16. Denis Minns and Paul Parvis, *Justin, Philosopher and Martyr, Apologies* (Oxford: Oxford University Press, 2009), 151, with n.4. They cite *Ref.* 10.19.2; Tertullian *AM* 1.11.3–7; cf. Epiphanius, *Pan.* 42.3.1. Miroslav Marcovich presents a similar text in *Iustini Martyris Apologiae pro Christianis* (Berlin: de Gruyter, 1994), 70. The fact that the manuscript says that Marcion posited a higher deity who made greater things than the creator is not an attempt to "depict Marcionite thought as muddled, obscure and inconsistent" (Matthijs den Dulk, *Between Jews and Heretics: Refiguring Justin Martyr's Dialogue with Trypho* (London: Routledge, 2018), 31n26.

17. Moll, "Justin and the Pontic Wolf," in *Justin Martyr and His Worlds*, ed. Sarah Parvis and Paul Foster (Minneapolis: Fortress, 2007), 145–151 at 147 ("who has done greater things"). Trobisch, *Origin of Christian Scripture*, 13: "has done greater works."

18. Tertullian, *AM* 1.15.1.

19. Tertullian, *AM* 1.16.1.

20. Tertullian, *AM* 4.7.1.

not deny that God created, only that God created "this" lower world.[21] The Marcionite Markus states that God has his own heavens, above the heavens made by the creator. These superior heavens are unborn and not made by hands.[22] These heavens would evidently be among the "greater things" made by the true God.

According to Ephrem of Nisibis, Marcion's God has heavens that have been created from nothing.[23] Jerome, as already observed, states that for Marcion the Good is "the creator of invisible things" (compare 2 Cor 4:18) while the lower creator makes "visible things."[24] Invisible things might include the realm of spirit, paradise, and so on. The sky's the limit, one might say—or rather, the starting point for God's superior creation.[25]

Tertullian may well be correct that Marcion's God did not *directly* make so much as a "single little chickpea," for a chickpea is an element of the lower, visible creation.[26] At the same time, the Good God's power feeds and funds even this lower creation. This means that God is not truly alien from the lower creation. The visible creation is still in God's power, otherwise Christ could not have controlled the waves and the wind (G 8:25), and the sun would not have darkened at his death (23:45). Creation responds to Christ—even in Marcion's Gospel. Christ was not alien to creation, and neither was his Father.

It is unnecessary to contrast Marcion's God of grace with a God of nature.[27] Jesus addressed his Father as "Lord of heaven" (G 10:21). The Lord of heaven is still presumably related to nature, at least by being over it. Heresiologists insisted that because Jesus came to heal bodies he was a representative of the *lower* creator. Not so. The higher creator could have power over bodies as well,

---

21. *Adamantius* 1.2 (805a): οὔτε δημιουργός ἐστι τῶν κακῶν . . . οὔτε ὁ κόσμος *οὗτος* ἐξ αὐτοῦ δεδημιούργηται (my emphasis).

22. *Adamantius* 2.19.

23. Ephrem in C. W. Mitchell, ed. *S. Ephraim's Prose Refutations of Mani, Marcion, and Bardaisan*, 2 vols. (London: William Norgate, 1912), 1.li.

24. Jerome, *Comm. Isa.* 12.45.

25. See further Cf. G. May, *Schöpfung aus dem Nichts*, AKG 48 (Berlin: de Gruyter, 1978), 60; Löhr, "Did Marcion Distinguish," 143.

26. Tertullian, *AM* 1.11.5.

27. Grant, *Heresy and Criticism*, 37.

even if he did not directly make them. Ironically, then, Tertullian's statement proves true, though not in the sense in which he meant it: Jesus is the Christ of the creator—meaning the *higher* one.

An "Alien" God?

Harnack believed that, for Marcion, the true God was more than just unknown. Lots of ancient people—in particular, philosophers—affirmed an unknown God. Altars "to unknown gods" are well attested in antiquity. Marcion's God, said Harnack, was "*alien* because there are simply no bonds and no obligation that connect him with the world and with humanity," not even with the human spirit.[28] In this way, Marcion's God was different from the "gnostic" God who was of the same substance as the human spirit.

Admittedly, the phrase "alien god" is attested early, probably in reference to Marcionite thought.[29] And to be sure, Ephrem regularly nicknamed Marcion's God "the Alien" or "the Stranger."[30] In the modern world, there is a certain frisson associated with the phrase "alien God." In a UFO or sci-fi culture, it gives the impression that God and his chief ambassador, Jesus, are something like extraterrestrials. Jesus suddenly appears on earth in a flesh suit like the alien in the movie *The Day the Earth Stood Still*.[31]

Yet if one examines Marcion's scriptures, they say nothing about God being alien to creation or to the human spirit. God still feeds the birds, and adorns the lilies (G 12:24–28). Moreover, Markus in the *Adamantius* says that God *did* send his own spirit into humanity, and it is this spirit that originally enlivened the human race (Gen 2:7).[32] Since Eden, the spirit has functioned as the true self of human beings, and it is this spirit that is saved (1 Cor 5:5).

Now one could say that Markus's views represent later Marcionite thought, in part because they contradict the views of his colleague Megethius (for whom the human soul, the inbreathing of the creator, is the subject of

---

28. Harnack, *Marcion*, 3.

29. Celsus in Origen, *Cels.* 6.54.

30. For example, Ephrem in Mitchell, *Prose Refutations*, 2.xxv.

31. *The Day the Earth Stood Still*, directed by Scott Derrickson (20th Century Fox, 2008).

32. *Adamantius* 2.8.

salvation).[33] And it is true that Markus's view about the human spirit seems to go back to Marcion's disciple Apelles (chapter 14).[34] Yet this point does not automatically imply that Megethius's position represents Marcion's view.[35]

Marcion's exact views on this question are unclear. It may be Tertullian who understands humanity made in God's image as humanity sharing the creator's substance.[36] The Carthaginian apparently does *not* know Marcion's exact position, because he is forced to use a hypothetical: "*if* humankind . . . is soul through the breathing of the creator . . ."[37] It is Tertullian himself who argues for the position that the soul is constituted from the creator's breath.[38] Harnack was motivated to accept this position as Marcion's because it helped him distinguish Marcion from "Gnosticism." Yet, even if it is granted that Marcion thought of the soul as breathed out by the creator, the creator still may have been unknowingly acting in accordance with the Father's will and power.

To be sure, the Father's radical mercy is something alien in this world of darkness, war, and sin. But if Marcion's God is also a creator—indeed, the "creator of everything" (Laod 3:8)—then the Good is not in fact alien to anything. Tertullian himself remarked, "How can there be anything alien to God when, if God truly is, he can have nothing alien to him?"[39] This is one of the rare cases where the Pontian would have concurred with the Carthaginian.

Heresiologists constantly infer that if the Father did not create this world, then he is alien to it and does not own anything in it. But these inferences are invalid. God can still come into rightful possession of this world even if God did not directly make it. The same is true for humans. God can "buy," or "buy back," humans from the creator even if God did not make their material bodies (chapter 12). Evidently, God felt *some* sort of connection with humans if he came to save them. That connection was not based on a common nature,

33. *Adamantius* 2.7.

34. Tertullian, *An.* 23.3; *Carn. Chr.* 8.2.

35. Harnack, *Marcion*, 271*–272*. See further Enrico Norelli, "Note sulla soteriologia di Marcione," *Augustinianum* 35 (1995): 281–305.

36. Tertullian, *AM* 2.5.1.

37. Tertullian, *AM* 5.6.11.

38. Tertullian, *AM* 2.9.1; cf. his *An.* 11.

39. Tertullian, *AM* 1.11.1.

perhaps, but there were still traits of the human spirit that resembled the true and good God, traits like goodness and love.

How Marcion actually imagined humanity's creation is unattested. He never denied that humans were created, on some level, in the Father's image. Perhaps he made a distinction between being in the material image of the creator and the immaterial likeness of the Father. One cannot know. At any rate, it seems mistaken to perpetuate Harnack's idiom by referring to Marcion's "alien" God.[40] Even Harnack observed that "the 'alien' God was only 'the Alien' because he appeared from what is alien."[41] It was not so much that God was "alien," but that humans made themselves alien to God (Laod 2:12).[42]

God as Judge

Heresiologists said that Marcion's God does not judge.[43] Harnack reaffirmed this position with force. "Marcion proclaimed with splendid assurance that *the loving will of Jesus (and, that is, of God) does not judge.*"[44] "God will not judge" and he "does not punish."[45] Harnack even claims that as a rule, Marcion "excised or emended the passages where the traditional text has the good God appear as a judge."[46]

But Marcion's scriptures punch back. The Pontian transmitted Romans 2:2 ("God's judgment is true"); Galatians 5:10 ("He who troubles you will bear his judgment"), Romans 2:16 ("In the day when God will judge the secrets

40. DeConick, *Comparing Christianities*, 36–37. According to DeConick, Marcion is to be credited with a theological innovation, "xenotheism," the "belief and worship of a God who is alien to our universe" (38).

41. Harnack, "Die Neuheit," 133 (*"Aber der 'fremde' Gott war nur 'der Fremde,' weil er aus der Fremde erschienen ist; durch sein Erscheinen wurde er 'der Vater'"*).

42. Tertullian says that Marcion in his *Antitheses* proves Christ a stranger (*alienum*) to the Law and the Prophets (*AM* 4.6.2), but he is not a stranger to humans.

43. Irenaeus, *Haer.* 3.25.2; Tertullian, *AM* 5.13.5 (*nec iudicat nec irascitur*); cf. *Adamantius*, 2.4.

44. Harnack, *Marcion*, 143, emphasis original.

45. Harnack, *Marcion*, 13, 81, 143.

46. Harnack, *Marcion*, 90.

through Jesus Christ"); and 2 Thessalonians 2:12 ("so that all who do not believe the truth may be judged").

One also finds passages in the Evangelion that portray God or Christ as a judge, such as 12:46: "the Lord of that slave will come on a day and hour he does not expect or know and cut him in two." And 13:28: "when you see all the righteous in God's kingdom but you confined outside—here there will be weeping and gnashing of teeth." Perhaps the clearest passages are these: "We must all be presented before the judgment seat of Christ" (2 Cor 5:10); "For we shall all stand before the tribunal of Christ" (Rom 14:10; cf. 2 Thess 1:6–8). In short, passages about divine judgment are relatively plentiful in Marcion's scriptures. Not all of them can be tied to the lower creator or explained by the idea that humans judge or condemn themselves by rejecting the gospel.[47]

Admittedly, Marcion and later Marcionites believed that God, as the Good, could not do evil to the extent that he does not directly engage in acts of revenge or punishment. But refusing to punish is not the same thing as refusing to judge. It is possible that Marcion's God left judgment to Christ and actual punishment to the lower creator.[48] Yet, insofar as Christ, who is also good, does engage in judgment, then one can argue that God judges through Christ.

The dogma of Marcion's non-judging God can be traced back to an inference of Tertullian, who concludes that because Marcion's God does not suffer passions (like rage and indignation), he cannot judge.[49] The Carthaginian clarifies (not naming his source), that for Marcionites, sinners are "cast away" out of sight on judgment day, and they are cast into the creator's fire.[50] It may be true that for Marcion, the creator devises the means of human punishment, but that does not mean that the true God does not judge. Tertullian makes a faulty inference. There is such a thing as a passionless, unvengeful judge.

Accordingly, Marcion was not the simplistic theological dualist as he is often portrayed. On *some* level, he had reconciled God's love and judgment. God does not become wrathful or vindictive, to be sure, but he *does* judge. Even

---

47. Norelli, "Marcione lettore dell'epistola ai Romani," 643, 646.

48. *Adamantius*, 2.5.

49. Tertullian, *AM* 1.27.5.

50. Tertullian, *AM* 1.27.6; 1.28.1.

Tertullian was forced to admit this: "But clearly he [Marcion's God] judges evil by not willing it and condemns it by forbidding it."[51]

One God, One Lord

With consummate oratorical skill, Tertullian writes that, "the principal, and consequently the entire, matter of discussion," in his battle against Marcion "is one of number, whether it is permissible to suggest the existence of two gods."[52] The Carthaginian claims that "the man of Pontus presents us with two gods, as it were the two Clashing Rocks on which he suffers shipwreck: the one the creator, whom he cannot deny, which is our God; the other, whom he cannot prove, a God of his own."[53]

The concept of two gods is often taken to be a stable part of Marcion's theology. One hears that, "The heart of Marcion's teaching is his assumption of two gods"[54]; that "Marcion maintained . . . that there were two different Gods,"[55] and that he upheld "ditheism."[56]

The problem is this: If Harnack and his heirs are serious that Marcion was a "biblicist," then they must admit that he believed the biblical teaching about divine oneness. A cavalier remark about Marcion's arbitrary twisting of the biblical witness is unfair and inconsistent.[57] If one takes seriously the language of Marcion's scriptures, then Marcion believed in "*One* Lord, one faith, one baptism, *one God and Father of all*" (Laod 4:5–6). If Marcion's Bible was also his rule of faith, then he—like virtually every other Christian of his day—affirmed one, single God, the only true God, the Father of Jesus

51. Tertullian, *AM* 1.27.1.

52. Tertullian, *AM* 1.3.1.

53. Tertullian, *AM* 1.2.1.

54. Gerhard May, "Marcion" in *Dictionary of Gnosis and Western Esotericism*, ed. Wouter Hanegraaff (Leiden: Brill, 2006), 765–768 at 765.

55. Bart Ehrman, *Studies in the Textual Criticism of the New Testament* (Leiden: Brill, 2006), 347.

56. Hoffmann, *Marcion*, 193. "Ditheism" is also used, e.g., by Moll, *Arch-heretic* 13n12; Still, "Shadow and Light," 96; Löhr, "Problems," 130.

57. Sebastian Moll, *Die christliche Eroberung des Alten Testaments* (Berlin: Berlin University Press, 2010), 33.

Christ. Having lived in the Greco-Roman world, of course, Marcion would have known that "there are those who are called 'gods,' whether in heaven or on earth . . . but for us there is one God, the Father, from whom (comes) all things" (1 Cor 8:5–6).[58]

Marcion was a Christian; as such, he would not have self-identified as a "ditheist," since ditheism is a form of polytheism. It was Marcion's *opponents* who consistently called both Marcion's supreme deity and the creator "gods." Marcion preferred the term "creator" and "cosmocrator" (that is, world governor) to designate the Judean lord.[59] Harnack observed that the creator was "not a full god."[60] But one can put the point more precisely: for Marcion, the creator was an intermediate being, not, properly speaking, a true God at all.

Patristic evidence supports this point. Justin indicates that Marcion explicitly taught people to deny that the lower creator is God.[61] Clement writes that Marcionites hastened toward the Good, but not toward the "god in a different sense."[62] This "god in a different sense" is evidently the lower creator, who is "god" only by a kind of poetic license.

Marcionites themselves were not consistent. They could speak of "God" in the proper sense (referring to the Good), and "god" in an improper sense (namely, the creator). Greek grammarians called this the "catachrestic" or improper employment of a word. That is to say, a Marcionite could call the lower creator "god" (as he is so frequently named in the Jewish Bible), but only by loosely extending the meaning of the term "god." Philo made the same argument about Moses. Scripture calls Moses a "god" (Exod 7:1), but that did not mean that he was, or that he replaced the supreme and true God who alone deserved this name in the proper sense. Likewise, Marcion's scriptures called the cosmocrator "god" by license of language. He is the "god of this

---

58. Attested in Tertullian, *AM* 5.7.9.

59. Tertullian, *AM* 1.2.1 (cf. 1.3.1; 1.6.1); Irenaeus, *Haer.* 1.27.2 (*cosmocratorem*); 3.12.12. Cf. Justin, *1 Apology* 26.5; *Ref.* 7.29.1; 7.30.3. See further René Braun, *Deus Christianorum: Recherches sur le vocabulaire doctrinal de Tertullian* (Paris: Études Augustiniennes, 1977), 374–375. McGowan points out that cosmocrator was generally used for pagan gods and Roman emperors ("Marcion's Love of Creation," 303).

60. Harnack, *Marcion*, 275* (*nicht voller Gott*).

61. Justin, *1 Apol.* 26.5; 58.1. See further Litwa, "Did Marcion Call?," 233–235.

62. Clement, *Strom.* 3.3.12.2.

world" (2 Cor 4:4), and the "god of generation" but that does not mean he is properly called "God."[63]

Accordingly, heresiological arguments that Marcion was a ditheist are mistaken. Irenaeus and Tertullian knew that Marcion did not typically refer to the creator as "God." When they said he believed in two gods, they aimed to make him look "pagan." But the argument is unfair, and its absurdity is shown by Tertullian's argument that Marcion actually taught that there were *nine* gods—"though he knew it not."[64] Tertullian's rhetorical question to Marcion, "Certainly you confess that the creator is a God?" is just that—*rhetorical*.[65] There is nothing certain about it. The Refutator reveals that Apelles, Marcion's disciple, was not willing to call the creator "god," and that he categorized the creator as an angel.[66] Here Apelles did not deviate from Marcion's teaching; rather, he clarified it.

It is true that some speak of Marcion's "ditheism" to affirm his dualism.[67] Marcion was a dualist if by dualism is meant that he opposed two superhuman beings. Yet in this sense, Marcion's dualism was not significantly different from the mitigated dualism upheld by a wide range of Christians during his time. Marcion discovered a lower, evil being lurking in what were considered to be scriptural texts. For most other Christians of his era, this being was Satan. For Marcion, it was the lower creator. The true God, however, always had far greater power than the creator, and over the lower creation.

* * *

This chapter shows what happens when one prioritizes the witness of Marcion's scriptures over heresiological reports. This simple strategy takes a hammer to common misconceptions about Marcion's theology. The view that Marcion's God is not a creator, for instance, is demolished by Marcion's scriptures and also by a close reading of the patristic evidence. Marcion's God *does* create.

---

63. The "god of generation" (*or* god of Genesis) is common in the *Adamantius*, e.g., 1.16 (814c.24–27).

64. Tertullian, *AM* 1.15.6.

65. Tertullian, *AM* 2.16.5.

66. *Ref.* 10.20.1.

67. On Marcion's dualism, see Dylan Burns, *Did God Care? Providence, Dualism and Will in Later Greek and Early Christian Philosophy* (Leiden: Brill, 2020), 137–149.

In fact, his God creates everything (Laod 3:8). Even if God does not directly create objects in the visible world, he is not alien to it, but exerts his power over nature and over the human body. In opposition to the view that the Good does not (or cannot) judge, Marcion's scriptures say that God judges through Christ. In judging, God is neither wrathful nor vengeful. Actual punishment is largely left to the lower creator, but God's judgment remains true and firm. Finally, Marcion's Bible destroys the view that he was a polytheist. The Pontian and his followers could on occasion call the creator "god" in an improper sense, but they clearly distinguished him from the Father, who is in the proper sense called "God." This God stands above other gods and lords as the "living God" (1 Cor 3:3) and, strictly speaking, the only one.

CHAPTER TEN

The Evil Creator

> If the gods do something foul, they are not gods.
>
> —Euripides

Deferred Demiurgy

It is said that Marcion "sundered the creator-God who spoke in the old Scriptures from the God revealed in Jesus."[1] From such language, one might infer that all Christians of Marcion's day automatically identified the true and highest God with the creator of this lower world. At some later point, some "renegade" theologians like Marcion and Saturninus came along and divided them. But such a reconstruction is inaccurate.

In the second century CE, there were basically two major theological options: either (1) a person could wholly identify the high God (the Father) with the creator of this world, or (2) distinguish them. Among intellectuals, the latter position, which can be named deferred demiurgy, was not uncommon. Deferred demiurgy had at least two sub-options. One could either (a) view the lower creator as working separately from the Father or (b) understand him as the Father's representative, the expression of the Father's mind.

Among Christians, the latter position (2b) can be called Logos theology. Such a theology, in short, views the Father as a powerful, immaterial mind. In eternity past, the Logos (or "Word") emerges from this mind as the expression of the Father's purely mental activity. The Logos then creates the lower world. The creative activity of the Logos can be referred back to the Father. The immaterial Father, in this theory, is still the creator of the material world, despite the fact that he creates nothing directly. The Father's creative activity is processed

1. Barton, *Holy Writings*, 42.

through his lower agent, the Logos. Logos theology allowed Christians like Justin to attribute creation equally to both Father and Son.

Marcion's view was different. The Pontian agreed that the Father was distinct from the lower creator. He simply viewed the creator as other and even as opposed to the Father's intentions for humanity. Marcion never explained where the lower creator came from. Perhaps he felt no need to explain it. Since he was focused on salvation, the Pontian seems to have been uninterested in the questions of high theology or cosmology.[2]

Like Justin, Marcion attributed creation both to the Father and to the lower creator. But he distinguished a lower creation (our world) from a higher one (the invisible world) (chapter 9). The creator, at least initially, was not aware of the Father or his higher creation. Thus he swore by himself that he was the only God (Isa 45:23).[3] Presumably, the creator revised his position after Christ revealed the Father in his ministry.

Both the Justinian and the Marcionite theories are still versions of deferred demiurgy. Creation, in both views, is not wholly and directly attributed to the Father. The creation of the material world, at least, is credited to the agency of a lower being, who is either connected to the Father (according to Justin) or initially ignorant of him (according to Marcion). Both versions of deferred demiurgy were equally valid in Middle Platonic philosophy, because they were both equally possible readings of Plato's *Timaeus*.

In the *Timaeus*, Plato attributed the creation—or one should say, organization—of the material world to a demiurge. It was a philosophical dispute whether Plato viewed this demiurge as the high deity—the Father or Good—or as subordinate to him. The Platonist Atticus, for instance, identified the demiurge with the high God,[4] while his contemporary Numenius distinguished them.[5] What was not disputed, however, was that the demiurge

2. Gerhard May, *Creatio ex nihilo: The Doctrine of 'Creation out of Nothing' in Early Christian Thought*, trans. A. S. Worrall (London: T&T Clark, 2004), 58. Here and below, I quote from this English translation.

3. Tertullian, *AM* 1.11.9; cf. 2.26.1.

4. Atticus, frag. 12 = Proclus, *On the Timaeus* 1.305.6–16.

5. Cf. Harpocration of Argos who made a distinction between a first and a second Zeus, the latter who functioned as a creator (Proclus, *In Tim.* 1.303.27ff). See further John Dillon, *Middle Platonists*, 2nd ed. (Ithaca: Cornell, 1996), 259–260.

used subordinates (the "young gods") to create aspects of the lower world, including the human body.[6] Thus the idea of deferred demiurgy as such was familiar to Platonists. They all believed that with regard to certain things, the high God did not "get his hands dirty," but delegated creation to subordinates.

One can fruitfully compare Justin's and Marcion's views with the thought of Numenius. Numenius (who thrived about 150 CE) lived in Apamea, Syria. He had an interest in confirming Platonic doctrines in "barbarian" philosophies (Syrian, Egyptian, Jewish, etc.). Following *Timaeus*, he distinguished the creator from the "primal God," also called "the Good itself," and "the primal Intellect."[7] Numenius believed in a triad of three principles: the Father and two aspects of the creator: the one who contemplates the Father, and the one divided by his alternative focus on matter. The primal God sowed the seeds of souls, and the creator planted them.

The Apamean valued Jewish theology, but he may have believed that the Jews mistook their lower creator for the primal Intellect. He himself comments on Plato's *Timaeus* 28c, "Plato knows that among men only the creator is known, while the primal Intellect, who is called Being itself, is completely unknown among them. For that reason he says this, as if someone would speak: 'O human beings, the Intellect which you focus on is not the primal Intellect, but there is another Intellect before it, superior and more divine.'"[8] This superior intellect was the Father. This particular view resembles the thought of Cerdo and Marcion in that the true Father was unknown by those who worshipped the lower creator.

Numenius could say that *both* the Father and the demiurge were creative agents. The Apamean called the Father "creator of being" whereas the

---

6. Plato, *Timaeus* 41a-d.

7. Numenius, frag. 12, 16 (des Places).

8. Numenius, frag. 17 (Des Places). Robert M. Van den Berg notes that "later Neoplatonic authors like Porphyry, the emperor Julian, and Proclus, take the Jews and the Christians to task for failing to see that their god is not the highest god" ("God the Creator, God the Creation: Numenius' Interpretation of Gen 1:2 (frag. 30)," in *The Creation of Heaven and Earth: Re-interpretations of Genesis 1 in the Context of Judaism, Ancient Philosophy, Christianity, and Modern Physics*, ed. George H. van Kooten [Leiden: Brill, 2005], 109–124 at 119).

demiurge was "creator of becoming."[9] In this model, the Father and the demiurge do not share a single act of creation; they create on distinct levels. The Father does not come into contact with matter. At the same time, the Father's intelligence provides the models for shaping the material world. This would make the Father, in Aristotelian language, the formal cause of the lower creation (the one who provides the model or blueprint), while the demiurge serves as the efficient cause (the actual maker).

Numenius's theory is both similar to and different from the positions of Justin and Marcion. Insofar as Numenius envisions the Father as creator of a higher essence ("being") and the demiurge as a separate entity who shapes matter ("becoming"), his position resembles that of Marcion. Insofar as Numenius envisions the creation and the Good as somehow working in tandem on the lower creation (as formal and efficient cause), his position resembles that of Justin.

Such entanglement shows that Marcion and Justin were competing in a common Platonic thought world in which the notions of deferred demiurgy were already available in the broader philosophical culture. After centuries of philosophers interpreting *Timaeus*, Platonic notions of demiurgy were "in the air." Marcion and Justin could effectively pick and choose which Platonic ideas they believed were most faithful to their scriptures. And of course they could adapt or modify aspects of these ideas to fit their biblical interpretations.

So there is both agreement and disagreement. Marcion and Justin agreed that there was a deferred demiurge; their chief disagreement was centered on his identity and character. For Marcion, the demiurge was the Judean lord; for Justin, he was the Logos who was allied to this lord.

This sketch of the Platonic intellectual context indicates that neither Justin nor Marcion would have admitted to "sundering" the lower creator from the Father or to "demoting" the demiurge.[10] In their minds, there was already (and from eternity) a distinction between the transcendent Father and the maker of this material world. Thus, by describing a subordinate creator (whether it be the Judean lord or Christ), they were, from their own perspective, describing ontological facts, not introducing new theories. From

9. Numenius, frag. 16 (Des Places).

10. Litwa, *Evil Creator*, 157–162.

within their Platonizing frameworks, they saw their own respective versions of deferred demiurgy as based in biblical texts.

Negative Demiurgy

Marcion's thought fits a basically Platonic philosophical culture. But Marcion was by no means a Platonist, since his position on demiurgy was, in the end, incompatible with any version of Platonism contemporaneous with him. Marcion disagreed with all Platonists by asserting that the *character* of the lower creator was evil. By contrast, every Platonist agreed with the clear statement of Plato in *Timaeus*: the demiurge was *good*, and out of his goodness, he created the best of all possible worlds.[11] Marcion bucked this view because his reading of the biblical witness overrode what Platonic philosophers understood as theologically appropriate. Marcion believed in an evil creator because he believed that this is what the Jewish scriptures revealed.[12]

Platonists had no loyalty to Jewish ("barbarian") scripture. Thus, they would have scoffed at a creator who said, "I am he who creates evils" (Isa 45:7 LXX). Today, these "evils" are sometimes translated by the words "woe" or "calamity." The underlying Hebrew term *rāʿ* includes disasters like famine, pestilence and war; but it also encompasses morally perverse actions. There is, for instance, the tree of the knowledge of good and *evil* (*rāʿ*) (Gen 2:17)—and in this case evil is taken in the broad sense to include moral evil (sin and disobedience). This same ambiguity between moral and physical evil is present in the Greek translation of *rāʿ* known to Marcion, namely *kaka*, "evils."[13] The lord who makes *kaka* is not only the maker of pestilence and plague, but—at least potentially—of morally wicked actions as well.

Isaiah 45:7 was not the only verse Marcionites used to associate the creator with evil.[14] In Jeremiah 18:11, the creator announced to his own people,

11. Plato, *Timaeus* 29e.

12. Litwa, *Evil Creator*, 67–89.

13. See further Thomas Römer, "The Origin and the Status of Evil according to the Hebrew Bible," in *Die Wurzel allen Übels: Über die Herkunft des Bösen und Schlechten in der Philosophie und Religion des 1.-4. Jahrhunderts*, ed. Fabienne Jourdan and Rainer Hirsch-Luipold (Tübingen: Mohr Siebeck, 2015), 53–66 at 63–65.

14. Origen, *Princ.* 4.2.1.

"behold I fashion evils (*kaka*) against you"; in Micah 1:12 it is said that "evils (*kaka*) have descended from the Lord against the gates of Jerusalem,"[15] and in Amos 3:6, the prophet asks, "Will there be evil (*kakia*) in the city which the Lord has not caused?" It is instructive also to note that the creator sends "an evil spirit" against his anointed king Saul in order to choke him (1 Kgdms 15:14).[16]

From the Judean lord's putatively wicked deeds, Marcion deduced that the creator himself was evil. It was not just that the creator did a few bad deeds to punish a stiff-necked tribe; no, his many and extensive evil acts revealed a basic flaw in his character. Marcion applied Jesus's saying to the Judean lord: a bad tree produces bad fruit (G 6:43). In short, his evil actions are not just anomalies; they emerge from an evil character.[17] Since the creator is wicked, and the true God revealed by Jesus could only be good, they had to be two different beings. One can call this solution radical, but for Marcion, it was the only honest reading.[18]

Of course, the Judean lord did many good things as well, at least for Judeans. Platonists had a name for a superhuman being who shows favoritism and does a mix of good and evil. Such a being was not a pure god, but a semi-divine being called a "daimon." Among Christians of the second century, however, the term "daimon" was already beginning to take on the negative nuances of its English transliteration—"demon" (e.g., 1 Cor 10:20).

Perhaps, then, one can understand why Ptolemy the Valentinian, in his letter to a Roman matron called Flora, reports how some people say that the devil gave the Mosaic Law. Ptolemy calls him the "opposing, corruption-making devil" who is also identified with the creator of this world.[19]

15. Jerome, *Comm. Micah* 1:12: "Both the Marcionites and the Manicheans use this scripture to show that the god of the Law is the creator of evil things" (trans. Thomas P. Scheck, *Ancient Christian Texts: Commentaries on the Twelve Prophets*, vol. 1, *Jerome* [Downers Grove: IVP Academic, 2016], 74).

16. Roughly equivalent to 1 Sam 18:10, a verse noted by Origen, *Cels.* 6.55; Cf. the "angel of the Lord" trying to kill Moses on his way back to Egypt (Exod 4:24). See further Räisänen, *Divine Hardening*, 47–52.

17. Tertullian, *AM* 1.2.1; Origen, *Princ.* 2.5.4; *Adamantius* 1.28; 2.20.

18. Lieu, *Marcion*, 256, 400; Matthew J. Thomas, *Paul's 'Works of the Law' in the Perspective of Second Century Reception* (Tübingen: Mohr Siebeck, 2018), 141–142.

19. Ptolemy, *Letter to Flora* 3.2.

If Ptolemy was describing the Marcionite view, he was inaccurate—since Marcion accepted the biblical idea of a devil separate from the creator.[20] Presumably, the devil was one of the creator's angels, as seen, for instance, in the book of Job (1–2). At the same time, one can see how Ptolemy could logically have connected Marcion's creator with the devil, especially if Marcion or his followers understood "the ruler of the authority of the air" (Laod 2:2), the "evil one" (Laod 6:16) and the "god of this world" (2 Cor 4:4) to refer to the creator.[21]

Harnack believed that, for Marcion, the lower creator was just, not evil. But the earliest evidence for Marcion indicates that—at least for the Pontian himself—the cosmocrator who creates evils has an evil character.[22] To be sure, the creator is just by his own lights. Yet, from the perspective of an entirely good God, the justice of the creator is cruel, savage, and vindictive—thus manifesting a perverse nature. The justice of the creator is like Roman justice—it worked to the imperialists' advantage. The cosmocrator is a shadow dictator, trying to enforce his regulations and laws on people, beginning with the people of Judea. But he is a slave master, a tyrant, only merciful to those who obey him, trying to control the narrative, opposing those who defy him or who try to escape his dominion.

A Jealous God

To exemplify the creator's bad character, Marcion pointed out that the creator was, by his own confession, jealous.[23] In the prevailing philosophy of Marcion's day, a God could not be jealous.[24] Plato had written: "There is no envy in the

---

20. Tertullian, *AM* 2.10.1–2 (the creator as originator of the devil). The devil is an angel of the creator in 5.16.

21. Litwa, *Evil Creator*, 90–108.

22. Irenaeus, *Haer.* 3.12.12; Tertullian, *AM* 1.2; *Ref.* 7.29.1; 7.30.2. See further Catherine Osborne, *Rethinking Early Greek Philosophy: Hippolytus of Rome and the Presocratics* (London: Duckworth, 1987), 100–108; Löhr, "Did Marcion Distinguish," 131–146. Moll, *Arch-Heretic*, 47–76, esp. 52.

23. This section adapts Litwa, *Evil Creator*, 74–77.

24. Tob 4:7, 16; 1 Macc 8:16; 3 Macc 6:7; Wisd 2:24; 6:23; 7:13; Sir 14:10; Philo, *Special Laws* 2.249; *That Every Good Person is Free* 13; *On the Creation of the World* 21, 77; *On the*

divine choir."[25] Aristotle made the same point: "the divine is not susceptible to jealousy."[26] True deity desires nothing for the simple reason that it lacks nothing. Jealousy assumes a certain insecurity due to lack. But God, according to Platonic theology, was perfect, complete, and self-sufficient.[27] Thus it was impossible for God to feel the flame of jealousy—in fact to feel any negative emotions at all.[28]

This widespread philosophical conception of God created a stumbling block for early Christians.[29] A famous passage in Jewish scripture has the creator declare himself to be a "jealous god." This declaration was memorable, given its place at the opening of the Ten Commandments (Exod 20:5; Deut 5:9). It was also emotionally loaded, because in context, the creator promised to punish the children of sinning fathers as far as the fourth generation.[30]

Cherubim 127; *Allegorical Interpretation* 1.80; 3.164, 203; *Questions and Answers on Genesis* 1.55; Irenaeus, *Haer.* 5.24.2; Clement of Alexandria, *Strom.* 5.4.24.1; 7.2.7.2.

25. Plato, *Phaedr.* 247a. Cf. *Timaeus* 29e; Musonius Rufus, *Discourses* 17 (Lutz); Celsus in Origen, *Cels.* 4.3; 8.21; *Corpus Hermeticum* 4.3. See further Ernst Milobenski, *Der Neid in der griechischen Philosophie* (Wiesbaden: Harrassowitz, 1964), 21–58; Thomas Rakoczy, *Böser Blick, Macht des Auges und Neid der Götter: Eine Untersuchung zur Kraft des Blickes in der griechischen Literatur* (Tübingen: Gunter Narr, 1996), 247–270; F. G. Herrmann, "φθόνος in the world of Plato's *Timaeus*," *Envy, Spite and Jealousy: The Rivalrous Emotions in Ancient Greece*, ed. David Konstan and N. Keith Rutter (Edinburgh: Edinburgh University Press, 2003), 53–84; Esther Eidinow, "Popular Theologies: The Gift of Divine Envy," in *Theologies of Ancient Greek Religions*, ed. Esther Eidinow, Julia Kindt, and Robin Osborne (Cambridge: Cambridge University Press, 2016), 205–232; Lieu, *Marcion*, 337–340.

26. Aristotle, *Metaphysics* 982a (οὔτε τὸ θεὸν φθονερὸν ἐνδέχεται εἶναι). See further Michael J. Mills, "ΦΘΟΝΟΣ and its related ΠΑΘΗ In Plato and Aristotle," *Phronesis* 30:1 (1985): 1–12.

27. Alcinous, *Handbook* 10.3; Apuleius, *Plato and His Teaching* 1.5.

28. Tertullian *AM* 4.31.5: "Marcion denies that his god is disturbed." Cf. 5.4.14: "the God of Marcion knows neither how to get angry nor take revenge." Marcion's God is connected to tranquility in *Praescr.* 7; cf. *AM* 4.29.10 Cf. Alcinous, *Handbook* 10.4; Aristotle, *Met.* 12.1073a11; Sextus Emp. *Hyp.* 1.162.

29. Lieu, *Marcion*, 338. In the LXX, jealousy (φθόνος) was already a negative attribute. See Tob 4:7, 16; 1 Macc 8:16; 3 Macc 6:7; Wisd 2:24; 6:23; 7:13; Sir 14:10. Irenaeus agreed that "jealousy is alien to god" (*Haer.* 5.24.2). Cf. Clement, *Strom.* 7.2.7.2; 5.4.24.1. See further Herbert Frohnhofen, *Apatheia tou Theou: Über die Affektlosigkeit Gottes in der griechischen Antike und be den griechischsprachigen Kirchenvätern bis zu Gregorios Thamaturgos* (Frankfurt am Main: Peter Lang, 1987), 143–57, 221–231.

30. Marcion criticized transgenerational punishment (Tertullian, *AM* 2.15.1–2; cf. 4.27.8).

Marcion and his followers underscored the creator's jealousy to undermine his claim to deity.[31] Jealousy indicates that the creator was morally flawed, subject to change, and thus a slave to corruption. If the creator was subject to corruption, then he could and would perish with every other being in the universe bound by the laws of decay.[32] Marcionites perhaps adapted this argument from philosophical skepticism: if god experiences any kind of distress, he is incomplete, and if he is incomplete, he desires change, and if he is changeable, he is also perishable, but a God cannot perish.[33] A god who can change and perish is in fact no God at all.

The Vain Claim

In the same chapter of Isaiah in which the creator confessed to making "evils," he announces: "I am the master, the god, and there is no other god besides me . . . I am the god and there is no other" (45:5, 22). The Greek practice of using a definite article (*the* god) was a way of signifying that the creator claimed to be the chief god—and in this case, the only one.

Perhaps in their original setting, these declarations sounded with a ring of comfort. Isaiah's creator cradled the world in his hands, invisibly tugging the strings of global politics. But to Marcion, the creator's words sounded ignorant. Any gentile in the ancient Mediterranean could look around and observe that the Judean daimon was hardly the only god; he was barely even heard of outside the confines of the province of Judea. This daimon was in every way a particular deity, dyed in local color, showing open favoritism for the Abrahamic clan. To the average Greek or Roman, there was nothing particularly unique about this deity, except his claim to be unique.[34]

---

31. Tertullian, *AM* 4.27.8. See further Ekkehard Muehlenberg, "Marcion's Jealous God," in *Disciplina Nostra: Essays in Memory of Robert F. Evans*, ed. Donald F. Winslow (Philadelphia: Patristic Foundation, 1979), 93–114.

32. Tertullian, *AM* 2.16.3.

33. Sextus Empiricus, *Against the Physicists* 1.157, 170. Carneades and Panaetius concluded that "what receives suffering must also accept death" (Cicero, *Nat. D.* 3.32; *Tusc.* 1.79). For the death of daimones, see Plutarch, *Decline of Oracles* 17 with Philippe Borgeaud, "The Death of the Great Pan: Problems of Interpretation," *History of Religions* 22:3 (1983): 254–283.

34. For example, Numenius frag. 56 (des Places): the Jewish god "considers no one worthy to share his honor."

Marcion did not assume the creator's uniqueness. To be sure, he believed, like other Christians, in a transcendent, loving Father revealed by Jesus. The creator's particularity and malice showed that he was not that transcendent, good deity. Marcion and his followers were thus led to interpret the creator's *claim* to be singular as a sign of his ignorance.[35] The creator was simply unaware of the true deity existing above him, so he foolishly declared that he alone was "god."

Yet, foolishness and ignorance were not the creator's only flaws. His trumpeted uniqueness sounded to Marcion's ears like arrogance—widely considered to be a vice in antiquity. The Epicurean philosopher Philodemus (about 110–40 BCE) defined arrogance as a disposition involving a sense of superiority and the haughty scorn of perceived competitors.[36] The competitors of the creator were the other deities worshiped by the nations (e.g., Exod 20:3; 34:14). The creator acknowledged that these competitors existed on some level.

A sign of the creator's arrogance, according to Marcion, was the fact that he swore by himself (Isa 45:22–23: "I am god; there is no other, I swear by myself").[37] In effect, the creator lacked evidence for his uniqueness, so he appealed to his own authority, employing a kind of self-authenticating and self-deifying rhetoric.[38]

Jewish scripture typically presented self-deifiers as arch-sinners suffering a swift demise. For instance, the personified city of Babylon proclaimed: "I am, and there is no other!" (Isa 47:10). The Judean lord himself responded to this proclamation with heated words: "Destruction shall seize you, though you don't anticipate it; there will be a pit into which you fall" (Isa 47:11). A

35. Tertullian, *AM* 1.11.9. Cf. Tertullian, *Flesh of Christ* 24.1–2: "Looking ahead to Marcion [the creator] said 'I am god and there is no other besides me." Cf. Ephrem: "acknowledge, O Marcion, the justice of him who said, I am god and there is none beside me!" (Mitchell, *Prose Refutations* 2.xxviii, modified; cf. 2.xliv).

36. Philodemus, "On Arrogance," 2.27, with Voula Tsouna, *The Ethics of Philodemus*, (Oxford: Oxford University Press, 2007), 145. See further Tsouna, "Aristo on Blends of Arrogance," in *Aristo of Ceos: Text, Translation and Discussion*, ed. William Fortenbaugh (London: Routledge, 2017), 279–292.

37. Tertullian, *AM* 1.11.9; cf. 2.26.1 and Eznik of Kolb, *A Treatise on God Written in Armenian by Eznik of Kołb (floruit c.430-c.450)*, trans. Monica J. Blanchard and Robin Darling Young (Leuven: Peeters, 1998), 358, 370.

38. M. David Litwa, *Desiring Divinity: Self-deification in Ancient Jewish and Christian Mythmaking* (Oxford: Oxford University Press, 2016), 47–65.

similar oracle was addressed to Lucifer the morning star: "You said in your heart, 'I will ascend to heaven . . . I will be like the Most High,' but now you go down into hell!" (Isa 14:12–14; cf. Ezek 28:1–10).

The most open and stubborn form of self-deification, however, was not perpetrated by Lucifer or Babylon. The most patent self-deifier in Jewish scripture was the creator himself, who repeatedly announced, "I am god and there is no other!" (Isa 45:22); "I am god, there is no one like me!" (Isa 46:9); "Behold, behold that I am, and there is no god except me!" (Deut 32:39).[39] When Marcionite Christians encountered this crowing creator, they made a logical conclusion: this "god" was not simply asserting his authority and control; he was infected with the vices of ignorance and arrogance.

Evil in Eden

For Marcion, the vice of the creator was showcased in the very first law legislated for humanity. The creator commanded Adam not to eat from the tree of the knowledge of good and evil (Gen 2:17). This unexplained rule seemed to many an arbitrary obstacle to humanity's education and growth. To quote the famous line from the *Testimony of Truth*: "What kind of god is this? First, he begrudged Adam's eating from the tree of knowledge . . . He has certainly shown himself to be a malicious envier."[40]

What struck Marcion, apparently, was that the creator commanded a law he knew the first humans would transgress. It was as if the creator foreknew that humans would run headlong off a cliff, but still set them playing like children by a precipice.[41] This precipice, moreover, was not some necessary evil, but the creator's own design. He deliberately crafted an object—a beautiful tree

39. Note also Isa 43:10; 44:6; 45:5–7, 18, 21–22.

40. *Testimony of Truth* (NHC IX,3) 47.14–48.4. See, Willem Cornelis van Unnik, "Der Neid in der Paradiesgeschichte nach einigen gnostischen Texten," in *Essays on the Nag Hammadi Texts in Honour of Alexander Böhlig*, ed. M. Krause (Leiden: Brill, 1972), 120–132; Miriam von Nordheim-Diehl, "Der Neid Gottes, des Teufels und der Menschen—eine motivgeschichtliche Skizze," in *Emotions from Ben Sira to Paul*, ed. Renate Egger-Wenzel and Jeremey Corley (Berlin: de Gruyter, 2012), 431–450.

41. The precipice image comes from Tertullian, *AM* 4.38.1. On the basis of *AM* 2.4.5–6 it can be gathered that Marcion(ites) cited Gen 2:17 to undermine the goodness of the creator.

with ripe and seductive fruit—and himself decreed the lethal punishment for eating from it (Gen 2:17). Given this scenario, Marcionites accused the creator not simply of carelessness, but of malice.

There were additional problems. Even if the creator is not the direct maker of evil, he still allowed it to enter and pollute creation.[42] He designed, as it were, a computer game in which many of the characters became evil. Evil, in short, must be traced back to the creator. If the creator is the creator of this entire world, that includes evil, even if it emerges indirectly through the will of his creatures. The creator is indirectly the maker of evils, since they would not have existed apart from his creation. The Marcionite logic is, in the end, straightforward. By shaping matter, the creator allowed the advent of evil, became its enabler, thereby proving that "he was himself evil."[43]

* * *

Marcion was, like all readers of the Bible, selective—perhaps culpably so. Yet, whereas most Christians today read Scripture to emphasize the creator's goodness, the Pontian underscored precisely the opposite—his wickedness. As it turned out, he hardly lacked material. Only a few topics have been discussed here: the creator as maker of evils, ignorantly boasting, designing temptation in Eden, and jealous.

It's evident from various sources, however, that Marcionites underscored other offenses of the creator. According to Tertullian, they emphasized the creator wiping out humanity with a flood, firebombing the cities of Sodom and Gomorrah, sending plagues against Egypt, hardening Pharaoh's heart, and killing the Israelites in the desert.[44] According to the report of Irenaeus, the creator "makes evils, is lustful for war, is inconstant in his judgments, and contradicts himself."[45]

---

42. Tertullian, *Herm.* 10.1.

43. Tertullian, *Herm.* 10.3. In the immediate context Tertullian mentioned "heretics" who, discovering the evil of the creator, concluded that there was "another supremely good god"—the trademark of Marcion.

44. All these episodes are mentioned by Tertullian, *AM* 2.14.4. Origen added the killing of the Israelites in the desert (*Princ.* 2.5.1). Cf. Jerome, *Comm. Micah* 1.9: "But if he [the creator] seems to us to be cruel, harsh and bloodthirsty, since he obliterated the human race in the flood, rained fire and brimstone upon Sodom and Gomorrah, drowned the Egyptians in the waters and made the corpses of the Israelites fall in the desert . . ." (trans. Thomas P. Scheck).

45. Irenaeus, *Haer.* 1.27.2.

The critique of the creator in the Pseudo-Clementine *Homilies* probably did not come from Marcion's *Antitheses*.[46] Nevertheless, it still usefully sums up the Marcionite critique of the lower creator: he lies, tempts people, flies into rage, changes his mind, becomes jealous, hardens hearts, blinds people, deafens them, counsels people to pillage, mocks people, shows weakness, creates evils; delights in war, shows no familial affection, and is not faithful to fulfill his promises.[47]

Now Marcion's opponents did their best to show how the characters of Christ and creator were compatible, with the creator, for instance, altering his salvific program in response to human maturation. But the enormity of the anti-Marcionite response from the second to the fifth centuries CE shows just how powerful and enduring Marcionite arguments were perceived to be.[48] Indeed, Marcionite arguments continue to crop up among people who do not know their Marcionite character. Marcion was the pathbreaker who first demonstrated *from the creator's own scriptures* that his justice was a form of cruelty, and that his repeatedly evil actions—which he himself admits (Isa 45:7)—proved him malign.

* * *

Coda
Marcion and "Gnosticism"

Clement of Alexandria wrote that Marcionites preach an alien "gnosis," or knowledge.[49] This is not a dig, since Clement himself spoke of "gnosis" in a positive sense throughout his work. Gnosis referred to deeper knowledge, and Marcion plausibly viewed the revelation of Christ—hidden from ages past—as a form of gnosis. Such views were common, however, and not enough to

46. *Pace* Harnack, *Marcion*, 278*.

47. Pseudo-Clement, *Homilies* 43–44. See further *Homilies* 3.38, where the creator is "without foreknowledge, imperfect, needy, not good, and a slave to countless horrid passions." Tertullian, addressing Marcion, listed some of the creator's passions: he becomes enraged (*irascitur*) and jealous (*aemulatur*), exalts himself (*extollitur*) and becomes irritated (*exacerbatur*) (*AM* 2.16.3); he is also "most pitiless/bitter (*acerbissimus*)" (3.4.2).

48. For the enormity of the anti-Marcionite response, see Harnack, *Marcion*, 99–103; Lampe, *From Paul* 250–251. See further Jason D. BeDuhn, "Biblical Antitheses, Adda, and the *Acts of Archelaus*," in *Frontiers of Faith: The Christian Encounter with Manichaeism in the Acts of Archelaus*, ed. Paul Mirecki and Jason BeDuhn (Leiden: Brill, 2007), 131–147.

49. Clement, *Strom.* 3.3.12.3.

classify Marcion as a gnostic in any technical sense (as a member of a self-named gnostic school). Yet the use of gnosis in reference to Marcion's movement opens up larger and perennial questions about Marcion and "Gnosticism."

Harnack famously said that Marcion was not a gnostic, though the historian's motives are generally recognized as apologetic. According to Harnack, Gnosticism was Christianity with cancer, a Christianity acutely affected with the malignant tumor of "Hellenism." Accordingly, the historian had to divorce Marcion from Gnosticism in order to portray Marcion as a Christian, a biblicist, a Paulinist, and something like a Protestant reformer. Scholars who do not see Christianity and Gnosis as opposed will not share Harnack's scruples.

Perhaps the best known twentieth-century student of Gnosticism, Hans Jonas, said that Marcion was a gnostic, and his discussion has become classic. Jonas had a typological view of Gnosticism based on his phenomenological method. A typological view says that Gnosticism has several key features, and if a system of thought has some or all of these features, then it can be called "gnostic" or (if one needs to hedge) "gnosticizing."

According to Jonas, some elements of Marcion's thought were gnostic, and some were not. Marcion, Jonas admitted, does not tick most gnostic boxes since "his teaching is entirely free" of "mythological fancy," since he had no apparent interest in telling the story of how the universe began, since he did not claim there was a divine spark in humanity. But Marcion was most certainly a gnostic by virtue of his "idea of the unknown God opposed to that of the cosmos, the very conception of an inferior and oppressive creator and the consequent view of salvation as liberation from his power by an alien principle."[50] Marcion was also "anticosmic" (opposed to the material world)—which was for Jonas another key gnostic trait.

Today, Marcion continues to be classed as a gnostic by virtue of such typological features. Some see a tension in Marcion between a redeemer God and the creator, a tension that is even more extreme than in most gnostics.[51] In addition to the idea of an inferior creator, scholars view Marcion as pessimistic about the world and the flesh. They attribute to him an inverse or contrarian interpretation of Old Testament stories.[52] Although Marcion is never said to

50. Jonas, *The Gnostic Religion: The Message of the Alien God and the Beginnings of Christianity*, 3rd ed. (Boston: Beacon, 2001), 137.

51. May, *Creatio ex nihilo*, 54.

52. Wilson, "Marcion and the Jews," 51.

have met Valentinus, or Basilides, or Saturninus, surely there must have been some cross-fertilization of ideas. He may have even met Valentinus personally in Rome.

What is Gnosticism?

If Marcion is classed as a gnostic based on typological definitions of Gnosticism, one can ask exactly how many traits he needs to have before being classed as a gnostic. A major problem here is that some categorize Marcion as a gnostic because they accept heresiological clichés about him as a docetist, a ditheist, a world-denier, and so on.[53] This book casts doubt on Marcion's acceptance of these dogmas. Still, it is clear that the Pontian supported "negative demiurgy"—the evil creator.[54]

It's useful to compare the details of Marcion's negative demiurgy with his presumed gnostic (or Sethian) contemporaries.[55] Marcionites and Sethians both agreed that the creator was evil. They emphasized the vain claim of the creator (permutations of "I am god and there is no other").[56] They both pointed out the evil in the garden of Eden, and the creator's jealousy manifest there and elsewhere.[57] Moreover, Marcion's idea that Christ redeemed Cain, the Sodomites,

---

53. Ugo Bianchi, "Marcion: théologien biblique ou docteur gnostique?" in *Selected Essays on Gnosticism, Dualism, and Mysteriosophy* (Leiden: Brill, 1978), 320–327.

54. Litwa, *Evil Creator*, 162.

55. David Brakke, *The Gnostics: Myth, Ritual, and Diversity in Early Christianity* (Cambridge, MA: Harvard University Press, 2010).

56. Cf. *Ap. John* (NHC II,1) 11.20–21; 13.8–9; *Hyp. Arch* (NHC II,4) 86.30–31; *Orig. World* (NHC II.5) 103.11–12; Irenaeus, *Haer.* 1.29.4; 1.30.6; *Ref.* 6.33; 7.25.3; Ps.-Clement, *Recognitions* 2.57.3; *2 Disc. Seth* (NHC VII,2) 64.20–26. See further Steve Johnston, "Le mythe gnostique du blasphème de l'Archonte," in *Les textes de Nag Hammadi: Histoire des religions et approaches contemporaines. Actes du colloque international réuni à Paris*, ed. M. Jean-Pierre Mahé, M. Paul-Hubert Poirier, and Madeleine Scopello (Paris: AIBL, 2010), 177–201.

57. See, e.g., Irenaeus, *Haer.* 1.30.7; *Ap. John* (NHC II) 13,5–13; *Reality of the Rulers* (NHC II,4) 96.3–6). The creator proclaims his jealousy in Irenaeus *Haer.* 1.29.4; *Eg. Gospel* (NHC III) 58.25–26. See further A. H. B. Logan, "The Jealousy of God: Exod 20,5 in Gnostic and Rabbinic Theology," *Studia Biblica* 1 (1978): 197–203; Muehlenberg, "Marcion's Jealous God" 93–114; Miriam von Nordheim-Diehl, "Der Neid Gottes, des Teufels und der Menschen—eine motivgeschichtliche Skizze," in *Emotions from Ben Sira to Paul*, ed. Renate Egger-Wenzel and Jeremey Corley (Berlin: de Gruyter, 2012), 431–450; Luttikhuizen, *Gnostic Revisions of Genesis*.

and the Egyptians resembles ideas that Irenaeus attributes to members of his "gnostic mob."[58]

But there are key differences between Sethian and Marcionite interpretations. The Sethians put the creator's vain claim in a set of new creation stories illustrating the creator's arrogance before his angels. Marcion, by contrast, emphasized the creator's ignorance: he swore by himself because he did not know there was a superior God.[59] Due to their interest in Genesis, Sethians took time to rewrite the Genesis story—especially its initial six chapters—whereas Marcion used Genesis as only one arrow in a full quiver of other "antitheses." Sethians also created new scriptures, such as the *Holy Book of the Great Invisible Spirit* and *The Secret Book of John*. On this score, Marcion is strikingly different, since he did not expand, but contracted the scope of scripture for his group.

With regard to the redemption of Cain and the Sodomites, Marcion was not supporting an inversion of traditional moral values.[60] "Old" Testament villains recognize their need for Christ's mercy. The patriarchs, by contrast, only remain in Hades because they think they are being tricked by the creator.[61] Abraham, Isaac, and Jacob are righteous, but poorly conditioned because of their loyalty to the creator. Marcion agreed with so-called Sethians that the Law and Prophets told the true (if partial) story of a false god. But if the Sethian style of interpretation can be called "inverse exegesis," this is not a fair description of Marcion's hermeneutics. The Pontian was in general a literal or historical reader of Jewish scripture, and it's not clear if he was directly opposing the interpretations of any discrete group.

Heresiologists sometimes associate Marcion's view of Christ's body with (eastern) Valentinian views. Eastern Valentinians said that Christ had a spirit body and an animate body.[62] Unfortunately, there is no clear statement as to how exactly Marcion described Jesus's body. Evidently, he would have followed his scriptures by envisioning it as something "like" human flesh—solid, to be

---

58. Irenaeus, *Haer.* 1.29.1; 1.31.1.

59. Norelli, "La funzione di Paolo" 580–81.

60. *Pace* Osborne, *Rethinking*, 107. See also Norelli, "La funzione di Paolo," 582–586.

61. See further Norelli, "Note sulla soteriologia di Marcione," 298–300.

62. Thomassen, *Spiritual Seed: The Church of the "Valentinians"* (Leiden: Brill, 2006), 62–71, 73–75, 79, 103, 124–128.

sure—but not exactly the same as mortal flesh. On a general level, it seems, these statements concurred with those of Valentinus. Valentinus considered Christ's flesh to be pure and incorruptible and so as something better than "default" human flesh.[63] Comparison is hindered by the fragmentary nature of the evidence. As in the case with Marcion, there is no clear statement from Valentinus himself that Christ's body was actually made up of something different from normal matter. Valentinians after Valentinus and Marcionites after Marcion more fully theorized the nature of Jesus's body (chapters 11 and 14).

Who Came First?

Jonas assumed that Marcion was shaped by preformed gnostic ideas.[64] But if one has a sociologically informed understanding of the gnostics, not just a phenomenological understanding of Gnostic*ism*, then one must try to pinpoint actual lines of influence. Marcion was very early in Christian history. What self-identifying "gnostics" did he actually meet? The obvious player here might seem to be Cerdo. If Marcion was connected to Cerdo, however, that would not make him gnostic, since Cerdo's intellectual pedigree is unclear. Irenaeus tries to connect Cerdo to Simon of Samaria, but the link seems invented.[65] Cerdo's connection with Syrian gnostics like Saturninus is an extrapolation from Epiphanius, who was the first to say that Cerdo came from Syria. Nevertheless, Cerdo's distinction between a just and a good God does not actually resemble the theology of Saturninus, given surviving reports.[66]

In the end, there is little evidence that so-called gnostics—including Valentinians and Sethians—preceded Marcion. Valentinus was a contemporary of Marcion, to be sure, but much of what came to be identified as Valentinian theology was the brainchild of his disciples. Second-generation Marcionites (Apelles, Lucanus, Prepon) interacted extensively with second-generation Valentinian thought as represented by Heracleon and Ptolemy. Ptolemy may

63. Valentinus, frag. 3 (Völker). See further Litwa, "Deification and Defecation: Valentinus Fragment 3 and the Physiology of Jesus' Digestion," *Journal of Early Christian Studies* 31, no. 1 (2023): 1–18.

64. Jonas, *Gnostic Religion*, 138.

65. Irenaeus, *Haer.* 1.27.1.

66. Irenaeus, *Haer.* 1.24.1–2.

have adapted Marcion's distinction between goodness and justice with reference to God; and Heracleon's idea of the Logos as lower creator might even be anti-Marcionite.[67] Yet if Valentinians were anti-Marcionite, Marcionites do not seem to have been anti-Valentinian. Apelles and Lucanus, it seems, adapted the notion of a just creator from Ptolemy and Heracleon, as opposed to Marcion's evil creator (chapter 14).

One cannot speak of named Sethians in Marcion's time, but one can point to a kind of "proto-Sethian": Saturninus. Saturninus was Marcion's contemporary, and, at first sight, they share many doctrines: an evil creator, an unknown Father, a Christ opposed to the creator, a rejection of the prophets, and an ethic of celibacy. But the devil is in the details. Marcion's Christ was a destroyer of the Law rather than of the creator specifically. Marcion did not reject the prophets as liars or attribute their prophecies to angels. The Pontian did not entirely forbid meat, and he did not enforce celibacy on all members of his communion. On present evidence, moreover, Saturninus had a more developed story of cosmology (a theory of angelic creation and the divine spark), as well as the notion that the creator himself was an angel. The creator as angel appears only with Marcion's disciple Apelles. These differences make it hard to prove any genetic connection between Saturninus and Marcion, though it would be hardly surprising if some Saturninian ideas percolated Rome in the 140s CE.

The earliest evidence for distinctly Sethian theology is the *Gospel of Judas*, which was probably written during Marcion's lifetime (between 130 and 170 CE).[68] Marcion agreed with the author of *Judas* that Jesus's disciples were flawed. But the virtual demonization of these apostles in *Judas* goes beyond Marcion.[69] Developed Sethian theology featuring Yaldabaoth, Barbelo, the Four Lights, the Selfborn, Adamas, and so on, seems to have evolved at least a generation after Marcion.

* * *

67. Markschies, "Die valentinianische Gnosis und Marcion—Einige neue Perspektiven," in May and Greschat, *Marcion und seine kirchengeschichtliche Wirkung*, 159–176 at 167–168.

68. David Brakke, *The Gospel of Judas: A New Translation with Introduction and Commentary* (New Haven: Yale University Press, 2022), 12–17.

69. Enrico Norelli, "Marcion et les disciples de Jésus," *Apocrypha* 19 (2008): 9–42 at 13.

If "Gnosticism" is only a reinscription of heresiological slander (Gnosticism = ditheism, docetism, and the deletion of scripture), then the term is best avoided for Marcion.[70] Nevertheless, one cannot artificially disassociate Marcion from his contemporaries like Saturninus and Valentinus. In comparing these "gnostic" contemporaries, one should prefer concrete evidence, details about a common cultural context, and disciplined social history over typological definitions and speculation on abstract ideas. The fact is, Marcionite Christians *did* overlap with their Sethian and Valentinian contemporaries on theological issues such as negative demiurgy and the nature of Jesus's body. To advance historical research, it seems best to focus on *these specific issues* rather than to debate whether Marcion fits a macrocategory of "Gnosticism." Once scholars have a clear definition of "Gnosis" or "Gnosticism," then they can reopen the debate about whether Marcion fits the category, and why such a classification is useful for creating knowledge, as opposed to reinscribing heresiological rhetoric.

70. See further Karen L. King, *What is Gnosticism*? (Cambridge, MA: Belknap Press, 2003).

CHAPTER ELEVEN

Marcion's View of Christ

> He is carried, he walks, wears clothes, duly sleeps, is brought to trial, suffers, is hung, and is buried. All this is evidence of a man who is transformed into a holy body.
>
> —*Carmen adversus Marcionitas* 1.98–100

HERESIOLOGISTS EMPHASIZED THEOLOGICAL differences in order to exclude Marcionites from their social groups. But it's useful first to examine points on which Marcion and his opponents agreed. Both Marcion and early catholics believed that Christ was God's son (Gal 4:4) who came to save people from their sins and from demonic forces. This Christ taught in Galilee, performed miracles, and had controversies with Jewish leaders. He died on a cross, rose on the third day, and showed his body to his disciples. In so doing, Christ freed gentiles from compulsion to practice Jewish Law in order to obtain inheritance in God's kingdom (Gal 5:1, 3; Rom 8:2).

Despite these basic overlaps, heresiologists underscored the differences between their views of Jesus and Marcion's. Reportedly Marcion did not believe that Christ was the son of this world's creator. Christ was not heralded by the Hebrew prophets. He was not even human, it is said; he only appeared in flesh, whereas he was actually a phantasm.[1]

Docetism?

Today, scholars continue to reinforce Marcion's supposed belief in the phantasmal nature of Jesus's body (a position called "phantasmal docetism").[2]

---

1. *Ref.* 10.19.3; Tertullian, *Carn. Chr.* 4.

2. For the varieties of docetism, see David E. Wilhite, "Was Marcion a Docetist? The Body of Evidence vs. Tertullian's Argument," *Vigiliae Christianae* 71 (2017): 4; Karen L. King, "Reconsidering Docetism," in *Nag Hammadi a 70 ans. Qu'avons-nous appris?*, ed.

Marcion's Jesus "was only apparently a man."[3] Marcion's Christ "inhabited a humanlike, ghostly form, like an angel, the same nonmaterial 'body' the elect will have in the resurrection."[4] "Marcion . . . thought that Jesus was a phantasm. He had not actually 'come in the flesh.'"[5] One could go on.[6]

In trying to disentangle the truth of these remarks, one should begin with Marcion's scriptures. All interpreters of Paul had to reckon with two verses:

> God, sending Christ in the likeness of sinful flesh (*en homoiōmati sarkos hamartias*) . . . (Rom 8:3)
>
> [Christ] emptied himself, taking a slave's form, becoming in the likeness of a human being (*en homoiōmati anthrōpou*), and being found in appearance as a human (*schēmati heuretheis hōs anthrōpos*) . . . (Phil 2:7).

Tertullian recognized that these verses reinforced the Marcionite point of view. He provides what appears to be a Marcionite commentary on the latter verse: Christ "took up the form of a servant—not in truth—and was in the likeness of a human—not in a human—and was found in appearance as a person—not in substance."[7]

Paul's consistent use of Christ's "likeness" or "appearance" in flesh is important. The Tarsian evidently thought that Jesus was "born of woman" (Gal 4:4) and that he had something that strongly *resembled* human flesh, but he was

---

Eric Crégheur, Louis Painchaud, and Tuomas Rasimus (Leuven: Peeters, 2019), 17–30; T. Christopher Hoklotubbe, "What is Docetism?" in *Re-making the World: Christianity and Categories: Essays in Honor of Karen L. King*, ed. Taylor G. Petrey (Tübingen: Mohr Siebeck, 2019), 49–71, esp. 58–59.

3. John Barton "An Early Metacommentary: Tertullian's *Against Marcion*," in *Reading from Right to Left: Essays on the Hebrew Bible in Honour of David J.A. Clines*, ed. J. Cheryl Exum and H. G. M. Williamson (Sheffield: Sheffield Academic Press, 2003), 38–49 at 41.

4. Dungan, *History of the Synoptic Problem*, 51.

5. Ehrman, *Studies in the Textual Criticism*, 348.

6. Vinzent, *Christ's Resurrection*, 122: "To Marcion Christ would not and even could not have added hollow matter to his spiritual body" (123). Peter Head claims that Marcion "regularly uses φάντασμα to describe Christ's body" ("Foreign God," 313). DeConick refers to "Marcion's idea that Jesus was an apparition" (*Comparing Christianities*, 40).

7. Tertullian, *AM* 5.20.3.

not *exactly* human in the way that all other humans were. One cannot expect the body of the incarnate son of God to be identical with the default flesh of common humanity. Being a god logically made a difference to one's bodily constitution—as seen in the Transfiguration story (where Jesus's flesh literally glows). At the very least, Christ's flesh was not tainted by human sin and throttled by base desires.[8]

At the same time, Marcion's Gospel repeatedly demonstrates that Christ's flesh was solid to the touch. Epiphanius points out that the hemorrhaging woman who touched Jesus "did not touch air, but tangible humanity." To confirm that real contact occurred, Jesus asked, "Who touched me? For I recognized power leaving me" (G 8:45–46).[9] For his part, Jesus could touch lepers and be jostled by a crowd. A woman could drench his feet with her tears, plant kisses on them, and wipe them with her hair (G 7:38).[10]

The greatest proof of Jesus's materiality is his death. Christ, according to Marcion's Gospel, was beaten, slapped, whipped, crucified, and buried.[11] He truly suffered, and it is important to emphasize these sufferings, because occasionally one still hears distortions such as the idea that, "Marcion claimed that Jesus . . . had not been crucified . . . nor did he die."[12] Even the heresiologists did not say this. Marcion's Gospel clearly portrayed the crucifixion (G 23:33–46) with no hint that it was a simulation.

The heresiologists were keen to emphasize that, even in Marcion's text, Jesus both predicted his suffering (G 9:22, 44) and actually suffered. Epiphanius observes, "So how is he captured and crucified if he is not subject to touch, according to your teaching, Marcion? . . . For you cannot define him as a phantasm."[13] Precisely. Again, Epiphanius urges (quite reasonably): "The one not having flesh cannot be crucified."[14] Finally, he adds: "A simulation or wind or spirit or phantasm cannot receive preparation for burial, a tomb, and

8. See further Francis Watson, "Pauline Reception and the Problem of Docetism," in *Docetism in the Early Church: The Quest for an Elusive Phenomenon*, ed. Joseph Verheyden, Reimund Bieringer, Jens Schröter and Ines Jäger (Tübingen: Mohr Siebeck, 2018), 61–66.

9. Epiphanius, *Pan.* 42.11.5, elenchus 14.

10. As pointed out by Epiphanius, *Pan.* 42.11.5, elenchus 10–11.

11. Admitted by Irenaeus, *Haer.* 4.33.2; Tertullian, *Carn. Chr.* 5.1; *AM* 3.11.8.

12. Dungan, *History of the Synoptic Problem*, 48.

13. Epiphanius, *Pan.* 42.11.5, elenchus 4.

14. Epiphanius, *Pan.* 42.11.5, elenchus 71.

resurrection."[15] After his resurrection, according to Marcion's Gospel, Christ showed his hands and feet. He openly denied that he was a spirit, and showed his body of bones. He even ate a piece of broiled fish (G 23:39–43).

Here one can lay to rest a common misinterpretation inspired by Tertullian. Tertullian was so baffled that Marcion's Christ showed his hands, feet, and bones, that the Carthaginian proposed that Marcion deliberately failed to omit this verse (G 24:39) in order to camouflage his other editorial omissions. Marcion did not omit everything that was against him, said Tertullian, in order to gaslight and confuse people, distracting them from his other omissions.[16] The logic is tortured, and Tertullian strains to preserve his own theory—that Marcion edited with a knife—in the face of a massive anomaly. If Marcion cut out anything, he should have cut out the resurrected Christ's hands, feet, and bones!

Tertullian's initial struggle with 24:39 in Marcion's text indicates that his later interpretation of it is not Marcion's view but his own, foisted upon the Pontian. It is Tertullian, that is, who twists 24:39 into a meaning that it did not have and that no one in the history of interpretation said it had: "you see me not having bones, just as a spirit."[17] It is astounding to hear a modern interpreter react to Tertullian's invention: "Obviously, word order argues against this reading, but the interpretation remains grammatically viable."[18]

The real question here is whether such a reading is permissible in its literary context. The context shows that Jesus is trying to prove—*against the supposition of the disciples*—that he is *not* a "spirit" (or, as Marcion had it, a "phantasm," G 24:37), not that he *is* a spirit who also happens to lack bones. Tertullian was happy to adjust the commonly-accepted meaning of scriptural texts elsewhere to fit his argument.[19] Knowing this tendency, one does well not to accept his (mis)translation as representing Marcion's point of view. Epiphanius, in this case, was more honest than Tertullian; he pointed out

15. Epiphanius, *Pan.* 42.11.5, elenchus 16.

16. Tertullian, *AM* 4.43.7; Epiphanius, *Pan.* 42.11.17 schol. 78.

17. Tertullian, *AM* 4.43.7.

18. Hays, "Marcion vs. Luke," 220.

19. Tertullian, *AM* 5.11.9 (on 2 Cor 4:4).

the plain meaning of the text: "after the resurrection he [Jesus] has bones and flesh, as he himself testifies, saying 'as you see me having.'"[20]

Regrettably, some scholars still choose to follow Tertullian in foisting his (mis)translation onto Marcion.[21] One researcher writes that the "Marcionite reading of the verse [24:39] is (just) comprehensible: inspecting Jesus's hands and feet will enable them to verify his identity and see that a spirit has no bones, *in just the same way as* they see he has."[22] Another says that Marcion reinterpreted 24:39, "in the interests of his docetic Christology to read: 'A spirit, such as ye see me to be, hath not bones.'"[23] To be sure, Marcion could have viewed the resurrected Christ as "a life-giving spirit" (1 Cor 15:45), but this spirit—according to Marcion's Gospel—still had bones.

Although Marcion's text lacked some words found in Luke 24:39, these unattested words do not mean that Marcion was a phantasmal docetist. Marcion's Christ invited the disciples to "see," but not to "touch" his body. But this is not a docetic reading, since the disciples only needed to use their eyes, not their hands, to see that he had bones. Marcion's text also did not apparently have the word "flesh." Christ says: "you behold me having bones" not "flesh and bones." But the word "flesh" is not technically needed to prove that Jesus had a solid body. If Jesus had bones, he had the most solid element of flesh, the very thing on which flesh hangs. One can easily imagine an early catholic editor later adding "flesh" to favor the resurrection of the flesh, but this addition would only clarify what Marcion's text already implied: even the postmortem Jesus—let alone Jesus before he died—had a solid body.[24]

Tertullian and Epiphanius of course knew the many texts in Marcion's Gospel that disproved docetism (he is touched, he eats, he sleeps, and so on).[25] It simply did not sink in that this material proves that Marcion himself was

20. Epiphanius, *Pan.* 42.11.17, elenchus 78.

21. Grant, *Letter and Spirit*, 118.

22. Carter, "Marcion's Christology," 558, emphasis original; cf. 565, 581.

23. Head, "Foreign God," 321, citing Harnack, *Marcion*, 239*. Cf. Vinzent, *Christ's Resurrection*, 121 and his "Der Schluss des Lukasevangeliums bei Marcion," in May and Greschat, *Marcion und seine kirchengeschichtliche Wirkung*, 79–94, esp. 85–86.

24. See further Daniel A. Smith, "Seeing a Pneuma(tic body): The Apologetic Interests of Luke 24:36–43," *Catholic Biblical Quarterly* 72, no. 4 (2010): 752–772, esp. 761–765.

25. For example, Epiphanius, *Pan.* 42.10.6.

no docetist. But the basic logic is not hard to grasp: if Marcion believed his scriptures, then he was not a docetist. Marcion believed his scriptures, therefore he was not a docetist.[26]

When one hears the heresiologists accusing Marcion of docetism, one is overhearing a debate about how to interpret scripture. The actual substance of the debate has been lost in the roar of repeated accusation, but the contours are still visible. Despite the impression heresiologists give, Marcion did not think that Jesus's flesh was insubstantial or spectral. Jesus had true and solid flesh before and after his resurrection; but it was not exactly like the decaying flesh of non-divine humans. If the substance of Jesus was "more recondite," according to Marcion, it was not phantasmal.[27]

Jesus's Birth

Tertullian claims that, at the beginning of Marcion's Gospel, Jesus descended straight from heaven to the synagogue at Capernaum.[28] "He was brought to birth out of heaven, at once full-grown, at once complete, Christ with no delay, spirit and power and god—and nothing more . . . devoid of body."[29] Both Tertullian and the Refutator claim that Marcion denied Christ's birth.[30] But he did so, the Refutator claims, for an Empedoclean reason, so that Christ would not be "subject to the bodily formation of destructive Strife."[31] This peculiar rationale should be a red flag to anyone taking this report at face value.

Nevertheless, one still reads scholars who say that "Jesus had never been born—he simply appeared out of the blue as a full-grown man in the synagogue at Capernaum."[32] Jesus "appears on earth fully grown," leaving some

---

26. Wilhite, "Was Marcion a Docetist?" 1–36.

27. Tertullian, *AM* 3.8.3.

28. Tertullian, *AM* 4.7.5 (cf. 3.23.7).

29. Tertullian, *AM* 4.21.11.

30. Tertullian, *Carn. Chr.* 1; *Ref.* 7.31.5.

31. *Ref.* 7.31.5.

32. Dungan, *History of the Synoptic Problem*, 48. A restatement of *Ref.* 7.31.5.

"ambiguity about whether Jesus is truly a human being."[33] One writer goes so far as to claim that Marcion "insisted" that, because Jesus was not born, he was not even Jewish.[34]

According to present evidence, Marcion never directly denied Jesus's birth.[35] Marcion's disciple Apelles did so, but Tertullian, at least, was able to distinguish their views on this very point.[36] To be sure, Marcion's Gospel lacked a birth story, but this fact does not constitute a denial of Jesus's birth. The Gospel according to Mark lacks a birth story. No one concludes that, for this reason, the author of Mark rejected Jesus's birth. Marcion should be treated no differently.

Tertullian's "from heaven to Capernaum" interpretation is flawed. The Carthaginian himself reveals that Marcion's Gospel actually read that Jesus "descended"—not from heaven, but—"into Capernaum a city of Galilee."[37] In other words, Jesus went down to this coastal town by the Sea of Galilee. He did not appear out of nowhere. There is no reason to think that Jesus, in Marcion's text, used anything more than his legs to move into Capernaum. "Descent" here means to go down in elevation, just as "ascending" to Jerusalem indicates a rise in elevation. With respect to birth, Marcion's Jesus seems to have been just as human as any other person.

In fact, another passage in Marcion's Gospel can be read to imply that Jesus was born: the existence of Jesus's physical mother and brothers (G 8:20).[38] The fact that in this passage Jesus redefines his family as those who "do his word" is not a denial that he had a birth mother and (at least half-)brothers.[39]

---

33. Gathercole, *Apocryphal Gospels*, 86.

34. Dungan, *History of the Synoptic Problem*, 48. See further Watson, *What is a Gospel?*, 199.

35. *Pace* Vinzent: "Marcion explicitly denied a human birth of Jesus Christ" (*Christ's Resurrection*, 130).

36. Tertullian, *Carn. Chr.* 1, 6. Some modern scholars don't make the same distinction (e.g., Watson, *What is a Gospel?*, 200).

37. Tertullian, *AM* 4.7.1.

38. Attested in Tertullian (*AM* 3.11.13). When Tertullian later comments on this verse (4.19.6), he attacks Apelles's position, not Marcion's.

39. *Pace* Wilson, *Marcion*, 100.

To be sure, If Jesus tried to establish a fictive kin group among his followers, he did not thereby deny that he was born. If Jesus had a physical mother who could visit him, then the assumption is that he was born. As Epiphanius puts it, the people around Jesus did not actually suppose Christ had "many mothers," but only one—the one who carried him in the womb.[40]

Other characters in Marcion's Gospel make the same assumption. A woman in Evangelion 11:27 raises her voice, "Blessed is the womb which bore you and the breasts which you sucked!" To be sure, Jesus offers a correction—"Blessed, actually, are those who hear and do God's word." Still, Jesus never contradicts the assumption that he was once in a womb and that he was breastfed. Tertullian rightly remarks that Jesus could not have transferred the blessing "away from his mother if he had had no mother."[41]

Marcion did probably deny that Jesus was *virgin* born.[42] The virgin birth was not an established doctrine during Marcion's lifetime. The theory seems to depend, for the most part, on the birth stories in canonical Luke, stories that are probably later than or at least independent of the Marcionite Gospel (chapter 3). Marcion, if he knew canonical Luke, would have viewed it as corrupt. Evidently, Marcion would have viewed the story of Jesus's birth from a virgin as an addition to and falsification of his Gospel.

Here one can also lay to rest Tertullian's slander that Marcion viewed the physical process of birth with disgust. "Make a speech," Tertullian orders Marcion (who was long dead) "against the nastiness of the generative elements within the womb, the filthy concretion of fluid and blood, of the growth of the flesh for nine months out of that very slime . . . You shudder, of course, at the child passed out along with his afterbirth and, naturally, caked with it."[43]

Tertullian's vivid imagery and rhetorical use of the second-person ("you") and "of course" are beguiling.[44] It's simply not obvious what Marcion said about

40. Epiphanius, *Pan.* 42.11.17, elenchus 12.

41. Tertullian, *AM* 4.26.13.

42. This is explicit in a source quoted by Jacob of Serugh. See Philip Michael Forness, "The Anonymous Source for Marcion's Gospel in British Library, Add. 17215: An Identification and Analysis," *New Testament Studies* 67 (2021): 541–559.

43. Tertullian, *Carn. Chr.* 4.1–2.

44. Scholars who seem to accept this rhetoric include Moll, *Arch Heretic*, 59, 132, 159; Vinzent, *Christ's Resurrection*, 111.

human birth, if anything. Tertullian constructs what he *thinks* Marcion should have said based on the premise that Marcion rejected everything made by the lower creator. But the premise is false: Marcion did not despise or reject creation as such. To recognize the creator as a lower being does not mean that one must hate the creation or the process of human birth.

Christ and the Law

According to Laodiceans 2:13–16,

> in Christ you who were far are near by his blood. For he is our peace, he who has made the two one, who has broken the dividing wall of hostility in his flesh, who has destroyed the Law of the commands by his teachings, so as to establish the two in himself as one new person, making peace, and to reconcile both to God in one body, having killed the hostility in it through the cross.[45]

The verb translated as "has destroyed (*katargeō*) the Law" is the same verb Paul used to describe the destruction of the world rulers who crucified Christ (1 Cor 2:6; 2 Thess 2:8), the discharge of the old self from the Law by death (Rom 7:6), and the destruction of death itself (1 Cor 15:26).[46] The tense of the verb indicates that Christ set about his work of destruction at a specific point in time—on the cross (Laod 2:16).

The object of destruction is clear: *ho nomos* (Laod 2:15)—*nomos* being Paul's customary word for the Mosaic Law.[47] In context, the Law is thought of as a wall dividing Jews and gentiles (2:14).[48] When Christ destroyed "the Law of the commandments," he reconciled Jew and gentile to form one new body. What fueled the war were the Law's commands. Once this Law was annulled, peace between Jews and gentiles was established on the basis of a new way of life.

45. The following section adapts Litwa, *Evil Creator*, 111–121.

46. In Heb 2:14, the one who held the power of death, the devil, is also destroyed (καταργήσῃ).

47. Räisänen, *Paul and the Law* (Tübingen: Mohr Siebeck, 1983), 16; Michael Winger, *By What Law: The Meaning of Νόμος in the Letters of Paul* (Atlanta: Scholars Press, 1992), 197.

48. Cf. *Ep. Aristeas* (about 150–50 BCE) §139.

Laodiceans 2:15 mentions "the Law of commandments in *dogmata*."[49] *Dogmata* could refer to the "decrees" of Law.[50] If *dogmata* refer to the rulings of the creator in the Law, one could understand them as describing the format of the commands: Christ "destroyed . . . the commandments (which are) in (the form of divine) decrees." When Megethius in the *Adamantius* says that Christ overthrew the decrees (*dogmata*) of the creator, he refers to the decrees of Law.[51] Nevertheless, *dogmata* was also a general term for "teachings." Thus many ancient interpreters understood *dogmata* instrumentally, referring to Christ's instructions. In this reading, Jesus destroyed the Law by his teachings.[52]

On the basis of Laodiceans 2:15, then, a Christian could legitimately claim that Christ came to destroy Jewish Law.[53] Marcion and his followers did claim this. The patristic evidence is consistent: "Jesus came down from another god to expose the creator and to destroy the Law."[54] "Christ came . . . and destroyed the Law of the creator."[55] Marcion "says that Christ has descended from on high for the salvation of souls and to convict . . . the Law."[56]

In fact, according to Marcion's Gospel, the Jews directly accuse Jesus of destroying the Law (23:2) in the "trial" before Pilate.[57] Several of these

49. Schmid, *Marcion*, 339. It is not clear if Tertullian's *sententiis* represents ἐν δόγμασιν or simply δόγμασιν. Only in P[46] and some manuscripts of the Vulgate is ἐν δόγμασιν omitted, probably by scribal error. C. J. Roetzel accepted the reading of P[46] and drew substantial conclusions from it ("Jewish Christian-Gentile Christian Relations: A Discussion of Ephesians 2.15a," *ZNW* 74 [1983] at 81–89 at 86).

50. Cf. Josephus, *Against Apion* 1.42; *Antiquities* 15.136; 3 Macc 1:3; 4 Maccabees 10:2; Philo, *Allegorical Interpretation* 1.54–55; *Giants* 52.

51. *Adamantius* 1.4. Similarly, certain "Cainites" according to Epiphanius believed that Christ "wanted to pervert the provisions of the Law" (*Pan.* 38.3.3).

52. See also BeDuhn, *First New Testament*, 253.

53. Irenaeus, *Haer.* 1.27.2.

54. Tertullian, *AM* 4.36.11.

55. *Adamantius* 2.10: ὁ ἐλθὼν χριστὸς . . . τὸν νόμον τοῦ δημιουργοῦ κατέλυσεν. Cf. 2.15, where Christ "annuls the Law (τὸν νόμον λύει), destroys the punishment and cancels the judgment."

56. Epiphanius, *Pan.* 42.4.2. Epiphanius claimed that Cerdo first took this position, along with many other sects (41.1.8). Cf. Celsus reported by Origen, *Cels.* 6.53: Christ destroyed the creator's creations (διαφθείρει τὰ τούτου δημιουργήματα).

57. Roth, 433 from Epiphanius, *Pan.* 42.11.6, scholion 69.

accusations stand in Luke 23:2. For instance, Jesus perverted the Jewish nation, forbade taxes to Caesar, and called himself a king. In Marcion's Gospel, the fictional Jews make this additional accusation: "We found this person (Jesus) . . . destroying the Law and Prophets."[58] Epiphanius claims that Marcion added this clause. It is, however, well attested in Old Latin witnesses to Luke, which indicates that it was a pre-Marcionite reading.[59]

This clause in Evangelion 23:2 corresponds well with Christ's deeds in the Gospel. In Evangelion 5:12, Christ touches and heals a leper. In doing so, Marcion, according to Tertullian, believed that Christ destroyed the Law.[60] The Law forbade people from touching lepers or from having any contact with them. According to Leviticus 13:45: "As for the leper . . . let his clothes be rags, his head uncovered, his mouth covered; he will call out 'Unclean!'" This ritual of self-isolation ensured that no one besides a priest came into contact with a leper. By reaching out to touch the leper, Christ violated the spirit and the letter of Jewish Law.

After making contact, Jesus tells the leper to appear before the priests as a testimony. According to the Evangelion, the testimony was not for the priests, but for the leper.[61] Priests had the duty of pronouncing lepers clean (Lev 13–14). But Christ proclaims the leper clean without priestly authority (G 5:13). Thus the "testimony" was, in effect, that Christ violated the Law.[62] The leper went to the priests, evidently, but to reveal that healing could be pronounced and accomplished without their authority.

---

58. Roth, 433: τοῦτον εὕρομεν . . . καταλύοντα τὸν νόμον καὶ τοὺς προφήτας. So also Klinghardt, 1.129–33.

59. Adolf Jülicher, *Itala: Das Neue Testament in altlateinischer Überlieferung* (Berlin: de Gruyter, 1954), XXIII, 256–257, though note the presence of "our" Law (*solventem legem* nostram *et prophetas*) in *b eff² i l q*. See also *The New Testament in Greek: The Gospel according to St. Luke*, Part 2, edited by the American and British Committees of the International Greek New Testament Project (Oxford: Clarendon Press, 1987), 204. BeDuhn points out that Jesus destroying the Law in Luke 23:2 was accepted in several editions of the Vulgate and passed without comment in Tertullian (*First New Testament*, 190; cf. Roth, *Text* 337).

60. Tertullian, *AM* 4.9.4.

61. ἵνα ᾖ εἰς μαρτύριον τοῦτο ὑμῖν attested by Epiphanius, *Pan.* 42.11.6 §1. Who the plural ὑμῖν refers to is disputed, but it presumably includes the leper. Cf. Tertullian, *AM* 4.9.10: *ut sit* vobis *in testimonium*. See further Roth, 413; Klinghardt, 2.543–49.

62. See further Tertullian, *AM* 4.9.11–1.

Similarly, when Jesus healed ten lepers (G 17.11–19), he commanded them to show themselves to the priests. According to Marcionites, Christ intended to cast scorn on the Law, for the lepers were healed apart from the Law's regulations.[63] Tertullian himself conceded that Christ, by healing the lepers, "went beyond the solemn rites of the Law."[64]

The Law forbids touching a woman who has an issue of blood (Lev 15:19); Christ not only permitted himself to be touched by such a woman, but healed her as well (G 8:43–48). In the report of Tertullian, it was first the bleeding woman who disobeyed the creator's Law by touching Jesus in a clandestine way.[65] The fact that Jesus healed her only reinforced his (later explicit) approval of her action and the breach of the creator's Law. Even if Jesus did not himself reach out his hand to her, he still involuntarily broke the Law, for anyone who touches a hemorrhaging woman "will be unclean" (Lev 15:19). Yet Jesus was not defiled. His purity and healing power showed that he was not under the Law's authority. Jesus approved the woman's faith, a faith that, according to Marcion, held the Law in contempt.[66]

In Marcion's Gospel 16:16, Jesus, after criticizing Pharisaic greed, says that "The Law and the Prophets were until John; from then the kingdom of God is being proclaimed as good news."[67] Here Jesus delimits two eras: the time when the Law was valid, and the time when it became invalid—the ministry of John the Baptist serving as the pivot.

Yet the following verse in Luke (16:17) contradicts the preceding: "It is easier for heaven and earth to pass away than for a single jot of the Law to fall." As seen in chapter 3, Marcion's Gospel had a different reading: "It is easier for the heaven and the earth to pass away than for a single jot of *my words* to

---

63. Roth, 427–428; Klinghardt, 2.990–96.

64. Tertullian, *AM* 4.35.4.

65. Tertullian, *AM* 4.20.9.

66. Tertullian, *AM* 4.20.9–10.

67. Roth, 426: ὁ νόμος καὶ οἱ προφῆται ἕως Ἰωάννου (ἐξ or ἀφ') οὗ ἡ βασιλεία τοῦ θεοῦ εὐαγγελίζεται (Klinghardt [2.962] prints ἀπαγγελίζεται). Matthew's version of the saying presented a different meaning. Instead of "the Law and the prophets [were] until John," Matthew used a different verb: "for all the prophets and the Law was prophesied until John" (Matt 11:13).

fall."[68] Tertullian accepts this latter reading without qualm.[69] The reading is consistent with Jesus's statement in Luke 21:33 (attested in the Evangelion): "heaven and earth will pass away, but *my words* will not." In short, Jesus heralded the end of the Law while proclaiming the eternity of his own teachings. Without mincing words, he opposes the temporary Mosaic Law to his own eternal revelation.

Perhaps the crowning violation of Jesus was his failure to keep the Sabbath. The Evangelion attests three of Jesus's Sabbath violations, two of which are shared with the Gospels of Mark and Matthew. The shared episodes are plucking grain (G 6:1–5 // Mark 2:23–28 // Matt 12:1–8), and the man with a shriveled hand (G 6:6–11 // Mark 3:1–6 // Matt 12:9–14). The Evangelion had another violation story: the crippled woman in the synagogue (13:10–17).

In Gospel 6:1–2, Jesus's disciples pick and rub heads of grain on the Sabbath. Some of the Pharisees inform them that this act is unlawful, since it is a form of harvesting, an act that was not permitted on the Sabbath.[70] The Pharisees were not just nitpickers. Both Irenaeus and Tertullian agreed that the act of harvesting performed in these verses was unlawful.[71] There was, moreover, no life-threatening need for the disciples to pluck the grain since, despite their hunger, they were in no danger of starvation.

Yet Jesus stoked the rhetorical fire. He justified his disciples based on the example of David who took—one might say stole—sacred and prohibited bread from the creator's tent shrine (1 Sam 21:1–6). Yet Jesus did not stop there. To ground his allowance of Sabbath violation, he presumed to call himself "Lord of the Sabbath."[72] Tertullian confessed that this claim put

---

68. Following Roth, 426: εὐκοπώτερον . . . τὸν οὐρανὸν καὶ τὴν γῆν παρελθεῖν ἢ τῶν λόγων μου μίαν κεραίαν παρελθεῖν. Cf. Klinghardt (2.962): ταχύτερον ἢ μία κεραία τῶν λόγων τοῦ κυρίου.

69. Tertullian, *AM* 4.33.9.

70. Exod 34:21: "on the seventh day you shall rest . . . in harvest you shall rest." Cf. Philo: "it is not permitted [on the Sabbath] to cut any shoot or branch, or even a leaf, or to pluck any fruit whatsoever" (*Mos.* 2.22).

71. Irenaeus, *Haer.* 4.8.3; Tertullian, *AM* 4.12.5.

72. Tertullian, *AM* 4.12.11; Irenaeus's claim that David was a priest is inaccurate (*Haer.* 4.8.3).

Jesus in apparent conflict with the Law.[73] Christ as Lord of the Sabbath was also "destroyer of the Sabbath."[74] Epiphanius concluded from the harvesting episode that "the Sabbath was abolished."[75] Eznik of Kolb affirmed that Christ, "like a lord of the Law, put a stop to the Law."[76]

Jesus did not only defend the Sabbath violation of others, he also transgressed it himself. He performed two Sabbath healings in synagogues before the astounded eyes of Jewish leaders. The first was a man with a shriveled hand (6:6–11); the second was a crippled woman (13:10–16). Both individuals did not need to be healed on the Sabbath since their conditions were not life threatening. In spite of this, Jesus publicly healed them in Jewish religious spaces. In each case, Jesus ignited a conflict, first by asking provokingly whether one can do good on the Sabbath (6:9), and secondly by calling his opponents hypocrites because on that same Sabbath they worked to untie farm animals (13:15).[77]

To be sure, there is no explicit law against healing on the Sabbath—only against work.[78] But the Sabbath disputes hinged on the idea that Jesus's healings were a form of labor. The Jesus of the gospels never disagreed that his healings were a form of work.[79] He even agreed with the charge of illegality in the grain rubbing episode. The disciples did something "unlawful" on the Sabbath (G 6:2), and were justified because David also did something in violation of Jewish Law. The use of "unlawful" and the fact that it is precisely the element of illegality that binds the two (otherwise rather different) incidents together, indicates that Jesus made no attempt to evade the charge that he worked on the Sabbath and that he approved of such transgression when others performed it.[80]

---

73. Tertullian, *AM* 4.12.1: the question concerning Sabbath violation, "could have no substance if Christ had not proclaimed himself lord of the Sabbath."

74. Tertullian, *Spectacles* 30.

75. Epiphanius, *Pan.* 30.32.3.

76. Eznik, *On God*, 392 (trans. Blanchard and Young).

77. Roth, 414, 425; Klinghardt, 2.578, 905.

78. A point made by Irenaeus, *AH* 4.8.2.

79. John 5:17 (where Jesus admits to working like his Father) implies that he took his Sabbath healing (John 5:8–9) to be a form of work.

80. The Mishnah equates practicing medicine with work (*m. Sabb.* 14:3–4). See further Robert Doldenberg, "The Jewish Sabbath in the Roman World," *ANRW* II.19.1 (Berlin: de Gruyter, 1979): 414–447 at 430–434.

For Marcionites, this was not merely an issue of interpreting the Law differently. The Gospel nowhere made the distinction between Law and human tradition as found in Mark 7:1–2; 10:2–3. The Jesus of the Gospel (the only Jesus Marcionites recognized) knew exactly what would be offensive to Jewish Law-observers, and performed it based on his own personal authority.[81]

According to Galatians 3:10, "As many as are under the Law stand under a curse." The wording indicates that the curse applies to all under Law, not just to those who fall short of it (for in that case the text would have read: "As many as *disobey* the Law are cursed").[82] The Law's value was nothing more than "dung" when compared with the righteousness gained by faith in Christ (Phil 3:8–9). The Law did not make people righteous, it revealed their sin. Paul wrote, "I would not have known sin except through Law," and "through the Law is the recognition of sin" (Rom 7:7; 3:20). Marcionites specifically highlighted the latter verse.[83]

The Law is Holy?

Yet, there's a tension within Pauline thought, since the Law that brings a curse is also "holy," and the commandment, "holy, just, and good" (Rom 7:12).[84] This verse is attested in Marcion's Apostolikon and requires explanation. Perhaps the "good" commandment refers to the law of the true God as opposed to the law of sin and death (Rom 7:25; 8:2). Maybe if the "holy" law refers to the Mosaic Law, its goodness is only relative to the lower creator. One could imagine a scenario in which the creator legislated what he thought was good, but it was not actually good when judged by the standards of the Good God. Perhaps Marcion, like Ptolemy the Valentinian, made distinctions

81. See further Dale C. Allison, *Resurrecting Jesus: The Earliest Christian Tradition and its Interpreters* (London: T&T Clark, 2005), 168.

82. "It is not with justice that he [the creator] spreads the curse" (Ephrem, *Hymns against Heresy* 51.12).

83. Clement, *Strom.* 2.7.34.4; Tertullian, *AM* 5.13.13–14; Origen, *Comm. Rom.* 3.3.10; 3.8.2. See further Winrich Löhr "Die Auslegung des Gesetzes bei Markion, den Gnostikern," *Stimuli: Exegese und ihre Hermeneutic in Antike und Christentum*, ed. Georg Schöllgen and Clemens Scholten (Münster: Aschendorff, 1996), 77–95 at 77–80.

84. Vinzent claims that Marcion "considered the Jewish law as 'just,' not good" (*Christ's Resurrection*, 126).

in the Mosaic law.[85] Some laws were unjust, but others were good and holy. Unfortunately, one does not know what Marcion thought because his interpretation of Romans 7:12 does not survive.[86]

Marcion, like everyone else, was a selective reader. Cognitively, humans selectively pick out data they resonate with and combine it to form a basic sense of what they consider to be valid. So, Paul called the Law holy, yes, and associated it with knowledge and truth (Rom 2:20). At the same time, he connected the Law with heightened sin (5:20), slavery (7:25; Gal 5:1), death (2 Cor 3:6–7; Rom 8:2), imprisonment (Gal 3:22), and cursing (Gal 3:10). Indeed, negative statements about the Law seem to overwhelm the positive, providing stumbling blocks for interpreters even today.[87]

Modalism?

Marcion believed that Christ embodies and reveals God, as did many Christians of his age. This doctrine does not mean that Marcion was a modalist.[88] Modalism means that one understands Christ as the manifestation of God on earth. It says that Christ and God are not really different persons, but different manifestations of the same being, that Jesus is, effectively, the Father in flesh.

Many Christian authors of Marcion's time could be understood in a modalistic way. Ignatius had no problem with calling Christ, "God," "my God," or "our God," and he made no systematic attempt to distinguish Christ

85. Ptolemy, *Letter to Flora* 4–5.

86. Tertullian's comments on Rom 7:12 (*AM* 5.13.15) mostly express his (not Marcion's) interpretation of the verse. Tertullian suggests that one could make a distinction, based on the verse, between a just and good God, but it is not clear that this is Marcion's interpretation of the verse, as opposed to a strawman target.

87. Löhr, "Auslegung des Gesetzes," 77–80; Klinghardt, "Gesetz bei Markion und Lukas," *Das Gesetz im frühem Judentum und im Neuen Testament: FS für Christoph Burchard zum 75. Geburtstag*, ed. Dieter Sänger and Matthias Konradt (Göttingen: Vandenhoeck & Ruprecht, 2006), 99–128; Bryan Blazosky, *The Law's Universal Condemning and Enslaving Power: Reading Paul, the Old Testament, and Second Temple Jewish Literature* (University Park: Eisenbrauns, 2019), 115–192.

88. *Pace* Muehlenberg, "Marcion's Jealous God," 108.

from the Father.[89] He referred to "the blood of God" and to the "suffering of God"—referring of course to Jesus.[90] The *Acts of John* (late second century) refers to "our God, Jesus Christ."[91] Earlier in the same work, the apostle John addresses "holy Jesus, for you alone are God and none else."[92] Melito of Sardis (also late second century) claimed: "He who hung the earth is hanging . . . he who fastened the universe has been fastened to a tree; . . . God has been murdered!"[93] According to Noetus of Smyrna (mid- to late second century), God in Christ was both visible and invisible, born and unborn, dying and not dying at one and the same time.[94] When God was born, he did not change his essence.[95] That is why Jesus could say, "I and the Father are one," and "the one who sees me sees the Father" (John 10:30; 14:9).[96]

Despite the apparent prevalence of modalism in Marcion's day, it is not clear that Marcion himself was a modalist. Jerome claimed that Marcion deleted "from God the Father" in Galatians 1:1 to make it seem that Christ raised himself from the dead.[97] Some scholars follow Jerome.[98] Yet in other verses (Rom 8:11; 1 Cor 6:14; Laod 1:20), Marcion had no problem saying that

---

89. Ignatius, *Ephesians* preface ("our God"); cf. 15:3; 18:2; *To Polycarp* 8:3. A similar phrase occurs twice in the preface to his letter *To the Romans*, but here it is also said that Christ is "Son of the Father." Cf. *Romans* 3:3; 6:3; *Smyrneans* 1.1.

90. Ignatius, *Eph* 1:1; *Rom.* 6:3. See further William R. Schoedel, *Ignatius of Antioch: A Commentary* (Minneapolis: Fortress, 1985), 20, 39; Reinhard M. Hübner, *Der Paradox Eine: Antignostischer Monarchianismus im zweiten Jahrhundert* (Leiden: Brill, 1999), 131–206.

91. *Acts of John* 107.

92. *Acts of John* 77, cf. 82.

93. Melito, *Pascha*, 96; cf. 66. Elsewhere Melito wrote of "God who is naturally God and human": "inasmuch as he begets, Father, inasmuch as he is begotten, Son" (*Pascha* 9). See further Hübner, *Paradox*, 1–38.

94. Most distinctly expressed in *Ref.* 10.26.

95. Similar language can be found in the *T 12 Patr.*, *T. Sim.* 6:5; *T. Naph.* 8:3; *T. Ash.* 7:3.

96. See further David K. Bernard, "The Development of Modalism in Early Church History," *Journal of Early Christian History* 9, no. 3 (2020): 70–84.

97. See T. Baarda, "Marcion's Text of Gal. 1:1: Concerning the Reconstruction of the First Verse of the Marcionite Corpus Paulinum," *Vigiliae Christianae* 42 (1988): 236–256.

98. Harnack, *Marcion*, 45; E. C. Blackman, *Marcion and His Influence* (London: SPCK, 1948), 44n2; Head, "Foreign God," 314.

the Father raised Jesus from the dead, indicating that the Father and Jesus were separate persons. Christ and the Father need to be separate beings for Marcion (chapter 9), because the Father performs his judgment through Christ. Christ is the manifestation of the Good, but not the Good itself. Thus, Jesus says, "Do not call me good; one is good, the Father" (G 18:19).

* * *

According to Marcion, Jesus was truly born; he grew in the womb and was breastfed as a baby. He truly lived, truly suffered, and truly died, and he was truly raised in a body with bones. If modern researchers continue to call Marcion a "docetist," then he was no more a docetist than the apostle Paul. Paul emphasized that Christ came in human "form" or "likeness." Marcion may have understood this to mean that Christ's flesh was made up of a special substance—his exact opinion isn't clear. It is evident, however, that even if Christ had special flesh, it was not phantasmal. Jesus could still be touched, handled, jostled, anointed, beaten, slapped, and nailed. In short, Christ inhabited a manifestly *human* body and lived a *human* life. During this life, he made himself an opponent of the creator's Law, and demonstrated his superiority over it. Christ manifested the wisdom and salvation of the Father, but he was not the Father in flesh. Marcion's scriptures show that Christ was neither docetic nor modalistic, and future reconstructions of Marcion's thought should take account of his scriptures before reinscribing (and reinforcing) the language of heresiological reports.

CHAPTER TWELVE

View of Salvation

Let Marcion correct himself;
Because he dares not introduce
Into the universe another name
Beyond the name of Jesus

—Ephrem, *Hymns against Heresy* 49.1

ACCORDING TO TERTULLIAN, the main tenet of Marcion's faith stemmed from the school of Epicurus: "a sluggish and indifferent God."[1] Yet the Good, by sending the Son to save the world, was anything but apathetic. Marcion's God did not "shun sinners."[2] The Father decisively intervened to liberate humanity. Tertullian apparently quotes a Marcionite—or perhaps Marcion himself—"Sufficient to our God is this one single work, that he has by his great and particular kindness, set humanity free."[3]

Marcion had to explain why the Good acted after thousands of years of human history.[4] But that was a problem faced by all Christians. In the long view of history, Jesus seemed to be tardy, allowing too many righteous people to descend and wither in Hades. The fact that Christ was prophesied, according to early catholic doctrine, did little to mitigate his late arrival. The question kept arising: What was God doing all that time when people were dying? Augustine reported the joke that he was creating hell for people who

1. Tertullian, *AM* 5.19.7.

2. Dungan, *History of the Synoptic Problem*, 50.

3. Tertullian, *AM* 1.17.1.

4. Tertullian, *AM* 4.26.9.

asked that question.[5] Such an answer would not have satisfied Marcion, for whom the cruelty of the creator was no joke.

On this score, Jerome was more accurate than Tertullian: Marcionites accepted the idea of divine providence and care, but they criticized the creator's lower providence.[6] In short, they recognized that the government of the creator was corrupt. It was, in effect, a cosmic tyranny. Therefore, the Good acted to redeem human beings from that tyranny—to transfer them from a wicked regime of darkness to a blessed kingdom of glorious light. The Good did so by sending his chief representative, Christ. Christ did not defeat the creator by the exercise of warlike violence, but by absorbing the creator's violence into himself. From this act of supreme love, Christ secured a lien on the creator's property: human souls.

Christus Victor

Marcion's view of salvation fits nicely into a soteriological paradigm commonly called Christus Victor—"Christ the champion."[7] That is to say, the Pontian did not emphasize Christ's death as a sacrificial propitiation, but as a victory. Early catholics agreed that Christ on the cross triumphed over the devil (Col 2:15). Yet, Marcion and his followers believed that Christ triumphed over the devil *and* the lower creator, for the creator was the chief archon apparently allowing Satan to run amok.[8] It was the Judean lord, ultimately, who convicted Christ, who cursed him as a Law-breaker, and who executed him according to his Law (Deut 21:23).[9]

---

5. Augustine, *Conf.* 11.12.14.

6. Jerome, *Comm. Is.* 7.9 on Isa 18:1–3. Marcion makes accusations "against the creator" and claims "that he went wrong in most of his works, and that he did not do as he ought to have done. For of what advantage to human beings are snakes, scorpions, crocodiles, fleas, bedbugs, and gnats" (trans. Thomas P. Scheck).

7. Gustaf Aulén, *Christus Victor: An Historical Study of the Three Main Types of the Idea of the Atonement*, trans. A. G. Hebert (London: SPCK, 1931); Riemer Roukema, "Salvation and Victory by Christ's Death and Resurrection in the Ancient Church," *Journal of Reformed Theology* 15 (2021): 304–326.

8. Tertullian, *AM* 2.5 (creator allows devil); 2.10 (creator creates devil); cf. 5.18 on Eph 6:12.

9. Litwa, *Evil Creator*, 109–156.

Christ's execution was a kind of transaction. Jesus allowed himself to be killed as the ransom price for human souls.[10] By his death, he literally "bought out" (*ex-agoreuō*) human souls from the creator (Gal 4:5). The idea has a good scriptural pedigree. "You were bought with a price," Paul writes to the Corinthians (1 Cor 6:20). And in Marcion's text of Galatians 2:20, Paul says not that Christ "loved me" but that he "purchased me." The creator owned human souls and, by virtue of his death, Christ became their new owner.

The church fathers confirm this basic picture. Epiphanius describes Marcion's point of view: "'Christ redeemed us from the curse of the Law, having become a curse on our behalf.' Indeed, he says, if we belonged to him, he would not have bought his own property. But having bought us for an alien world, he came to redeem us, ... For we were the product of another being and for this reason he bought us for his own life."[11] Ephrem spoke of a "bargain" between Christ and the creator.[12] Eznik summed up Marcion's doctrine: believers "are the price of the blood of Jesus."[13]

Eznik tells a more detailed tale, much later than Marcion, but still useful for illustrating how concretely Marcionites envisioned salvation. According to this story, the resurrected Christ goes to trial with the creator. Since the creator committed murder (by killing Christ), he is sentenced to death by his own Law. To avoid this fate, the creator agrees that Christ take believing humanity as a ransom (the creator posted bail, as it were).[14] By his crucifixion, Christ "purchased humankind."[15]

Salvation, in short, was salvation *from the creator*.[16] According to Tertullian, Marcion applied the parable of the strong man to the creator

10. For ransom language, see Ephrem in Mitchell, *Prose Refutations* 2.96.28–32; cf. 2.90.27–44.

11. Epiphanius, *Pan.* 42.8.1–2.

12. Ephrem in Mitchell, *Prose Refutations*, 2.xli. See further Lieu, *Marcion*, 169–173.

13. Eznik, *On God*, 386.

14. Eznik, *On God*, 358.

15. Eznik, *On God*, 387. See further Wolfgang Hage, "Marcion bei Eznik von Kolb" in May and Greschat, *Marcion und seine kirchengeschichtliche Wirkung*, 29–38; Harnack, *Marcion*, 288*; BeDuhn, *First New Testament*, 267. See also Moll, *Arch-heretic*, 70–71.

16. See further Robert P. Casey, "The Armenian Marcionites and the Diatessaron," *Journal of Biblical Literature* 57, no. 2 (1938): 185–194.

(G 11:21–22).[17] A strong man (the creator) can protect his property (human beings). But when someone stronger than him arrives (Christ), he overcomes his opponent and takes his property. Like a divine warrior, Christ came to fight the cosmic lord. He fought him by undermining his Law and by removing humans from his dominion. He won the battle not by violence, but by self-sacrifice. This act of self-giving gave Christ the right of purchase, a purchase performed "in humble fashion."[18]

Marcion reportedly told a story in which the resurrected Christ came in triumph to Hades.[19] When he arrived, Cain and those like him, the Sodomites, the Egyptians, and all sinful nations, collectively ran to the redeeming lord. By embracing the triumphant master, they were taken up into his kingdom of light. Ironically, the patriarchs of old—men like Abel, Enoch, Noah, Abraham, and the prophets—did not run to embrace Christ. They knew the creator all too well. The creator tempts people in order to discern their loyalty (witness the infamous call to sacrifice Isaac, Gen 22). Apparently they imagined that the creator sent Christ to see if they would remain loyal to him and not to this unheralded champion. So they stayed put in Hades—though not, apparently, without comfort in the "bosom of Abraham" (G 16:22).[20]

One wonders how Marcion developed this myth. Usually Christ's descent to Hades is devised from passages like 1 Peter 3:19–20: "he went and made a proclamation to the spirits in prison who in former times did not obey." This passage was not in Marcion's Bible, but he probably knew it (1 Peter was addressed, in part, to Christians in Pontus). The phrase that Christ "descended to the lower parts of the earth" (Laod 4:9) is unattested in Marcion's Apostolikon. But the phrase "he led captivity captive" (Laod 4:8) was there. It certainly made sense for Christ, who redeemed tax collectors and prostitutes, to focus his post-resurrection redemptive mission on sinners. And since the prophets and patriarchs did not foresee the Christ of the Good God, logically they would not have recognized him in Hades.

---

17. Tertullian, *AM* 5.6.7.

18. Ephraim in Mitchell, *Prose Refutations*, 2.lx. See further H. J. W. Drijvers, "Christ as Warrior and Merchant," *Studia Patristica* 21 (1989): 73–85.

19. Irenaeus, *Haer.* 1.27.3. The source for the story is perhaps the elder mentioned in 4.27.1–2. Cf. Epiphanius, *Pan.* 42.4.3.

20. Marshall, "Misunderstanding the New Paul," 22.

To most modern people, "redemption" is a dead metaphor, but Marcion understood it literally. To redeem means "to buy back." One must admit, however, that this image of salvation does not jibe well with modern sensibilities. At root it indicates that salvation is a transfer of property (human beings) between two slaveholders (God and the lower creator). The creator once owned humans as his property; now the Good is their master. Salvation is the transfer from a cruel lord, with his harsh legal system, to a good and kind master. In view of this theory, Tertullian likened Marcion's Christ to a kidnapper.[21]

Marcionites did not perceive Christ as kidnapper, but as liberator. Nevertheless, the process of salvation does assume that humans are and continue to be slaves. Once they were slaves of the creator; now they are slaves to God and Christ. This result of salvation might sound strange to modern ears, but it is faithful to Paul, who consistently identified himself as a "slave" of God and thought of his converts as slaves as well (for instance, 2 Cor 4:5). Even for Marcion, there is no strictly "law-free" gospel. Freed from the Law of the creator, believers now follow the "law of God," and the "law of the Spirit of life" (Rom 7:25; 8:2).

Theft?

The chief argument used by heresiologists to attack Marcion's model of salvation was the theft argument: Christ stole the creator's property, showing that he and the Good were not so good after all. The argument is clever, since Marcion had criticized the creator who commanded Israel to despoil the Egyptians. Yet ultimately the heresiological rebuttal misses the mark, since, according to Marcion, Christ did not steal human beings from the creator. To be sure, Marcion used the scriptural metaphor of salvation as theft (G 12:39; 11:21–22), but he believed that Jesus paid a fair price for humanity—the ultimate price, his blood.[22] A deal wrought by death allowed for a genuine transfer of property. Humanity became Christ's, and Christ transferred them to the Father.

Heresy writers protest that, since the Good did not create human bodies (or souls), he had no right to possess them. Yet this objection would not have fazed

21. Tertullian, *AM* 1.23.7 (*plagiator*).

22. DeConick, *Comparing Christianities*, 41.

Marcion, since most things people own, they do not make. Slaveowners in the ancient world did not make their human property. Humans in antiquity, like today, owned cats, dogs, and horses without forming them in the womb. They owned houses without building them; they came to own land, though they did not create its soil, trees, and rocks. In terms of legal practice, then, there is nothing odd or unlawful about the Good coming to own human beings whom the Good did not directly make. Later Marcionites, moreover, came to argue that the Good *did* in fact create the human spirit—an essence distinct from body and soul—and that this is the true subject of redemption (chapter 14).

What is Flesh?

Heresiologists assert that Marcion denied salvation to the flesh. This time, their testimony is borne out by Marcion's scriptures and by Marcion's own Platonic mindset.[23] But this mindset, arguably, had already been shaped by Paul. In the Apostolikon, Paul affirms that "flesh and blood do not inherit God's empire, neither (does) corruption (inherit) incorruption" (1 Cor 15:50). He delivers a man's flesh to destruction so that his "spirit" is saved on the day of the Lord (1 Cor 5:5). He says that, "We think well of being absent from the body and present to the Lord" (2 Cor 5:8). The apostle writes, "no good dwells in my flesh" (Rom 7:18), and "I have the desire to be released from the flesh and to be with Christ" (Phil 1:23). Marcion's scriptures distinctively read in 2 Corinthians 7:1, "Let us cleanse ourselves from all pollution of flesh and blood, for these do not attain God's kingdom" (cf. 1 Cor 15:50).

There are other Pauline passages, however, in which salvation is not described as departing from flesh, but as its transformation. "We shall be changed" (1 Cor 15:52) into an incorruptible body (15:42, 50), one that is characterized by spirit (15:44), glory, and power (15:43). In Philippians 3:21, Christ "will transform our abased body to conformity with his glorious body" (compare 1 Cor 15:49; 2 Cor 3:18; 4:16). It is a debated question whether flesh so radically changed can still be called "flesh." To be sure, other interpreters of Paul, like Irenaeus and Tertullian, used these same passages to affirm the resurrection of the flesh. Yet, they acknowledged that resurrected flesh is not the vulnerable, mortal stuff it now is—plagued by everything from cancer to the common cold.

---

23. Alcinous, *Handbook*, 23–25; Plutarch, *Is. Os.* 396e.

On the topic of transformation, Tertullian wrote that Marcion's God promised believers the "true substance of angels."[24] It's not exactly clear, for Marcion, what constituted angelic substance, though Tertullian indicated that it was bodies made up of "spirit," and heavenly fire.[25] In short, Marcion envisioned a future physical transformation into angelic substance (a form of angelification).[26] This would imply that believers still, in heaven, inhabited bodies. The bodies were, however, not made of mortal flesh, but endowed with an angelic constitution. The new, angelic bodies did not need food or sex, and were not subject to death.

In short, there was an inner-Christian dispute about the salvation of the flesh because "flesh" was a floating signifier—it could mean the decaying skin suit (Marcion), but also the "glorious body" believers will inherit in heaven (Irenaeus and Tertullian).[27] Irenaeus and Tertullian made a "heretic" out of Marcion, but it is better to describe their argument as an in-house Christian debate about how to interpret Pauline teachings about salvation and resurrection. It may have become unorthodox for Christians to deny final salvation to corruptible flesh, but in effect it was and remains a common Christian belief. A Christian today who refers to her deceased grandpa "in heaven" still acknowledges that his actual corpse is in the ground, at least for the time being. Whether theologically correct or not, the invisible self is first to inherit salvation.

Marcion on Matter

Denying final salvation to the flesh raises the more philosophical question about Marcion's view of matter. This is not a question that naturally arises

24. Tertullian, *AM* 3.9.4.

25. Tertullian, *AM* 3.9.7, citing Ps. 103:4 LXX; cf. 2 Enoch 29:3.

26. Tertullian agrees that "we shall be changed in a moment into angelic substance, by virtue of that supervesture of incorruption (combining 1 Cor 15:52; 2 Cor 5:2), and be translated into that heavenly kingdom" (*AM* 3.24.6).

27. Outi Lehtipuu, "Flesh and Blood Cannot Inherit the Kingdom of God': The Transformation of the Flesh in Early Christian Debates Concerning Resurrection," in *Metamorphoses, Resurrection, Body, and Transformative Practices in Early Christianity*, ed. Turid Karlsen Seim and Jorunn Økland (Berlin: de Gruyter, 2009), 159–180; Taylor Petrey, *Resurrecting Parts: Early Christians on Desire, Reproduction, and Sexual Difference* (New York: Routledge, 2015).

from scripture. Marcion's Bible did not reflect on the nature and destiny of matter (*hylē*). Our earliest witnesses, Justin and Irenaeus, make no mention of Marcion's reflections on matter, probably because Marcion himself did not use overtly philosophical language.

Matter becomes a point of debate only with Clement and Tertullian (early third century). Clement says that for Marcionites, nature is evil because it was created out of "evil matter."[28] Tertullian states that Marcion believed in eternal matter and that he imputes unborn and unmade evil to matter.[29] (The Carthaginian says that Marcion took his idea of matter from the Stoics, but for Stoics, matter was passive, not evil.[30]) According to the Refutator's summary report (which contradicts his main report), Marcionite matter serves as an evil principle alongside the good and just.[31] Some of Marcion's disciples, however, proposed four principles: good, just, evil, and matter—thus disassociating matter from evil.[32] Ephrem opposed Marcionites who made matter one of three "roots."[33] Matter technically opposes the creator, yet he still makes everything from it.[34] These reports are not exactly consistent.

One could accept the idea that Marcion's believed in preexistent matter and judged it negatively.[35] This would make Marcion agree with Numenius, who thought of matter as "openly harmful."[36] On present evidence, however,

---

28. Clement, *Strom.* 3.3.12.1. In May's early work (*Creatio ex nihilo* 56, 61), he accepted Clement's views that for Marcion, matter was evil.

29. Tertullian, *AM* 1.15.4–5.

30. Tertullian, *AM* 5.19.7.

31. *Ref.* 10.19.1. Contrast *Ref.* 7.29.1.

32. *Ref.* 10.19.2.

33. Ephrem, *Hymns against Heresy* 3.6.4; 48.1.4.

34. Ephrem, *Hymns against Heresy* 14.8–9. Edmund Beck opines that Ephrem's sources were Marcionite splinter groups who proposed a doctrine of three gods. The majority of Marcionites in Ephrem's time and place still spoke of the creator and the Good ("Die Hyle bei Markion nach Ephram," *Orientalia Christiana Periodica* 44 [1978] 5–30 at 30).

35. Schüle, "Der Ursprung des Bösen bei Marcion," 36, citing Tertullian AM 1.15; McGowan, "Marcion's Love of Creation," 301.

36. Numenius, frag. 52 (Des Places) from Calcidius, *Timaeus*, ed. J. H. Waszink (London: Warburg Institute, 1975), 298.

Marcion never said that matter or nature were evil; and he never claimed that the human body is evil in itself.[37] Marcion's belief that human beings are raised to incorruption does not imply that he despised the current mortal platform. A newly-hatched bird that leaves its shell does not hate the shell or complain that the egg is not preserved.[38]

What passes for Marcion's doctrine of matter is the elaboration of his later disciples. When Clement attacks Marcion, for instance, he switches between attacking Marcion and his followers, assuming that the followers represent the master. The Alexandrian wrongly assumes that for the Pontian, the world is evil and therefore he jumped to the conclusion that for Marcion, matter must be evil. Marcion's actual position was that the *creator* is evil, not the world.[39] Marcion was imbued with Platonist values, but he did not express himself in philosophical terms. The Pontian was a Paulinist; Pauline writings expressed considerable skepticism about flesh, and Marcion followed suit. Paul, however, said nothing against "matter" as such, and neither did Marcion.

Later Marcionites became interested in the topic of matter. Syrian Marcionites, for instance, had a common myth of how the creator made the world, paradise, and humanity from matter.[40] In the more elaborate Marcionite myth reported by Eznik, matter becomes a personal agent and effectively the creator's wife.[41]

One must be careful not to import these later reflections back into Marcion's time. One could infer, of course, that if for Marcion the flesh is not

---

37. McGowan, "Marcion's Love of Creation," 299. Tertullian accused his enemies (not specifically Marcionites) of castigating the body, and even calling it an "evil thing" (*malum*) (*Res.* 5). But if they pointed out the mortal body's inferiority to the spirit or soul, they did not necessarily hate it.

38. Ephrem, *Hymns against Heresy* 52.6; cf. 52.9.

39. May, "Marcion in Contemporary Views," 25.

40. Michel Tardieu, "L'imitation du monde selon Marcion d'apres les auteurs orientaux," in *Ressembler au monde: Nouveaux documents sur la theorei du macor-microsme dans la'antiquite*, ed. Philippe Gignoux (Turnhout: Brepols, 1999), 41–53.

41. This particular myth has striking parallels with Justin's *Book of Baruch* (*Ref.* 5.23.1–27.6), for which see Michael Williams, *Rethinking Gnosticism: An Argument for Dismantling a Dubious Category* (Princeton: Princeton University Press, 1996), 18–23; Litwa, *Found Christianities*, 247–255. Cf. Ephrem, *Hymns against Heresy* 48.1 (the pact between matter and the creator).

saved, then neither is matter. Matter is the stuff of the lower creation, while the point of salvation is to transcend the creator's realm. All this is true. But to leap to the conclusion that Marcion hated creation or despised matter as such goes beyond the evidence.

* * *

Although Marcion did not deny other models of salvation, he emphasized what is now called the Christus Victor model. He viewed salvation concretely as the Good's act of purchasing human souls from the lower creator. God did not steal human souls from the creator. He paid a fair price, the blood of his Son. By redeeming human souls, the Good demonstrated the purity of his love. In denying salvation to the flesh, Marcion did not deny that in some sense flesh could be transformed such that humans inherited a higher substance—the substance of angels—after death. His denial of salvation to mortal and decaying flesh did not necessarily mean or even imply that Marcion hated creation, matter, or human bodies in particular.

CHAPTER THIRTEEN

Going to Church with Marcion

> He says, "this is my body and blood which is poured out for you" always commanding what later will happen. With what substance do you suppose bread and wine are his own body and blood? What must we confess? Did he not prove himself by deeds to be maker of the world and to bear a body of both flesh and blood?
>
> —*Carmen adversus Marcionitas* 5.192–96.

MARCION'S GOD LOVES those who are alien, or rather alienated, from God (Laod 2:12). This kind of love is not the love owed to self, neighbors, and kin. Such is the love of the lower creator, which fulfills the creator's law (Rom 13:8–10). The love shown by the true God comes with no obligation. It is a pure and perfect love of strangers given without any obligation of kinship.[1] It is a love vibrant even in the face of hate (G 6:36).

By contrast, the love of neighbor is human love; love rightly lauded, but natural. One's neighbors are those most proximate. Those most proximate are family, friends, and fellow citizens. It's rational and dutiful to love them, for they will return that love and offer benefits in return. To love family is wonderful, but ordinary. They are flesh and blood, they share our identity and extend it to the world. The sacrificial love of one's children is heartwarming and beautiful, but instinctual, written into our genetic code.

The true God calls for a different, "super-natural" kind of love: a love beyond that of neighbor; love for the person far away, love for a person who is other, even hostile, who hates, insults, and curses (G 6:27–28).[2] That sort of love goes beyond the creator's Law. It is this superordinate love that Jesus

1. Tertullian, *AM* 1.23.3.

2. Tertullian, *AM* 1.23.3.

recommends: the love that gives to everyone with no hope of receiving; that takes a slap yet holds no anger; the love that accepts theft and verbal abuse without understanding them as shame or loss (G 6:29); the love that prays for the persecutor, and truly wishes good upon them, not just as a psychological trick. This is the love of the golden rule—treat others as you wish to be treated (G 6:31). Here there is no limitation, no near and far. *All* people must be treated this way, no matter how many times they have betrayed you, insulted you, wounded you, killed you or members of your family.

There are two kinds of life, and two kinds of love. When Jesus dialogues with a law expert who asks how to inherit life, he tells him to obey the Law, and to love the creator who benefits those who obey him (G 10:25–28). But when he tells another man how to inherit *eternal* life, then he gives a different response: "sell all you have and give to beggars . . . then come follow me" (18:22). One mode of behavior secures a good and long life on this earth. The other mode secures poverty now, but a rich and everlasting life in the celestial kingdom.

In short, the heart of Jesus's ethics, according to Marcion, goes beyond Jewish law. Jesus was Jewish, of course, but he was not thereby a follower of Mosaic Law. He demanded that people go beyond the Law, to realize an ethical way of life not controlled by a written code. Truly good people do not need a written code to be ethical. This position is not antinomianism but "transnomianism," adherence to a transcendent law.

Bodily Discipline

Heresiologists are famous for accusing their opponents of all manner of sins, from eating their own semen in sexual rites, to using love potions, to invoking demons to inspire dreams, and so on.[3] But the mouth of these same heresiologists was stopped when they came to Marcion. They simply could not convincingly accuse him or his followers of any sort of immorality.

Origen observed that "the most dangerous heretics are those whose lives are good."[4] Early catholic writers were manifestly threatened by Marcion not only because he lived by a higher standard, but because his whole church

---

3. Knust, *Abandoned to Lust*; Litwa, *Carpocrates, Marcellina, and Epiphanes*, 113–119.

4. Origen, *Hom. Ezekiel* 7.3.

attempted to follow suit. Marcion's text of Galatians distinctly called the church "holy" in 4:26, and Marcionite Christianity was, in sociological terms, a sectarian movement with clear demands of holiness for its members. In short, the Marcionite church was ascetic, with practices of sexual and dietary abstinence that were more rigorous than competing assemblies.

The heresiological strategy, was to undermine Marcion's asceticism by poisoning its motives. Marcionite self-discipline was smeared as world-hatred.[5] The inference seems to have been this: Marcion hated the creator; therefore he must have hated the creation.[6] This inference quickly led to some absurd conclusions: If Marcion hated the creation, then his followers must have tried to abstain from created elements—like bread and water—despite the fact that they needed these elements to survive.

The patristic evidence is consistent in this regard. According to the Refutator, Marcion leads his disciples into a Cynic-like lifestyle. By this means, he "supposes he can grieve the creator by abstaining from his products and ordinances."[7] Tertullian uses the technique of showing an absurd consequence logically following from assumed premises. Addressing an imagined Marcion, he cried, "You are hostile to the sky, yet in your houses you plan for a free view of the sky. You despise the earth, from which was born that flesh of yours which you hate, yet you forcibly extract all its richness for you to feed on. You disapprove of the sea, yet stop short of its contents, which you account a holier kind of food."[8]

Theodoret (about 393–457 CE) tells a story of a Marcionite man in his nineties who at dawn was in the habit of washing his face with his own spit. When asked the reason, he answered that he did not want to stand in need of the creator's water. When the bystanders asked, "How then do you eat, drink, clothe yourself, sleep, and perform your accustomed sacraments?" He responded that he did this by necessity because otherwise he could neither live nor perform the sacraments.[9] If this man was an actual Marcionite (and

5. Clement, *Strom.* 3.3.12.2. See further Muehlenberg, "Marcion's Jealous God," 108.

6. May, *Creatio ex nihilo*, 55, 59.

7. *Ref.* 10.19.4.

8. Tertullian, *AM* 1.14.4.

9. Theodoret, *Fab.* 1.23.5.

not some radical ascetic of another stripe), he had diverged considerably from the man of Pontus.

Tertullian cites what could be taken as a quote from Marcion to prove his supposed anticosmism: "Sufficient to our God is this one single work, that he has by his great and particular goodness set humanity free, a goodness of more value than all locusts."[10] From such a remark one might deduce that Marcion disliked locusts. Tertullian explicitly says that Marcion scorned "tiny animals."[11] The Carthaginian seems to have adapted such arguments from Academic polemic against Stoics.[12] One should not accept such remarks at face value. At best, they only prove that Marcion despised bugs, not the world. Christ himself said to his disciples, "How much more valuable are you than birds?" (G 12:24). Jesus did not hate birds, let alone the world. One should be willing to give Marcion the same charity.

Nevertheless, sometimes modern writers outdo the heresiologists in highlighting Marcion's supposed world-hatred. Harnack spoke of Marcion's "unsurpassable disgust directed at 'flesh,' procreation, and birth."[13] More recently, it is reported that "Marcion's soul appears to be infested by a fanatical hatred of the world," a hatred that is "irrational."[14] The Pontian "seems to have had an enormous, and again slightly pathological, disgust for sexuality as such."[15]

This particular comment is based on the all-too-common acceptance of Tertullian's slanders (that Marcion supposedly called the womb a sewer, site of a "filthy concretion of fluid and blood"[16]). But Tertullian considered such "vilification of the flesh" to be common coin among both "heathen" and "heretics." It was Tertullian who decorated his own language with tawdry descriptions such as "the flesh, . . . unclean from the beginning as from the dregs of the soil,

10. Tertullian, *AM* 1.17.1.

11. Tertullian, *AM* 1.14.1.

12. Chrysippus in *SVF* 2.1048, Galen, *De forma foet.* 6; Lactantius, *De ira Dei* 13.11.

13. Harnack, "Die Neuheit," 140–141 (*Marcion zeigt einen Abscheu gegen das 'Fleisch,' die Zeugung und Geburt, der nicht überboten werden kann*).

14. Moll, *Arch-heretic*, 59, 159.

15. Moll, *Arch-heretic*, 132.

16. Tertullian, *AM* 3.11.7; *Carn. Chr.* 4.1

more unclean from the mud of its seed, worthless, weak, guilty, burdensome, and . . . doomed to lapse back to its origin, the earth."[17]

It's not actually clear that this rhetoric came from Marcion. Thus, it is not wise to opine that "Only in expressions dealing with feces and the anus can Marcion speak about marriage, procreation, pregnancy, birth, and childhood."[18] Nor can one plausibly claim that "Marcion was a serious sexual neurotic," that he was "repressed" and had a "bug phobia."[19] Such psychologizing comments are typically inferred from Tertullian's rhetoric. They do not advance knowledge since they are reinscriptions of heresiological slander.

Another way to poison Marcion's motives was to attribute his ethics to spite against the creator.[20] Clement says that Marcionites do not want to fill the world with children in order to oppose the creator. "So they are abstinent not by an act of will but through hatred of the creator and the refusal to use any of his products."[21] Scholars rephrase this point with characteristic color: in his "ascetic practices, Marcion believed he was taunting the evil Creator and flouting his rule over the realm of matter."[22]

Truth be told, it is not clear that Marcion *hated* the creator (an emotional state), let alone the creation. Marcion certainly opposed the creator of this (lower) world, but it's not clear whether this opposition involved an actual attitude of abhorrence. Ephrem accuses later Marcionites of hating the creator.[23] But the evidence is late, embedded in a poetic hymn, and based on Ephrem's

---

17. Tertullian, *Res.* 4 (trans. A. Souter).

18. Jörg Woltmann, "Fremden Gott," 38, quoting Harnack, *Marcion*, 277* (*Nur in Fäkal- und Analausdrücken kann Markion über Ehe, Zeugung, Schwangerschaft, Geburt und Kindheit sprechen*).

19. H. J. Schoeps, *Aus frühchristlicher Zeit: Religionsgeschichtliche Untersuchungen* (Tübingen: Mohr Siebeck, 1950), 257n2 (*Marcion ein schwerer Sexualneurotiker und Verdrängertyp gewesen ist . . . Seine . . . Ungezieferphobie ist in der Tat einer psychiatrischen Untersuchung wert*).

20. Clement, *Strom.* 3.4.25.1; followed by Moll, *Eroberung*, 40–41.

21. Clement, *Strom.* 3.3.12.2.

22. Dungan, *History of the Synoptic Problem*, 51, citing *Ref.* 10.15 (which does not refer to Marcion). McGowan, in my view, too quickly assents to the proposition that Marcion and disciples believed that they were spurning the creator and his works when they rejected meat and wine ("Marcion's Love of Creation," 305).

23. Ephrem, *Hymns Against Heresies* 33.2.1.

inference. There were other attitudes a Marcionite could exhibit toward the creator such as cold indifference or benign neglect. We cannot reconstruct Marcionite emotions, only their teachings.

Marcion and Marriage

There is both a more logical and a more charitable motive for Marcionite celibacy in his Bible, and in particular in Gospel 20:34–36.[24] In this passage, the Sadducees question Jesus about a woman with seven successive husbands. The resurrection, they imply, would necessitate a woman's marriage with multiple men, because the woman would belong to seven men. Jesus immediately bursts the framework of the debate. He says, "the children of this aeon marry and are given in marriage, but those whom the God of that aeon deems worthy even of the resurrection from corpses, they do not marry nor are they given in marriage. For they do not die any longer. For they are equal to angels and are children of God, being children of the resurrection."

This passage has clear implications for marriage and celibacy. In 20:35, Marcion's text (agreeing with canonical Luke) uses the present tense: people "*do* not marry nor *are* they married."[25] The present tense is important, because it shows that Jesus's observation has ethical meaning for the present, not just for some celestial future. Jesus was not, or not only, saying that *in heaven*, believers will not marry. He was saying that *because* of a future reality, believers now, in the present, *do* not marry.

Marcion's text (as well as Luke) also employs the present in 20:36: "they *are* equal to angels."[26] The present tense suggests present action. Christian readers of 20:34–36 were not at liberty to say that *after death* marriage would cease. No, in this life, marriage should cease, for in this life, Christians *are* already equal to angels. They are not *actually* angels,

24. M. David Litwa, "Equal to Angels: The Early Reception History of the Lukan ἰσάγγελοι (Luke 20:36)," *Journal of Biblical Literature* 140, no. 3 (2021): 601–622.

25. Roth, *Text* 172.

26. As Roth points out (*Text* 173), Marcion's use of the present is confirmed by Tertullian's persistent change to the future tense ("they *will be* equal to angels") when citing Luke 20:36 (*AM* 3.9.4, 4.39.11, 5.10.14; *Mon.* 10.5; *Res.* 36.4–5, 62.1, 62.4). Cf. Justin Martyr, *Dial.* 81.4.

but they are *equal* to them (*isaggelos*), and that status has present ethical implications.[27]

Tertullian approaches this view when he writes that "already on earth, by not marrying," women "are considered part of the angelic household."[28] One can also compare the *Acts of Paul and Thecla*, where Paul, who periodically has the face of an angel, preaches: "Blessed are they who fear God, for they shall become angels of God."[29] Fear of God is expressed by celibacy, which in this text is the backbone of Paul's ethics.

Jesus himself was celibate, and his advocacy of celibacy is consistent with what Marcion found in Paul. The Pontian probably took as Pauline the opening line in 1 Corinthians 7: "It is good for a man not to touch a woman"—meaning, not to have sex. Paul wished that everyone was as he was, that is, celibate (1 Cor 7:7). It is hard to avoid the conclusion that these passages promote celibacy—and not only for a particular class of Christians, but for all of them.

Mandatory Divorce?

Despite his recommendation of celibacy, however, Paul was not issuing a command to divorce. Jesus openly forbade divorce according to Marcion's Gospel (16:18), and so did Paul. "To those who have married, I instruct a wife—not I, but the Lord—not to separate from a husband . . . and (I instruct) a husband not to divorce a wife" (1 Cor 7:10–11).[30] At the same time, Paul recommended that those with spouses live as though they had none (v.29). This is not exactly a clear directive, but it could easily be taken as a recommendation for celibacy. Those who live "as though" unmarried do not, by mutual agreement, have sex.

Occasionally heresiologists accuse Marcion of dissolving marriage, but if Marcion followed the advice of his Bible, then, not only did he refuse to require

27. See further David Aune, "Luke 20:34–36: A Gnosticized Logion of Jesus?" *Geschichte-Tradition-Reflexion, Festschrift für Martin Hengel*, ed. Hubert Cancik, Hermann Lichtenberger and Peter Schäfer, vol. 2 (Tübingen: Mohr Siebeck, 1986), 198–199.

28. Tertullian, *Ux.* 1.4.4.

29. *Acts of Paul and Thecla* 3, 5.

30. Tertullian, *AM* 5.7.6.

divorce, he also forbade it.[31] Marcion was no Ezra, requiring the mass divorce of all married couples who joined his movement (Ezra 9–10). If anything, he implemented Paul's advice for these couples to stay married but live as though they were not. For Marcion, this would have meant celibate marriage, the situation in which two people shared life and property without having intercourse.

For couples who applied for baptism, Marcion required celibacy.[32] Even this does not mean that married couples had to divorce before baptism; they only had to agree to be celibate. Tertullian says that Marcionites baptized married couples who swore—not to divorce—but to have no children: "You do not admit to the sacrament of baptism and the eucharist persons married elsewhere, *unless* they have sworn to each other against the fruit of marriage."[33] Note the "unless." The implication is that Marcion *did* allow married couples—not only to join his church—but to celebrate its sacraments *as long as* they agreed not to engage in intercourse.

This implies that there were married couples in Marcion's community, and that some (not all) of them agreed to be celibate. Those who did not agree to be celibate did not have to leave Marcion's assembly. They could simply remain unbaptized, participating in the services as "hearers" or catechumens. This hypothesis would imply that Marcionite churches had something like a two-tiered membership consisting of those married without a commitment to celibacy, and those with a commitment to celibacy (whether married or not). Marcion officially discouraged marriage—like Paul—but he did not exclude married couples. He recommended celibacy, well knowing that not all his congregants could attain it.

Marcion followed his own interpretation of Paul. He probably considered his church the only one that maintained these pure Pauline standards. Other churches—which encouraged and valorized marriage—he considered unPauline and as falling short of Gospel truth. In the language of his Gospel, Marcion distinguished between the "children of this aeon who marry" (including early catholics) and God's children counted worthy of the resurrection who do not marry (initiates in the Marcionite community).[34]

---

31. *Ref.* 7.30.3–4; Tertullian, *AM* 4.24.5. In the latter passage, Tertullian assumes that Marcion, on the basis of Jesus's prohibition of divorce, would or should have forbid it himself.

32. Tertullian, *AM* 1.24.4; 1.29.1.

33. Tertullian, *AM* 4.34.5, emphasis added.

34. Tertullian *AM* 4.38.8.

The author of the Pastorals may have targeted Marcion when he said that his opponents "forbid marriage" (1 Tim 4:3), but Marcion—if he followed his own Bible—could not have absolutely forbidden matrimony. The undisputed Paul had written, "let each man have his own woman and each woman have her own man" and "a woman . . . is [free] to be married" (1 Cor 7:2, 39). The exhortation to married couples in Laodiceans 5:21–22 ("subject yourselves . . . wives to their own husbands") also assumes that most adult Christians would have been married. Marcion probably made the same assumption. If the Pontian only accepted single people, widows, and the divorced into his church, his assembly would have never grown, and it would never have posed a threat to anyone.

As it turns out, heresiologists reinscribed the Pastor's language in claiming that Marcion forbade marriage outright.[35] Some scholars have followed them.[36] Significantly, however, it is only with Tertullian that heresiologists begin to make this claim. Irenaeus, who had access to Justin's writings against Marcion, never mentions Marcion's supposed prohibition of marriage, though he openly objected against such views in Tatian and others.[37]

Even if Marcion (like Paul) recommended against physical marriage, he could have endorsed theological marriage (as seen among those who take holy orders today). If so, Marcion could have recommended something like a collective marriage to Christ. Christians owed both purity and chastity to Christ (2 Cor 11:3), and Marcion's Apostolikon spoke of a "great mystery," the marriage of Christ to the church" (Laod 5:22). When the Refutator says that for Marcion, marriage is corruption, he was equating marriage and sex and was probably confusing Marcion with Tatian.[38]

In sum, it is more likely that Marcion discouraged marriage because Jesus and Paul told him so, not for his supposed hatred of the creator or of the world. Marriage as such was pure, as indicated by Christ himself who took the church as his bride.

35. Tertullian, *Praescr.* 33; *Marc.* 1.29.1, 5; 4.11.8; *Ref.* 7.30.3–4.

36. For example, DeConick, *Comparing Christianities*, 43.

37. Irenaeus, *Haer.* 1.28.1.

38. *Ref.* 10.19.4. For Tatian, see Irenaeus, *Haer.* 1.28.1; *Ref.* 8.20.1–2. Irenaeus distinguished between Marcion and "Encratites" who did forbid marriage and meat.

Sacred Worship

Heresy writers tend to depict their enemies as creating schools, not churches. If Marcion created a church, he would have to be viewed as a church father. If he created a school, then he could be dismissed as a philosopher, or as a philosophically inspired teacher. A school had traditions, but a church had rites of worship. A school focused on a human teacher; a church was centered on God.

Marcion was a teacher, to be sure, but he was also a church leader; and later Marcionites called him their bishop.[39] The kind of institution he created was not just a center of learning, it was a space for liturgy, where hymns were sung and rites were performed. In fact, Marcion's church is a witness to many distinctive rites practiced by Christians, rites that predated those performed in Roman Catholic or Byzantine liturgies.

Marcionite Christians did not read the Hebrew scriptures in their liturgy. It might be tempting to think that they cut out these readings from their "lectionary" (to use modern language). In fact, there is no reliable data telling us whether or how often the Hebrew scriptures were read in Christian services between, say, 50 and 140 CE. Judging from Paul's description of Corinthian worship (1 Cor 12–14), there was no formal reading of Scripture, but a more charismatic, Spirit-inspired message given by a variety of people. Pliny the Younger's description of Christian worship in the area of Pontus when Marcion was growing up (about 110 CE), does not mention scriptural readings. By Justin Martyr's time, readings from the Prophets had been added in his church. By not adding readings from the Jewish Bible, Marcionites may have been liturgically conservative.[40]

Generally speaking, Tertullian describes a Marcionite liturgy that looked very much like his own catholic one. Marcionite Christians used hymns, prayers, the sign of the cross on the forehead, sacraments, and "pure sacrifices" (evidently referring to consecrated elements in the Eucharist).[41] They baptized, spread out their hands toward the sky in prayer, bowed down to the ground

39. *Adamantius* 1.8.

40. McGowan, *Ancient Christian Worship: Early Church Practices in Social, Historical, and Theological Perspective* (Grand Rapids: Baker, 2014), 83.

41. Tertullian, *AM* 3.22.7. Psalms and hymns appear in 1 Thess 5:19 and Maruta refers to independent Marcionite hymns (Arthur Vööbus, trans. *The Canons Ascribed to Mārūtā of Maipherqat and Related Sources* [Leuven: Peeters, 1982], 18–19).

(apparently another prayer gesture), and gave charity to the poor.[42] One scholar of early Christian liturgy observes, "In a second-century context there was no difference between Marcionite and catholic sacred meals; both avoided meat, both employed bread and water, both employed wine, both knew the use of a variety of foods, both used the language of antitype and likeness to explain the relationship between the foods they consumed and the presence of Jesus."[43]

Prayer

Prayer was important among Marcionites. The Marcionites opposed by Ephrem claimed to pray more than the prophet Daniel.[44] The Marcionite version of the Lord's Prayer had five petitions:

> *Father, let [your] holy Spirit come upon us . . .*
> *Let [your] kingdom come.*
> *Give to us your daily* [or: *supersubstantial] bread every day.*
> *Forgive us our sins.*
> *And do not let us be drawn into temptation. (G 11:2–4)*[45]

In this version, the name of the Father is not hallowed, but the Father is asked to send a hallowed Spirit. For Marcionites, this Spirit was a Spirit of holiness who inspired and empowered their ascetic commitments to celibacy. Like other Christians, they awaited a regime change brought about by divine power. They asked for bread to sustain them each day, and the adjective "supersubstantial" (*epiousios*) hints at a deeper, spiritual nourishment for their souls or spirits. They begged for forgiveness, showing an awareness of sin and an attitude of humility. Marcionites did not think that the Good would actually lead them

42. Tertullian, *AM* 1.23.9.

43. Alistair Stewart, "Bread and Fish, Water and Wine: The Marcionite Menu and the Maintenance of Purity," in May and Greschat, *Marcion und seine kirchengeschichtliche Wirkung*, 208–220 at 220. Everett Ferguson also observes that Marcionites "did not deviate that much [in terms of ritual practice] from the church which excluded them" (*Baptism in the Early Church: History, Theology, and Liturgy in the First Five Centuries* [Grand Rapids: Eerdmans, 2009], 276).

44. Ephrem in Mitchell, *Prose Refutations*, 2.xxxi.

45. Reconstructed from Tertullian, *AM* 4.26.3–4.

into temptation—that was the job of the devil. Accordingly, they prayed not to be *allowed* to be led into temptation.

Baptism

Early Marcionites, at least, did not baptize using a Trinitarian formula (as found in Matt 28:19). They used the simple phrase, "in the name of Jesus Christ."[46] Epiphanius says that the Marcionite churches of his day allowed three or more baptisms. He heard this via various oral reports.[47] Whether multiple baptisms represented Marcion's *original* rule is not certain. If the practice went back to the second century, one would think that Irenaeus or Tertullian would have mentioned it. Perhaps there was a development of Marcionite views on baptism in fourth-century Syria. Since Marcionite baptism required celibacy, Marcionites had to devise a rule for those who failed to keep their commitments. It would not be surprising if married Marcionite couples who committed to celibacy occasionally failed to maintain it. In this system, multiple baptisms would have been logical.[48]

As is customary, Marcionites rooted their practice in scripture. They pointed out texts that Epiphanius found treacherously persuasive, observing that though Jesus had already been baptized by John, he still referred to "another baptism" he wished to complete, and "another cup" he wished to drink (G 12:50).[49] This verse would seem to indicate multiple baptisms even for Jesus—a view authorizing multiple baptisms for Christians.

Since baptism was the main means of forgiveness, allowance for multiple baptisms would have accentuated God's unlimited grace. Repeated baptism is

---

46. Heinrich Kayser-Afferde, "Zur marzionitischen Taufformel," in *Theologische Studien und Kritiken* 108 (1937–38): 370–386 at 386.

47. Epiphanius, *Pan.* 42.3.6.

48. According to Eve-Marie Becker, Marcion emphasized the ethical-anthropological implications of baptism in contrast to its soteriological and eschatological aspects ("Taufe bei Marcion—eine Spurensuche," in *Ablution, Initiation, and Baptism: Late Antiquity, Early Judaism, and Early Christianity*, vol. 2, BZNW 176, ed. David Hellholm, Tor Vegge, Øyvind Norderval, and Christer Hellholm (Berlin: De Gruyter, 2011), 889).

49. Epiphanius, *Pan.* 42.3.10.

not a sign of moral laxity, since those applying for further baptisms had to go through a period of penance.[50] Grace was always given, but it did not come cheap.

According to Tertullian, Marcionites anointed people with oil, presumably after they were baptized. He also says that they used milk and honey, but it is unclear whether they gave them to the baptized, distributed them during the Eucharist, or both.[51] Ephrem indicates that Marcionites used milk and honey in their Eucharist.[52] In the second and early third century, bestowing milk and honey was common among early catholics as well.[53] During this time, Naassene Christians evidently tasted honey and milk to become "perfect," "kingless," and to share in the Fullness.[54]

Eucharist

According to Marcion's Gospel, Jesus waited until after the Last Supper to bless a piece of bread, break it, and share it with his disciples: "This is my body given for your sake." Similarly, he took the cup, saying, "this cup is the covenant in my blood" (G 22:19–20).

The Marcionite Eucharist is the best refutation of Marcion's supposed docetism. As Tertullian pointed out, "there can be no blood except from a body which is flesh."[55] Ephrem sung in one of his hymns, "Where the real body is, there is also real blood."[56] The hymn is against Marcion, but Marcion would not have disagreed with this point. Christ was no phantasm. Jesus had a real body and real blood, and Marcionites consumed these real elements

---

50. Epiphanius, *Pan.* 42.3.8.

51. Tertullian, *AM* 1.14.3.

52. Ephrem, *Hymns against Heresies* 47.6; cf. Tertullian, *AM* 1.14.3. Cf. Barn. 6:17.

53. Tertullian, *Cor.* 3.3. See further McGowan, *Ascetic Eucharists: Food and Drink in Early Christian Ritual Meals* (Oxford: Oxford University Press, 1999), 107–115, 253; McGowan, *Ancient Christian Worship*, 160–163.

54. *Ref.* 5.8.30.

55. Tertullian, *AM* 4.40.5.

56. Ephrem, *Hymns against Heresies* 47.1.

every time they celebrated their sacred meal. They broke true bread, which represented the body of Christ.[57]

The Marcionite Eucharist probably featured a meal before the rite (1 Cor 11:21). After the meal, Marcionites shared a consecrated loaf of bread and a common cup.[58] They considered the cup to be a participation in the blood of Christ, and the bread to be a participation in Christ's body (1 Cor 10:16). The exact words of institution (1 Cor 11:23–35) are not securely attested in Marcion's Apostolos. Thus, it's unclear if Marcionites ate in memory of Christ's death. According to Tertullian, Marcion upheld the bread as a "figure" of Christ's body.[59] This was also language used in Tertullian's own church.[60] It implies, as Tertullian observed, that Jesus had a real body. Marcion had every right to use the creator's elements (bread and wine), since he did not hate the creation.[61]

One could follow Epiphanius in asserting that Marcionites avoided wine in their Eucharist,[62] but Eznik records the use of wine among Marcionites, and Ephrem says that they have a liquid that looks like blood.[63] Tertullian refers to the sealing of the covenant in the wine, which represented Christ's blood.[64] Possibly some Marcionites used water in their Eucharist while others used wine. One cannot expect heresiologists to pay too close attention to the details of Marcionite practice. They only criticized what disagreed with their own rituals, and these rituals evolved over time.

---

57. Ephrem, *Hymns against Heresies* 47.1–2, 8.

58. Jason David BeDuhn, "New Studies on Marcion's *Evangelion*," *Journal of Ancient Christianity* 21, no. 1 (2017): 22.

59. Tertullian, *AM* 4.40.3.

60. Stewart, "Bread and Fish," 210.

61. Tertullian, *AM* 1.14; Ephrem, *Hymns against Heresies* 47.6.

62. Epiphanius, *Pan.* 42.3.3. McGowan, *Ascetic Eucharists*, 164–167, notes the absence of wine in *AM* 1.14.3: "He certainly has not even yet rejected the creator's water, for in it he washes his own, nor the oil with which he anoints them, nor the compound of milk and honey on which he weans them, nor the creator's bread by which he makes manifest his own body."

63. Stewart, "Bread and Fish," 212–213, citing Eznik, *On God*, 409; Ephrem, *Hymns against Heresies* 47.3, 8.

64. Tertullian, *AM* 4.40.5–6.

Epiphanius says that the Marcionite Eucharist was performed openly before catechumens.[65] For this practice, Marcion had a biblical basis: "let the catechumen who learns the teachings share in all things with the one who catechizes" (Gal 6:6). Jerome comments: "Marcion interpreted this verse to mean that catechumens and the faithful ought to pray at the same time and that the teacher must share in prayer with his disciples."[66] These reports suggest less hierarchism in Marcionite assemblies. There was no hard distinction, that is, between teaching priests and the laity who were taught, between the as yet unbaptized and the fully initiated.[67] Although the practice of catechumens watching the eucharistic consecration had become strange among catholics by the fourth century, it was the custom of most Christians in the second.[68]

Avoidance of Meat?

Some heresiologists report that Marcion forbade meat.[69] They do not specify whether this was a perpetual rule or meant only for the eucharistic meal. It was not uncommon, in fact, for Christians to avoid meat during their ritual meals.[70] Nevertheless, the Refutator and Epiphanius both depict Marcion as a Pythagorean, prohibiting meat because human souls abide in animals.[71] But the support for a Marcionite doctrine of reincarnation is weak.

It is unlikely that Marcion issued a blanket prohibition on meat, largely due to statements in Marcion's scriptures. Christ spoke of a son who asked for fish, implying that fish was something good for a father to give. Christ ate not only fish (G 24:41–42), but lamb as well, if he was eager to eat the Passover with his disciples (G 22:15). Paul said, "Eat everything that is sold in a meat

65. Epiphanius, *Pan.* 42.4.5.

66. Trans. Andrew Cain, who believes that the comment "presumably goes back to Origen" (*St. Jerome: Commentary on Galatians* [Washington, DC: Catholic University Press of America, 2010], 253n268).

67. Cf. also Tertullian, *Praescr.* 41.1–4.

68. Stewart, "Bread and Fish," 209.

69. Tertullian, *Jej.* 15; *Ref.* 7.30.3–4.

70. Stewart, "Bread and Fish," 214.

71. *Ref.* 7.30.4; Epiphanius, *Pan.* 42.11.17, elenchus 24.

market" (1 Cor 10:25).[72] Presumably, however, Marcion would have followed Paul's rule of strategic limitation out of love: "It is well not to eat meat or to drink wine or (do anything) by which your sibling stumbles" (Rom 14:21).

If Marcion discouraged meat eating in his sacred meal, he evidently allowed fish. Tertullian said that fish, for Marcion, was a holier sort of food, and Eznik directly says that Marcionites consumed fish.[73] Eating fish in the sacred meal was not a deviant practice but was, again, well-known from contemporaneous Christian rites.[74]

Marcion's Gospel envisioned fasting as implemented after Jesus's departure (G 5:35). According to Epiphanius, Marcionites fasted on Saturdays. It is not clear how (as the heresiologist claims) this practice spited the creator who rested on Saturday.[75] If Marcionites fasted on this day, it would at least have underscored the difference between Marcionite and Jewish practice.

Female Leadership

Tertullian refers to the saintly women of Marcion's church.[76] One would love to know their stories. Presumably, righteous widows would have found Marcion's assembly attractive. In this assembly, widows, young and old, would be honored for their celibacy. Epiphanius says that the Marcionites of his day allowed women to baptize.[77] Tertullian refers to bold women who teach, argue, perform exorcisms, effect cures, and "perhaps" baptize, but it's unclear whether he was referring specifically to Marcionites.[78]

Despite these remarks, Marcion's church was probably not the vanguard for female liberation. Marcion's Bible still preserved 1 Corinthians 11:10, which required women to wear veils as a sign of authority over their heads. It also kept 1 Corinthians 14:34: "women/wives should keep quiet in an

72. Tertullian, *AM* 5.7.14.

73. Tertullian, AM 1.14.4; Eznik, *On God*, 407.

74. Stewart, "Bread and Fish," 215.

75. Epiphanius, *Pan.* 42.3.

76. Tertullian, *AM* 5.9.12.

77. Epiphanius, *Pan.* 42.4.5.

78. Tertullian, *Praescr.* 41.5.

assembly, for it has not been permitted for them to speak, but let them keep themselves subordinate."[79] If Marcion allowed women to preach and to baptize, however, he was indeed distinctive. Jerome says that Marcion sent a female missionary ahead of him to Rome.[80] Unfortunately, this report is isolated and unconfirmed. If true, however, Marcion did allow women to preach and had them in his inner circle.

* * *

Much of what is known about Marcionite ethics and liturgy has to be inferred from defamatory and rhetorically charged reports. Still, a basic picture emerges. Marcion created a church (not just a school) that was, in general, more ethically rigorous than early catholic counterparts. He demanded celibacy for higher members and he likely prohibited red meat in his sacred meal. There is little reason to think that Marcion enforced this ethic out of hatred for the world or to spite the lower creator. As on most issues, the Pontian followed his scriptures. Scripture provided a guideline for the Marcionite liturgy, its form of prayer, its baptismal rite (which featured anointing with oil), its Eucharist (which involved milk and honey and probably did not exclude wine). There is evidence that Marcionite churches exhibited less hierarchism than early catholic ones. Catechumens were able to see the performance of the mysteries, even if they did not partake of the consecrated elements. There is also some evidence for an increased presence of female leadership in Marcionite communions. There was at least one female Marcionite martyr of the mid-third century. Her name is unfortunately unknown, along with the names of any saintly Marcionite woman in the Marcionite church network. The only exception may be Philumene (see the following chapter), though she is never explicitly called a Marcionite.

79. Epiphanius, *Pan.* 42.12.1, scholium 15 and 23; Tertullian, *AM* 5.8.11; *Adamantius* 2.18.

80. Jerome, *Ep.* 133.4.

CHAPTER FOURTEEN

Marcion's Disciples

> What you leave behind is not what is engraved in stone monuments, but what is woven into the lives of others.
>
> —Pericles

MARCION HAD MANY disciples. Some are named, though most are not. Justin says that Marcion convinced people of every nation to follow his views.[1] Tertullian imagines Marcion's church as thriving "all over the world" and his statement that Marcionites build churches "like wasps build combs" illustrates their industry and organization.[2] Epiphanius says that in his day (the late fourth century), Marcionite churches existed in Rome, greater Italy, Egypt, Palestine, Arabia, Syria, Cyprus, the Thebaid (in Egypt), in Persia, and other places.[3] These churches must have had leaders.

The histories of most of these leaders are unrecorded because their very existence was despised by their early catholic opponents. Only in rare cases did ecclesiastical historians and heresiographers take notice of certain independently minded Marcionites—in part because they wanted to show how far they had strayed from their master. In spite of themselves, however, the heresiologists provide windows into the lives and teachings of later Marcionites.

Marcionite Martyrs

Eusebius of Caesarea records a persecution that he says occurred in second-century Smyrna. On this occasion, a Marcionite presbyter named

---

1. Justin Martyr, *1 Apol.* 1.26.5.

2. Tertullian, *AM* 4.5.3; cf. 5.19.2.

3. Epiphanius, *Pan.* 42.1.2.

Metrodorus was burned to death.[4] It is likely, however, that this particular execution took place about a hundred years later under the emperor Decius. Metrodorus was crucified and burned side by side with a catholic martyr named Pionius.[5] In the ensuing Valerian persecution (257 CE), an unnamed Marcionite woman was thrown to the wild beasts in Caesarea on the coast of Palestine. She was joined by three others.[6] In the year 310, Asclepius, a Marcionite bishop, was burned at the same city.[7] Asclepius was burned alongside a young catholic confessor named Peter.

One wonders how much theological differences would have mattered to the Marcionite and catholic martyrs who were tied down and torched together. The fact that these leaders died side by side (in at least two documented cases) indicates that the Romans, at least, did not make too much of a distinction between different types of Christians. Early catholics were willing to die for their commitment to Christ, and so were Marcionites.

Lucanus

Lucanus (Greek: Loukianos) was one of those rare Marcionite leaders mentioned by heresiologists.[8] And even they admit that, in the main, Lucanus proved faithful to Marcion's teachings.[9] Yet Lucanus did make one important modification. He did not portray the creator as evil, but as righteous. Lucanus thus distinguished the creator from an unambiguous figure of evil, whom early Christians typically identified with Satan or the devil.[10] Deemphasizing the

4. Eusebius, *Hist. eccl.* 4.15.46.

5. *Martyrdom of Pionius* 21.6 in Herbert Musurillo, ed., *The Acts of the Christian Martyrs* (Oxford: Clarendon, 1972), 165.

6. Eusebius, *Hist. eccl.* 7.12.1.

7. Eusebius, *Martyrs of Palestine* 10 in *The Ecclesiastical History and the Martyrs of Palestine*, vol. 1, trans. H. J. Lawlor and J. E. L. Oulton (New York: Macmillan, 1927), 378.

8. The following discussion adapts Litwa, *Found Christianities*, 226–236.

9. *Ref.* 7.37.2; Ps.-Tertullian, *AAH* 6.3; Epiphanius, *Pan.* 44.1.3 (κατὰ πάντα . . . κατὰ τὸν Μαρκίωνα δογματίζει); cf. Filastrius, *Diverse Heresies* 46 (18).

10. Epiphanius, *Pan.* 43.1.4.

evil of the creator was perhaps an adaptation toward Valentinian Christian thought, which flourished in the 160s and 170s CE.

At the same time, Lucanus maintained Marcion's negative attitude toward the creator. He emphasized two different prophetic maxims: "The one who serves the lord is foolish (or impious)" (Mal 3:14), and "They opposed god and were saved" (Mal 3:15).[11] The "god" and "lord" in these verses was taken to be the lower creator. Those early catholics who worshiped him were foolish; those who defied the false deity were redeemed. The fact that Lucanus was reading the prophet Malachi indicates that he, like Marcion, was happy to use the Jewish Bible. The "word of the lord" (namely, the Judean lord) could still be used against him.

According to Epiphanius, Lucanus hardened Marcion's ascetic teaching by prohibiting marriage—not just discouraging it. To enter Lucanus's church, reportedly, one had to be single, divorced, or widowed. Celibacy was required, and Lucanus himself modeled this way of life. His motive for sexual abstinence was not simply moral purity. Producing children was the creator's will ("Be fruitful and multiply!" Gen 1:28). By cutting off reproduction, Lucanus opposed the creator's designs.[12]

Lucanus's philosophical education shines through his doctrine of resurrection. He proposed three basic human components: the flesh (made by the lower creator), the soul (also made by the creator), and the mind or *nous* (coming from the good God).[13] This tripartite humanity is Pauline (1 Thess 5:23). In the resurrection, both body and soul are dissolved. Only mind or deep consciousness (*nous*), the true self, rises pure and free to heaven.[14]

Aristotle was one of the first to develop a theory of the perduring human *nous*, but Lucanus was probably more directly dependent on second-century Platonists. Plutarch, for instance, told a myth of two deaths. The first death occurs when the soul separates from the body on earth. The second death happens on the moon, when the purified mind separates from the soul and

11. Epiphanius, *Pan.* 43.1.4.

12. Cf. *Test. Truth* (NHC IX,3) 29.26–30.17.

13. This basic division can already be seen in Plato, *Tim.* 30b.

14. Tertullian, *Res.* 2.12.

goes to live in the sun (symbol of the intelligible world).[15] The survival of the pure mind, which early Christians tended to call "spirit" (*pneuma*), became a widespread idea among Christian intellectuals of Lucanus's time, among both early catholics and Valentinians.

Prepon

All that is known about the Marcionite leader named Prepon comes from the Refutator. Prepon lived in the eastern Roman empire (Syria) during the early third century CE.[16] He attacked Bardaisan, and perhaps specifically Bardaisan's treatise against Marcion. He agreed with Lucanus that the creator was righteous rather than evil.[17] The creator thus mediates between a good principle (the true God of Jesus Christ) and an evil one (Satan). Prepon is evidence for the existence of Marcionite Christianity in Syria, which became the heartland of Marcionite Christianity in the fourth and fifth centuries.

Apelles

Lucanus and Prepon were important disciples of Marcion, but they were both outshone by Apelles. Apelles was a student of Marcion perhaps at Rome in the late 140s or early 150s CE. Yet, Apelles did not remain in the capital. After instruction from his teacher, he traveled to Alexandria.[18] There he remained for as long as twenty years, absorbing the intellectual culture of the Egyptian metropolis—one-time home of Valentinus, Carpocrates, and Basilides.

Apelles was and remained celibate, honored for his temperate way of life.[19] Tertullian's claim that Apelles's sexual lapse led him to travel to Alexandria is

15. Plutarch, *Fac.* 941a–945d. See further William A. Beardslee, "De Facie quae in Orbe Lunae Apparet (*Moralia* 920A–945D)," in *Plutarch's Theological Writings and Early Christian Literature*, ed. H. D. Betz (Leiden: Brill, 1975), 286–288; Deuse, "Plutarch's Eschatological Myths," in *On the* Daimonion *of Socrates*, ed. Günther Nesselrath (Tübingen: Mohr Siebeck, 2010), 184–186.

16. *Ref.* 7.31.1–2.

17. *Ref.* 7.31.2.

18. Tertullian, *Praescr.* 30.5.

19. Eusebius, *Hist. eccl.* 5.13.

ad hominem and unvalidated.[20] Spreading such rumors were common polemical tactics. Epiphanius made a similar, unsubstantiated claim about Marcion himself.[21]

Apelles's sojourn in Alexandria could reasonably have occurred anytime between 150 and 180 CE when Julius Cassianus flourished there along with Prodicus, Isidore, Epiphanes, and Theodotus.[22] Evidently Apelles successfully established a Christian group there, since Origen called him "father of a sect."[23] Alexandria's vibrant intellectual culture inspired Apelles to push Marcion's thought in new directions.[24]

God is One

Marcion's theology was (and is) widely misrepresented as ditheistic (chapter 9). Apelles made it harder for heresiologists to make this charge. He underscored the oneness and single rule of the good God, Father of Jesus Christ. Apelles agreed with Philo that God as first principle could not be demonstrated by arguments.[25] God was the presupposition upon which theological arguments could be built.

Apelles clarified the ontological status of the creator, categorizing him as an angel, not a god. He agreed with Lucanus and Prepon that the creator was not evil but righteous.[26] Perhaps from the Valentinians, Apelles understood the creator to be progressing toward the good. His bodily substance was made up of fire, an idea probably based on Deuteronomy 4:24, "The lord . . . is a consuming fire."[27]

---

20. Tertullian, *Praescr.* 30.

21. Epiphanius, *Pan.* 42.1.4.

22. M. David Litwa, *Early Christianity in Alexandria* (Cambridge: Cambridge University Press, 2024), 91–149.

23. Origen, *Cels.* 5.54.

24. Alfons Fürst, *Christentum als Intellektuellen-religion: Die Anfänge des Christentums in Alexandria* (Stuttgart: Katholisches Bibelwerk, 2007), 25.

25. Eusebius, *Hist. eccl.* 5.13.6–7; Philo, *Post.* 167.

26. *Ref.* 7.38.1. *Exc.* 7.5; Cf. Tertullian, *Praescr.* 34; *Res.* 5; *An.* 23.

27. *Pace* Katharina Greschat (*Apelles und Hermogenes: Zwei theologische Lehrer des zweiten Jahrhunderts* [Leiden: Brill, 2000], 90–96) and Meike Willing ("Die neue Frage des

Angelic Creation

According to Apelles, the creator-angel made both the world and the fleshly body.[28] The notion of angelic creation goes back to Jewish tradition and was supported by Valentinus.[29] (The Refutator, who distinguished Apelles's creator-angel from a separate fiery angel and another malignant angel, unnecessarily multiplied divinities.[30]) Apelles's creator-angel functioned like Plato's craftsman. The craftsman made this world for the glory of the unborn and good God. He made it according to the model of the upper world.[31]

This lower creator could not make the world perfect and so felt remorse (Gen 6:6).[32] This remorse is similar to the repentance Wisdom felt after her fall in Valentinian sources.[33] Apelles called the creator "the lost sheep"—another image used for Wisdom in Valentinian lore.[34] In both cases, the lost sheep was found by the searching shepherd (whether God or Christ). Apelles's creator-angel asked the good God to send Jesus in order to correct the world.[35] The creator was apparently not ignorant of the true God before Christ's advent.

According to Apelles, the creator was the god of the Mosaic Law and of Israel.[36] The idea that Jews worshiped a lower lord would have distinguished

---

Marcionschülers Apelles—zur Rezeption marcionitischen Gedankenguts," in *Marcion und seine kirchengeschichtliche Wirkung*, 221–231 at 221), it is not advisable to follow the Refutator (*Ref.* 7.38.1; 10.20.1) and distinguish the angelic creator from yet another fiery angel who created the human body. The Refutator shows a tendency to multiply divine beings unnecessarily.

28. Tertullian, *Resurrection* 5.2; *Flesh of Christ* 8.

29. Justin, *Dial.* 62.3.

30. *Ref.* 7.38.1; 10.20.

31. Ps-Tertullian, *AAH* 6.4.

32. Tertullian, *Carn. Chr.* 8.1.

33. Irenaeus, *Haer.* 1.4.1–2.

34. Irenaeus, *Haer.* 1.8.4; Tertullian, *Carn. Chr.* 8.3. See further Greschat, *Apelles und Hermogenes*, 88–89.

35. Origen *Epistle to Titus* via Pamphilus, *Apology* 33 in René Amacker and Éric Junod, *Pamphile et Eusèbe de Césarée apologie pour Origène suivi de Rufin d'Aquilée Sur la falsification des livres d'Origène.* SC 464 (Paris: Cerf, 2002), 80.

36. Tertullian, *Praescr.* 34.4.

the Apellian Christian circle from early catholics. At the same time, Apelles did not excoriate the Judean lord nor did he, in what survives, attack Jews themselves. Apelles affirmed Marcion's idea that Christ alone, not the Hebrew prophets, was sent by the true God to redeem humanity.[37]

Christ's Body

Like the Valentinians, Apelles theorized about the nature of Jesus's body.[38] When Christ descended through the heavens, he generated his own body out of stellar or ethereal substance.[39] With this starry body, Christ blended in with heavenly beings, as seen in other second-century texts.[40] When he arrived on earth, he wove his body from the four "essential constituents of the universe (that is, from the hot, cold, moist, and dry)."[41] Heresiologists tended to conflate Christ's sidereal and elemental bodies, but they are probably different. One body was adapted to heaven, the other to earth.[42] Apelles's Jesus employed a body with the same elements as all human bodies.[43] This elemental body was evidently true flesh, made of solid material elements.[44]

Because Christ generated his own body, there was no need for him to be born from a virgin. Valentinians said that Jesus was born through Mary but he did not inherit flesh from her. Jesus passed through Mary like water through a tube.[45] Apelles took it one step further. According to him, Jesus

---

37. Origen, *Cels.* 5.54; Origen, *Comm. Titus* via Pamphilus, *Apology* 33.

38. Tertullian, *Res.* 2.

39. Tertullian, *Carn. Chr.* 6.3; 8.5.

40. *Ref.* 7.38.3. Cf. *Asc. Isaiah* 10; *Epistle of the Apostles* 13:1–2; Simon of Samaria in Epiphanius, *Pan.* 21.2.4.

41. *Ref.* 7.38.3; Epiphanius, *Pan.* 44.2.3.

42. See further Greschat, *Apelles und Hermogenes*, 102–109.

43. Galen, "Medical Definitions," 31 in *Claudii Galeni Opera Omnia*, vol. 19, ed. K. G. Kühn (Leipzig: Knobloch, 1821–33), 356.

44. Tertullian, *Carn. Chr.* 6.3.

45. Irenaeus, *Haer.* 1.7.2. See further Michel Tardieu, "À travers un tuyau: Quelques remarques sur le myth valentinien de la chair céleste due Christ," in *Colloque international sur les textes de Nag Hammadi*, ed. Bernard Barc (Quebec City, QC: Université Laval, 1981), 151–177.

was not born at all. Though Jesus was not an angel, he appeared in flesh just as angels appeared to Abraham of old (Gen 18).[46] They could eat and drink, though they were not born. The fact that Jesus did not have a mother was proved by the story of those who told Christ that his mother and brothers were standing outside. Jesus asked: "Who are my mother and brothers?" (G 8:20–21).[47] The question was not rhetorical, according to Apelles. It signified that Jesus rejected any physical kin. This interpretation of the passage is different from that of Marcion.

Christ's Suffering and Resurrection

According to Apelles, Jesus's body truly suffered, was truly crucified, and truly rose from the dead.[48] Agreeing with Marcion's Gospel (24:39), Apelles said that Christ showed his resurrected flesh to his disciples.[49] The resurrection body was no phantom; but when Christ rose to heaven, he stripped away the earthly elements of his body and rose as a pure spirit on high.[50]

The theory is similar to Philo's description of Moses's final ascent to heaven. Moses did not die like other people. His fleshly elements spun away and Moses ascended as pure consciousness (*nous*) to heaven, bright like the sun.[51] Philo, Apelles, and Lucanus agreed that the fleshly body made by the creator was not the subject of redemption. Only the intelligible core of humanity is saved.

Souls

When Christ came to save souls, according to Marcion, he removed them from the creator. Heresiologists thus accused Marcion's Christ of theft—filching souls that did not belong to him. Apelles solved this problem by arguing that souls were offspring of the true God, thus true possessions of God.[52] These souls preexisted the fleshly bodies made by the creator. They were enticed

---

46. Tertullian, *Carn. Chr.* 6.3.

47. Tertullian, *Carn. Chr.* 7.1; cf. *AM* 4.19.7.

48. Epiphanius, *Pan.* 44.2.7.

49. Epiphanius, *Pan.* 44.2.7.

50. *Ref.* 7.38.4–5; Pseudo-Tertullian, *AAH* 6.5.

51. Philo, *Vit. Mos.* 2.288.

52. Greschat, *Apelles und Hermogenes*, 95.

by the "earthly foods" of this world sometime before or after the creator fused them to flesh.[53] Here again, Apelles moved in a Valentinian direction. Valentinians viewed the soul as the direct offspring of Wisdom. It was thus something divine and not the creator's possession.[54]

Syllogisms

Apelles was perhaps most famous for writing his *Syllogisms*, a mammoth work that advanced and expanded the project of Marcion's *Antitheses*.[55] A syllogism, to define it simply, is form of reasoning in which a conclusion logically follows from premises.[56] Using syllogisms, Apelles contended that if the stories and prophecies of the Old Testament were taken as true, absurd conclusions about God would follow.[57] Specifically, the *Syllogisms* set out to prove the discord and mythic quality of passages in the Law and the Prophets.[58] Its surviving fragments focus on logical problems in the Garden of Eden story and the narrative of Noah's flood.[59]

Apelles's *Syllogisms* was dependent on a long tradition of literary criticism in antiquity.[60] Most educated Greeks of the time could not believe everything in ancient mythology. It was incredible, for instance, that the Trojan horse contained three thousand armed soldiers, all undetected as the horse was hauled

---

53. Tertullian, *An.* 23.3.

54. Clement, *Exc.* 2.2.

55. The name of this work is preserved in Pseudo-Tertullian, *AAH* 6.6; book thirty-eight is mentioned by Ambrose, *Paradise* 5.28.

56. Cf. Alcinous, *Handbook* 6.3.

57. Éric Junod's idea ("Les attitudes d'Apelles, disciple de Marcion a l'égard de l'Ancien Testament," *Augustinianum* 22 [1982]: 113–133 at 131–133) that Apelles changed his view of the Old Testament between the writing of the *Syllogisms* and the *Manifestations* is not based on sufficient data. There are no fragments of the *Manifestations* to adequately judge its contents, nor is there hard evidence that it was written later than the *Syllogisms*.

58. Ps.-Tertullian, *AAH* 6.6

59. Litwa, *Found Christianities*, 233–235; Greschat, *Apelles und Hermogenes*, 45–72.

60. Greta Hawes, *Rationalizing Mythology in Antiquity* (Oxford: Oxford University Press, 2014); M. David Litwa, *How the Gospels Became History: Jesus and Mediterranean Myths* (New Haven: Yale University Press, 2019), 1–21.

into Troy.[61] Apelles presents a similar critique regarding the myth of Noah's ark (Gen 6–7). The ark, Apelles contended, could not contain two of *every* unclean animal on earth and fourteen of *every* clean animal. Aristotle distinguished at least 550 species of animals in his works (as is known today, there are millions more). No zoo could have the space or budget to feed so many animals over the course of a year. Apelles estimated that the ark, despite its large dimensions, could only store enough food to feed about four elephants annually.[62]

Apelles zeroed in on more logical and theological problems in the Hebrew scriptures. The book of Genesis spoke of Adam and Eve in Eden. According to Genesis 2:7, the creator enlivened Adam by breathing into him the breath of life. Later, the creator drove Adam and Eve out of the garden to prevent them from eating the tree of life (3:22–23). Apelles asked why the tree of life had more power to bestow life than the creator's own breath. What more could the true God have given to bestow life other than his own breath? If the Judean lord was the true God, his breath should have provided eternal life at the beginning—but it did not.[63]

The first couple died because they ate of a tree. But it was not the tree that killed them. If this was the case, then a tree would have more power than the life-giving breath of the creator. No, it was the creator who killed Adam and Eve by his own punishment. Given this fact, either the creator lacked goodness—since he refused to pardon the first couple's fault—or he was morally weak because he was unable to forgive.[64]

The creator forbade the first couple from eating the fruit of knowledge (Gen 2:17). From this story, Apelles inferred that the creator himself knew good and evil. The Marcionite reasoned that if it was good for the creator to know these things, then it was good for human beings as well. Nevertheless, the creator prohibited humans from sharing his knowledge. The prohibition indicated that the creator not only made an unfair ruling, but also begrudged humanity something good.[65]

61. This is the figure given in the *Little Iliad*, frag. 22 in W. W. Allen and D. B. Monroe, *Homeri opera* (Oxford: Clarendon, 1912–1946). See further Dio Chrysostom, *Oration* 11.123, 125, 128.

62. Origen, *Hom. Genesis* 2.2; cf. Origen, *Cels.* 4.41. See further Grant, *Heresy and Criticism*, 85–88.

63. Apelles in Ambrose, *Paradise* 5.28.

64. Apelles in Ambrose, *Paradise* 7.35.

65. Apelles in Ambrose, *Paradise* 6.30. See further Greschat, *Apelles und Hermogenes*, 54–56. Cf. Theophilus of Antioch, *Autolycus* 2.25–26; Irenaeus ("god did not envy him the tree

Tertullian cites an Epicurean argument showing that the creator was not good, not foreknowing, or not strong enough to prevent Adam's Fall.[66] One might assume that the argument comes from Marcion, but its syllogistic form suggests that it derives from Apelles.[67] Given current evidence, Marcion did not devote much reflection to the strength or foreknowledge of the creator; he was only concerned to deny his goodness. To do this, he juxtaposed passages from the Bible, and did not depend on raw philosophical logic. Apelles used more of the tools of logic and focused more directly on the opening chapters of Genesis.

The creator, said Apelles, wrongly condemned Adam and Eve. These freshly created humans had no idea what good and evil were. Like children, they had no notion that disobeying a command was evil. A true (good) God, according to Apelles, would never have punished Adam and Eve with the extreme penalties of banishment, affliction, and death.[68]

The pain and suffering inflicted on humanity's first parents was only an example of a broader phenomenon. The continuing and uncorrected disorders of the world (death, plague, natural disaster), Apelles urged, showed either that the creator was physically weak or—if he had the power—was evil because he did not care to rid the world of its flaws.[69]

Canon

Apelles's criticisms might lead one to think that he rejected everything in the Hebrew scriptures—but that is not so.[70] Apelles prided himself on following

of life, as some dare to declare," *Haer.* 3.23.6). Cf. *Life of Adam and Eve* 18:4 (the serpent speaking to Eve): "god knew that you would be like him, envied you and said not to eat from it" in J. Tromp, ed., *The Life of Adam and Eve in Greek: A Critical Edition* (Leiden: Brill, 2005); *Testimony of Truth* IX,3 47.14–48.4: by begrudging Adam the fruit of the tree of knowledge, the creator proves himself to be a malicious envier. See further May, "Marcions Genesisauslegung," 89–98; Williams, *Rethinking Gnosticism*, 68–72.

66. Tertullian, *AM* 2.5.1–2.

67. Gager, "Marcion and Philosophy," 55–56.

68. Apelles in Ambrose, *Paradise* 6.31–32.

69. Apelles in Ambrose, *Paradise* 8.41.

70. *Pace* Moll, *Arch-heretic*, 152, 155–156, who reinscribes Pseudo-Tertullian, *AAH* 6.6; *Ref.* 7.38.2. See Origen, *Comm. Titus* via Pamphilus, *Apology for Origen* 33 in René Amacker and Éric Junod, *Pamphile et Eusèbe de Césarée apologie pour Origène* 80 (§33).

Christ's reputed advice to "be approved money changers"—to detect, that is, the good and discard the bad.[71] Following Marcion's example, Apelles trained himself to preserve what was useful in Hebrew prophecies, even if he rejected the Jewish Bible as Christian scripture.[72]

It is never explicitly said that Apelles used any other canon beyond Marcion's Gospel and Apostolikon. At the same time, he appealed to more authorities. He apparently used several Gospels and at least one unwritten saying of Jesus. He inscribed the sayings and visions of the virgin prophetess Philumene. There is no evidence, however, that Apelles viewed these "private readings" as scriptural or that he actively sought to add to Marcion's Bible.[73] Being open to new revelations was part of Marcion's scriptural logic: "Don't quench the spirit. Don't despise prophecies" (1 Thess 5:19–20). Being a prophet was the gift of the holy Spirit (1 Cor 12:28). Perhaps Apelles's openness to new revelations was also in response to Montanism, which flourished in the late second century.[74] Valentinians emphasized prophetic gifts as well.[75]

---

71. Clement, *Strom.* 1.28.177.2; Origen, *Comm. Matt.* 28 in E. Benz, ed. *Origenes Matthäuserklärung 2. Die lateinische Übersetzung der Commentariorum Series*, GCS 38 (Leipzig 1935), 51. Epiphanius, *Pan.* 44.2.6; cf. *Ref.* 7.38.4. Ps.-Clementine, *Homilies* 2.51.1 (1.55.17 Rehm/Strecker).

72. Cf. Epiphanius, *Pan.* 44.2.6; cf. *Ref.* 7.38.4; Ps.-Clem., *Hom.* 2.5.1. See further J. S. Vos, "Das Agraphon 'Seid kundige Geldwechsler!' bei Origenes," in *Sayings of Jesus: Canonical and Non-canonical. Essays in Honour of T. Baarda*, ed. W. L. Petersen, Johan S. Vos, and Henk J. de Jong (Leiden: Brill, 1997), 227–302; Giovanni Bazzana, "'Be Good Moneychangers': The Role of an Agraphon in a Discursive Fight for the Canon of Scripture," in *Invention, Rewriting, Usurpation: Discursive Fights over Religious Traditions in Antiquity*, ed. David Brakke, Jörg Ulrich, and Anders-Christian Jacobsen (Frankfurt am Main: Peter Lang, 2012), 297–312. Origen seems to have quoted the Συλλογισμοί explicitly and all the surviving fragments are transmitted by him directly or via Ambrose's treatise *On Paradise* (Gianmarco Cerreti, "Osservazioni sulle fonti sui Συλλογισμοί del marcionita Apelle," *Augustinianum* 62, no. 2 [2022]: 297–329).

73. Ps.-Tertullian, *AAH* 6.6 (*privatas . . . lectiones*).

74. May, "Apelles und die Entwicklung der marcionitischen Theologie," in *Gerhard May: Markion. Gesammelte Aufsätze*, edited by Katharina Greschat and Martin Meiser (Mainz: Philipp von Zabern, 2005), 93–110 at 99.

75. For example, Irenaeus, *Haer.* 1.13.3.

Jerome's statement that Apelles wrote his own gospel is isolated and unsubstantiated.[76] The report cannot be saved by the theory that Apelles's "Gospel" refers to his own edited version of Marcion's Gospel. Origen suggested that Apelles "continued the text critical work of Marcion" by "purging" the Gospel and Apostolikon.[77] The statement cannot be dismissed out of hand. But note that Origen here only makes a passing remark and cites no actual evidence that Apelles's scriptures differed from Marcion's. The Refutator, an older contemporary of Origen, does not accuse Apelles of altering his scriptures, only of selecting his doctrines from the Gospel and Paul.[78] Epiphanius claims that Apelles showed which sayings are actually spoken by Jesus and in which scripture, and which sayings come from the creator.[79] Whether or not this accusation is true or false, it does not indicate that Apelles edited or changed Marcion's scriptures.[80]

The Great Debate

As an old man, Apelles returned to Rome.[81] He likely arrived sometime after 180 CE, since Irenaeus, who wrote *Against Heresies* about this time, did not mention Apelles. While in Rome, Apelles attracted followers. Yet, his new teachings and ideas proved controversial, and he had to compete with already-established Marcionite leaders.

The Marcionite church in Rome, like the early catholic church of the time, was diverse. Different assemblies supported a variety of leaders with diverse

---

76. Jerome's *Comm. Matthew, CCSL* 77.1.1, ed. Hurst/Adriaen; Pseudo-Tertullian, *AAH* 6.6. For different opinions, see Junod, "Les attitudes d'Apelles" 114; Greschat, *Apelles und Hermogenes*, 31–33.

77. Löhr, "Editors and Commentators," 81–82, citing Rufinus, *On the Falsification of Origen's Books* 7 (SC 464:301–302. This view goes back to Bardenhewer and Harnack, who are cited in Wilhelm Schneemelcher, ed., *New Testament Apocrypha*, vol. 1, trans. R. McL. Wilson (Louisville: Westminster John Knox, 1991), 400.

78. *Ref.* 7.38.2.

79. Epiphanius, *Pan.* 44.2.6.

80. *Pace* Blackman, *Marcion and His Influence*, 48; Bokedal, *Formation*, 185, 188.

81. Rufinus called Apelles Marcion's "successor" (*On the Falsification of Origen's Books* 7 [SC 464:302]).

views. About 185 CE, Rhodon identified what he thought were three different Marcionite branches in Rome. The first was led by Apelles. Apelles emphasized a single God as the principle from whom all reality developed. A second church was co-led by Potitus and Basilicus. Reportedly, they emphasized a more dualistic system in which good and evil were opposing principles. Syneros, a third Marcionite leader, putatively proposed three principles.[82]

Rhodon aimed to make Marcionite Christians seem hopelessly conflicted. When one looks beneath the surface, however, one finds basic theological continuities. The "three principles" of Syneros, for instance, seem to be nothing more than the good God, just creator, and evil angel (that is, devil) proposed by Apelles, Lucanus, and Prepon.[83] One could combine, that is, pseudo-divine entities (the creator and the devil) with a true God existing on a higher plane. Despite Rhodon's language, these were not considered *co-equal* principles.

Heresiographers made it seem as if Apelles rebelled against Marcion and set up an opposing church, but neither point seems accurate.[84] Apelles formed his own ecclesial network, to be sure, but he showed no antagonism toward Marcion; nor did he oppose other Marcionite assemblies in Rome. Apelles agreed with Marcionite teaching on major points. For instance, the good God and Father of Jesus Christ was different than the creator; the creator was not good; Christ truly suffered, and so on. Apelles employed Marcionite scriptures, maintained Marcion's criticism of the Hebrew scriptures, and practiced Marcionite sacraments.[85] He continued Marcion's policy of discouraging marriage.[86] Apelles ate no meat and remained celibate.[87] He did not despise the flesh,

---

82. Rhodon in Eusebius, *Hist. eccl.* 5.13.2–4.

83. Marcionite three-principle systems appear in *Adamantius* 1.2; Epiphanius, *Pan.* 42.3.1; 43.1.4. Cf. the good God, just Sabaoth, and evil Yaldabaoth in *Nat. Rulers* II,4 86.27–96.17.

84. Tertullian, *Praescr.* 30.6; *Carn. Chr.* 1. See further May, "Apelles und die Entwicklung," 96–97.

85. Cyprian referred to the baptisms of Marcion and Apelles in a single breath (*Epistle.* 74.7). Almost two hundred years after Apelles died, Marcellus of Ancyra "quoted" Apelles to the effect that Marcion deceived people by introducing two principles (*On the Holy Church* 17, in Alistair H. B. Logan, "Marcellus of Ancyra (Pseudo-Anthimus), '*On the Holy Church*' Text, Translation and Commentary," *Journal of Theological Studies* 51, no. 1 [2000]: 81–112 at 93).

86. Tertullian, *Pr. Haer.* 33, claimed—I think wrongly—that Apelles absolutely forbade marriage.

87. Rhodon in Eusebius, *Hist. eccl.* 5.13.

but rejected its final salvation. In line with Lucanus, he preached that resurrected humans, following Christ, ascend to heaven in spirit bodies.[88] To be sure, Apelles developed Marcionite thought, but for this he was no less a Marcionite.

* * *

The Christian movement inspired by Apelles rippled out from its epicenters in Rome and Alexandria. By about 200 CE, it was established in North Africa and Palestine. Tertullian wrote a lost treatise against Apelles and his followers about 205 CE. Between 200 and 250, Origen undertook journeys in order to combat Apellian Christianity in various cities of the East.[89] He also wrote against Apelles's *Syllogisms*, as did Ambrose in Milan about 375 CE.[90] In Rome between 254 and 257 CE, bishop Stephen I did not require former Marcionite or Apellian Christians to be rebaptized—a stance that indicates their continued presence in the capital.[91]

What unites Lucanus, Prepon, and Apelles is their attempt to make Marcionite theology intellectually respectable in their time.[92] They succeeded in softening the harsh "good God vs. evil creator" paradigm of Marcion. They depicted the creator as a just being mediating between the good God and an evil figure (the devil). For Lucanus and Apelles, there was one true God—the Good. They therefore preserved the rule of a single divine being, while attributing evil to a third principle, Satan. They also revised Marcion's apparent view that the soul was made from the creator's breath. For Apelles, the human soul comes from the good God, the higher creator, and Lucanus said something

88. Attempts to emphasize a firm break between Marcionite and Apellian theology depend on Harnack's reconstruction of Marcionite thought. Willing claims that Marcion's "split between the creator and the redeemer god" and his "differentiation of the just Law and good gospel" are not transmitted by Apelles, but there is no evidence that Apelles disagreed with these points ("Die neue Frage," in May and Greschat, *Marcion und seine kirchengeschichtliche Wirkung*, 231).

89. Arnobius iunior, *Praedestinatus* 1.22. The success of the church movement fostered by Apelles shows that he did not form a mere school (*pace* Greschat, *Apelles und Hermogenes*, 38–44, 123).

90. Origen, *Hom. Genesis* 2.2.

91. Cyprian, *Letters* 74–75, in ed. Von Hartel, 810–813.

92. Willing, "Die neue Frage," in May and Greschat, *Marcion und seine kirchengeschichtliche Wirkung*, 221–231.

similar, clarifying that the God-sent part of the soul was the mind or higher consciousness (*nous*).

Long after the leadership of Lucanus, Prepon, and Apelles, Marcionite churches continued to thrive, especially in the East. Cyprian's letters reveal that Marcion continued to have a strong following in third-century Africa.[93] About the mid-fourth century, Cyril of Jerusalem warned members of his church that, if they visited a different town, they should not just ask for the "church," because they might be led to the Marcionite congregation.[94] In the fifth century, Theodoret boasted that he converted eight Marcionite villages.[95] During this time, a five-book poem against Marcionites (*Carmen adversus Marcionitas*) was written in the Latin West.[96] Traces of Marcionite groups are found in Arabic sources as late as the tenth century.[97] Al-Nadīm (author of the *Fihrist*), for instance, says that there are many Marcionites in the Khurasan region of northeastern Iran, "their cause being openly known."[98]

93. Kayser-Afferde, "Taufformel," 375.

94. Cyril, *Mystagogic Catecheses* 18.26.

95. Theodoret, *Ep.* 81, col. 1261. See further Arthur Vööbus, *History of Asceticism in the Syrian Orient: A Contribution to the History of Culture in the Near East*, vol. 1 (Leuven: CorpusSCO, 1958), 45–54; René Roux, "Antimarcionitica in the Syriac *Liber Graduum:* A Few Remarks," *Augustinianum* 53 (2013): 91–104.

96. Karla Pollmann, ed., *Das Carmen adversus Marcionitas* (Göttingen: Vandenhoek & Ruprecht, 1991), 33. Moll (*Arch-heretic*, 21–23) puts the *Carmen* in the mid-third century, in part because he assumes that Marcionism did not pose a real threat beyond the third century. It is better, however, to let the text itself tell us whether and when Marcionite Christianity was still powerful in the Latin west. Moll is right that the poem treats Marcionite Christianity as a living and active force, but it could well be a living and active force in the age of Augustine. It is inadequate to say that other Christian sects are attacked under the cover of fifth-century (neo-)Marcionism. The only sect mentioned in the poem is the Marcionite one, and there is every indication it was alive and well at the time of writing.

97. Here I adopt the language of Räisänen, "Marcion," 101, who rightly cites Marco Frenschkowski, "Marcion in arabischen Quellen," in May and Greschat, *Marcion und seine kirchengeschichtliche Wirkung*, 39–63.

98. Bayard Dodge, ed., *The Fihrist of al-Nadīm: A Tenth-century Survey of Muslim Culture*, vol. 2 (New York: Columbia University Press, 1970), 807.

Conclusion

Rejecting Biblical Violence

> [O]ne can only wish that in the confused choir of the God-seekers today, Marcionites also be found.
>
> —Adolf von Harnack

MARCION IS NOW officially a Christian saint, having been beatified in Corinth, Greece on June 8, 2023. His feast day is July 15, taken to be the day he published the first Christian Bible in Rome in 144 CE. This, at least, is what is reported by the Marcionite Christian Church.[1] The Church claims that Marcion's ecclesial network became the largest Christian denomination until the emperor Constantine issued a "*damnatio memoriae*" (a purge from memory) in 332 CE, "intended to erase all history of The Very First Bible."[2] It further asserts that the catholic counter-Bible (combining twenty-seven New Testament books with the Old Testament) was ratified in a council at Rome in 382 CE.[3] The Marcionite Church constructs a life of its founder based mainly on the reports of Epiphanius and Tertullian, as filtered through the Harnackian paradigm. Indeed, it is arguably Harnack's heroic portrait of Marcion that makes "St. Marcion" possible.

There are in fact two Marcionite churches active today, the Marcionite Christian Church (MCC) and the Marcionite Church of Christ (MCoC). Although not organizationally connected, they make similar claims about church history, emphasizing a conflict model between Marcionites (who

---

1. See https://medium.com/@prenicene/saint-marcion-canonized-holy-day-announced-bd61c9c7c773

2. *The Very First Bible: Original Scriptures Transcribed by Saint Marcion of Sinope in 144 A.D.* (Marcionite Christian Church: 2020). 247, 249. https://www.marcionitechurch.org/saintmarcion.html

3. *The Very First Bible*, 247.

were initially in the majority) and the increasingly powerful catholics. The Marcionite churches claim originality, purity, and apostolicity for the Marcionite tradition. They both publish lengthy, defined liturgies with a strong claim to revive ancient practices and formulae. It is difficult to estimate the size of these movements (the MCC supports a house-church model with independent leadership and seemingly little oversight). But if they lack physical property, they recruit energetically online.

The MCC's *The Very First Bible* introduces Marcion's Pauline letters with the Marcionite prologues and includes a reference and study guide at the end—a sort of modern *Antitheses* compiled by A. W. Mitchell. The guide explains why the Marcionite Bible does not contain the Old Testament. It then contrasts passages from the Old and New Testaments in chart form, asking "Is This the Same God? You Be the Judge." Following these discussions come more theological and historical summaries called "Assessing the Damage of the Old Testament," "First Shots Fired by Constantine, Council of Nicaea," "Roots of the Very First Bible," and "Rebirth of the Marcionite Christian Church."

The MCoC publishes a Bible called *The Testamentum: The First Christian Holy Bible* as "compiled and transcribed by Marcion" in 130 CE. This Bible has a 28-page historical introduction to Marcion and his movement.[4] It presents Marcion as born about 70 CE, dying at the age of ninety, as son of a bishop, "Philologus" (a name taken from Rom 16:15), who was one of the Seventy disciples and a companion of Paul.[5] Marcion was not a "myth-oriented" Gnostic, but a man determined by the canon, who became the most successful second-century Christian preacher.[6] The Pontian did not preach docetism, despite the fact that Christ descended from heaven as a mature man.[7] Marcionites are not dualists, they do not prohibit marriage, alcohol, or meat.[8] MCoC Marcionites, at least, are Trinitarian.[9]

---

4. Marcionite Church of Christ, *The Testamentum: The First Christian Holy Bible. Original Scriptures Compiled & Transcribed by Marcion of Sinope in 130 C.E.* (Amazon Digital Services, 2022), 5, 7.

5. Marcionite Church of Christ, *Testamentum* 1.

6. Marcionite Church of Christ, *Testamentum* 7.

7. Marcionite Church of Christ, *Testamentum* 4, 9. "Timeline," Marcionite Church of Christ, accessed May 6, 2024, https://marcionitechurchofchrist.org/#timeline.

8. Marcionite Church of Christ, *Testamentum* 23.

9. Marcionite Church of Christ, *Testamentum* 10.

Both the MCC and MCoC churches view Marcion's Gospel as the only original one.[10] Both affirm that Marcion himself retraced the route of Paul's missionary journeys, collected his letters, and organized them into a single work.[11] The MCoC, however, adds reconstructed versions of the Pastoral Epistles and the letter traditionally called Hebrews (identified with the epistle to the Alexandrians) as deuterocanonical (allowing their occasional liturgical use).[12] It also reconstructs a "Psalmicon," dated to about 134 CE, from the *Odes of Solomon*.[13]

The MCoC offers a maximalist reconstruction of the Evangelion and Apostolikon, which is to say that it uses the Gospel according to Luke and John (with bits of Matthew) to produce a continuous text.[14] Although the MCoC denies that its Gospel is a harmony, it reads, in large part, like an amalgam of Luke and John in the language of the King James Bible.

For its Evangelion, the MCoC admits dependence on the translation of James Hamlyn Hill (1891), which is based on the 1823 reconstruction by August Hahn.[15] Hill's text is in the public domain (gnosis.org). In this online version, Hill's text has been updated by Daniel Mahar "to reflect the reconstruction done by Theodor Zahn [later in the 19th century]."[16] The MCoC lists two other editors, namely David Inglis, and Stephen Huller, who used the reconstructions done by Gustav Volkmar,[17] Zahn, Charles B. Waite,[18] and André Wautier.[19] All these reconstructions are now outdated.

10. Marcionite Church of Christ, *Testamentum* 14.

11. Marcionite Church of Christ, *Testamentum* 15.

12. Marcionite Church of Christ, *Testamentum* 17–18.

13. Marcionite Church of Christ, *Testamentum* 20.

14. Marcionite Church of Christ, *Testamentum* 27.

15. James H. Hill, *The Gospel of the Lord: An Early Version* (Guernsey: John Whitehead, 1891). For another English translation of Marcion's Gospel, see P. L. Couchoud, *The Creation of Christ: An Outline of the Beginnings of Christianity*, vol. 2 (London: Watts & Co., 1939), 321–423.

16. http://www.gnosis.org/library/marcionsection.htm; Theodore Zahn, *Geschichte des N.T. Kanons*, 2 vols. (Erlangen: A. Deichert, 1888–1892).

17. Gustav Volckmar, *Das Evangelium Marcions: Text und Kritik* (Berlin: Weidmann, 1852).

18. Charles B. Waite, *History of the Christian Religion to the Year Two Hundred*, 5th ed. (Chicago: C. V. Waite, 1900), 276–286.

19. André Wautier, *Comment naquit le Christianisme* (Bruxelles: self-published, 1981).

For the Apostolikon, the MCoC depends on the work of David Inglis, who utilized the reconstructions of the Apostolikon by Harnack (*History of Dogma*, 1894), Paul-Louis Couchoud (*La première edition de St Paul*, 1928), and Jason BeDuhn (*First New Testament*, 2013). To reconstruct their version of the Pastorals and Hebrews, the MCoC uses the 2016 dissertation of Maegan C. M. Gilliland (*The Text of the Pauline Epistles and Hebrews in Clement of Alexandria*, 2016), along with quotations of early church fathers (from Philip Schaff's *Ante-Nicene Fathers*, 1885).

By contrast, the MCC does not provide any guidance for how it reconstructs Marcion's Gospel and Apostolikon. (Perhaps this is intentional, to present the Scriptures as the work of God and not of human editors.) One suspects, however, that the MCC also makes use of Hill's translation as updated by Mahar. It updates the archaic English of the KJV ("thee" and "thou" is changed to "you," for instance), though much archaic grammar and vocabulary remains. The MCC's Evangelion lacks passages from John, though it does fill in language from canonical Luke.[20]

Marcionism as Evangelical Foil

Today one can become a Marcionite Christian by becoming a member of a Marcionite church. Among conservative theological circles, however, it takes even less to be called a "Marcionite." All one must do, in fact, is to express skepticism or dislike for the "Old" Testament.[21] Yet the use of "Marcionite" as a stigma obscures the deeper and more persistent problem: "texts of terror"—from "Old" and New Testaments—continue to drive Christians (and some non-Christians) toward "Marcionite" positions.

Today, theologically conservative writers spend great energy defending the "hard sayings" of Scripture. For example, there is a book on the market today telling people how (not) to read the Bible so that they can make

20. It is concerning that both Marcionite churches depend, at least in part, on nineteenth-century translations of Marcion's scriptures, which are derived in turn from outdated and problematic reconstructions of Marcion's Greek text. Although there is mention of BeDuhn for the Apostolikon, there seems to be no knowledge of more recent and reliable reconstructions of the Evangelion by BeDuhn, Bilby, Klinghardt, and Roth.

21. Räisänen, "Marcion," 64; Eric A. Seibert, *Disturbing Divine Behavior: Troubling Old Testament Images of God* (Minneapolis: Fortress, 2009), 64–67.

sense of the antiwoman, antiscience, proviolence, proslavery, and other "crazy-sounding parts of scripture." It acknowledges that the fast-track to atheism is reading the Bible itself. It helpfully concedes that many Christians "pick and choose by taking the nice-sounding Bible verses and claiming they are true and applying them to our lives, while skipping past the negative-sounding ones."[22]

These are the words of Dan Kimball, who represents a genre of (primarily American) Evangelical literature defending the "Old" Testament, largely, but also some troubling parts of the New.[23] Kimball urges his audience to avoid—not the Bible—but "dangerous ways of reading" it.[24] He recommends a hermeneutical procedure that does not reflect church tradition so much as modern historical and literary criticism: people should read the Bible not as a book, but as many book*s* written by many humans to other humans in history over a 1,500-year period, and they should read them in context.[25] The advice is sound, though not specifically Christian, and it does not answer the fundamental question why the "crazy-sounding" parts of Scripture are there and (more importantly) why they still *should* be there.

Late in the book, Kimball depicts what might be called the orthodox encyclopedic portrait of Marcion. The Pontian, "felt the Old Testament God was violent and was all about killing people, which didn't align with how he understood the God of Jesus in the New Testament."[26] Therefore Marcion began "teaching that the Old Testament was not true . . . and even removed several sections from the New Testament. He took out anything he felt was inappropriate or too violent, passages about God's judgment or hell, and edited

---

22. Kimball, *How (Not) to Read the Bible: Making Sense of the Anti-women, Anti-science, Pro-violence, Pro-slavery and Other Crazy-sounding Parts of Scripture* (Grand Rapids, MI: Zondervan Reflective, 2020), 36.

23. Walter C. Kaiser Jr., Peter H. Davids, F. F. Bruce, and Manfred T. Brauch, *Hard Sayings of the Bible* (Downers Grove: IVP Press, 1996); Manfred T. Brauch, *Hard Sayings of Paul* (Downers Grove: IVP Press, 1989); Peter H. Davids, *More Hard Sayings of the New Testament* (Downers Grove: IVP Press, 1991); Charles Siegel and Mitchell Mackinem, *Did He Say That? The Difficult Words of Jesus* (Eugene, OR: Wipf & Stock, 2016).

24. Kimball, *How (Not) to Read the Bible*, 34.

25. Kimball, *How (Not) to Read the Bible*, 15–60, with summary on 26.

26. Kimball, *How (Not) to Read the Bible*, 265.

and shaped a new Bible with just the nice things about God (from his own perspective)."[27]

By now, readers should be inoculated against these oft-repeated half-truths. Marcion did understand the Hebrew god as violent, as do millions of people and hundreds of biblical scholars today. For Marcion, however, this being was "god" in name only. The Pontian believed that the Jewish Bible was historically and theologically accurate, and that was, perhaps, the most troubling thing about it. He did not remove things from a preexisting "New Testament"; instead, he forged his own distinctly Christian canon, which was arguably the first one. In this Gospel plus Apostolikon he left in passages about God's judgment, since he did not feel at liberty to change what was for him an inspired text.

It is important to correct errors about Marcion to prevent apologists from continuing to use him as a foil—a whipping boy illustrating how *not* to read Scripture. But Marcion's way of reading the Bible is just as Christian as the modern Evangelical way of reading it. In fact, Marcion's mode of interpretation is extremely early in Christian history, demonstrably more original than "orthodox" readings, and arguably more honest.

It might seem that Marcion would disagree with statements like, "Jesus has a backstory called the Old Testament" and "we need the Old Testament to understand the New."[28] In fact, Marcion read the Jewish scriptures in a similar way, though with a twist. They provided the negative backdrop for understanding the positive message of the Gospel. True, Marcion would not have agreed that that everything in the "Old" Testament points to Jesus.[29] But he did believe that it provided the necessary backstory for understanding the newness and radicality of Jesus's message.

Kimball himself sounds rather Marcionite when he says that the Gospels "might" sound as if Jesus "was erasing the Old Testament laws, rituals, and dietary restrictions and starting over from scratch. "But," he assures us, "that's not what happened." He then proposes time-worn solutions that, in many permutations, have served churches for centuries: some things in the Hebrew Bible are abolished and some are not, and Christians (or rather Christian

27. Kimball, *How (Not) to Read the Bible*, 266.

28. Kimball, *How (Not) to Read the Bible*, 43.

29. Kimball, *How (Not) to Read the Bible*, 26.

leaders) get to choose (though, as it turns out, they choose differently). God is ever faithful, but there "is a change in how God relates to people after Jesus."[30] There is a "broader storyline" in the Bible that theologians select out by blurring many of the Bible's violent and frankly horrifying details.[31] (Kimball even recommends "proper" cherry-picking that follows "good Bible-study methods."[32]) The end of God's complicated story justifies the violence in the middle: "There will be a new creation, a new heaven and a new earth where God will dwell and live with those who have believed the good news."[33]

Descripturalizing Divine Violence

Kimball struggles the most with passages manifesting divine violence, admitting that he did not want to write chapters on this topic. He also discloses that it is this material that, if anything, could make him an atheist.[34] In the end, Kimball undermines his own ethos, however, by accepting the accounts of divine violence, though in mitigated form. In the Bible, God does not engage in mass killing, Kimball says, but in "a series of strategic attacks for God to have the people who had rejected his guidance and his purposes removed from interrupting his plan."[35] God does commit murder, just not mass murder; he does slaughter people, just not ruthlessly or mindlessly. God had a plan for the Canaanites, to remove "what didn't belong in his land."[36] "Phrases like 'utterly destroy,' 'drive them out,' and other language we find in the Bible were common war rhetoric," not reality.[37] But fiery rhetoric can incite violent reality, and Kimball never addresses how individual Canaanites ever consciously rejected God's plan and guidance before being attacked by Jesus's putative precursor (and namesake) Joshua.

---

30. Kimball, *How (Not) to Read the Bible*, 267.

31. Kimball, *How (Not) to Read the Bible*, 288.

32. Kimball, *How (Not) to Read the Bible*, 80.

33. Kimball, *How (Not) to Read the Bible*, 290.

34. Kimball, *How (Not) to Read the Bible*, 255–256.

35. Kimball, *How (Not) to Read the Bible*, 285.

36. Kimball, *How (Not) to Read the Bible*, 283.

37. Kimball, *How (Not) to Read the Bible*, 283.

Such admonitions can only serve as palliative care, while the root cancer of divine violence remains in the marrow of "orthodox" faith. If people accept the reality of divine violence, they err about God and seriously diminish their claim to moral uprightness. No apologetic work—even one ten thousand pages long—justifies stories of God killing people, or ordering them to be killed, strategically or not. "God only uses violence as a last resort, when he is provoked to anger."[38] This is not an excuse. Stories of divine violence simply get God wrong, and apologists need to face this fact—without apology.[39]

It is not just that Christians are misinterpreting their sacred texts by taking them out of context or perverting them to justify violence. Violence lives in the hearth of these texts, and violent people cite them to justify their violent deeds.[40] Patriarchy, violence against children, and violence against women is not just read into Scripture. It is already there. "God *is* represented as abuser and killer of children; God *is* said to command the rape of women and the wholesale destruction of cities, including children and animals. To shrink from making such statements is dishonest."[41]

Modern people know that many passages of the Bible cannot be applied; instead of avoiding such passages, it is best to confront them, to name them as morally and theologically problematic.[42] One does not have to overthrow biblical authority, since one can always blame the interpreter's lack of understanding. But one should at least be honest that some passages are still, demonstrably, incitements to evil. It is fine to uphold biblical authority, but one

---

38. Claude Francisco Mariottini, *Divine Violence and the Character of God* (Eugene: Wipf & Stock, 2022), 373.

39. Eric A. Seibert, *The Violence of Scripture: Overcoming the Old Testament's Troubling Legacy* (Minneapolis: Fortress, 2012), 24–26, 160. Research on divine violence is extensive; for recent works, see Rhiannon Graybill, *Texts after Terror: Rape, Sexual Violence, and the Hebrew Bible* (New York: Oxford University Press, 2021); Monica Jyotsna Melanchthon and Robyn J. Whitaker, *Terror in the Bible: Rhetoric, Gender, and Violence* (Atlanta: SBL Press, 2021); Adi M. Ophir, *In the Beginning Was the State: Divine Violence in the Hebrew Bible* (New York: Fordham University Press, 2023); Helen Paynter and Michael Spalione, eds., *Global Perspectives on Bible and Violence* (Sheffield: Sheffield Phoenix Press, 2023).

40. Nelson-Pallmeyer, *Is Religion Killing Us?*, xv, emphasis original.

41. Terence E. Fretheim and Karlfried Froehlich, *The Bible as the Word of God: In a Postmodern Age* (Minneapolis: Fortress Press, 1998), 99–100, emphasis original.

42. John J. Collins, *Does the Bible Justify Violence?* (Minneapolis: Fortress, 2004), 31–32.

should be very concerned about the human ability to interpret or rationalize biblical violence.

Most Christians search for interpretive strategies to mask, blunt, or transcend biblical violence.[43] One of these, allegory, is no longer considered convincing. The Canaanites are not internal vices; they were real people, or at least imagined to be real in the biblical narrative.[44] Another reading strategy can be called "historical-critical." This is a form of active reading that involves questioning and critiquing biblical violence.[45] But any sort of ideological criticism will inevitably chip away at inerrancy and thus be unsatisfying to conservative readers, since it underscores biblical inconsistency. For some parts of the Bible (the love commands, for instance) one allows oneself to be shaped by the text; but for the violent bits of the Bible, a modern, more ethical framework is introduced to understand the text. For some biblical stories, one reads from the margins with the minor characters; in others, one rejoices with and embraces the voice of the protagonists.

It's high time to stop defending biblical "texts of terror."[46] This includes the strategy of deeming violent Scriptures useful because they "raise awareness." Violent biblical texts do not usually invite violent people to reevaluate their violent behavior.[47] Violent people read Scripture like all other people—with their cognitive biases. They do not stop to peruse a scholarly handbook on how to read nonviolently. Rather, they underscore the violence because it reinforces their authoritarian predisposition. Violence is valorized in Scripture. The towering authority of the Bible means that, practically speaking, most of its main audience (devout Christians) will not read it with the tools of ideological criticism.

Having refused to defend scripturalized violence, one must find a better way to approach it. Harnack found such a way, and he is often quoted—not without a faint gasp of horror and contempt:

---

43. Seibert, *Violence of Scripture*, 3.

44. Collins, *Does the Bible Justify Violence?*, 29–30.

45. Seibert, *Violence of Scripture*, 62–67, 76–87.

46. Phyliss Trible, *Texts of Terror: Literary-Feminist Readings of Biblical Narrative* (Minneapolis: Fortress, 2022).

47. Siebert, *Violence of Scripture*, 88.

> To reject the Old Testament in the second century was a mistake which the Church rightly repudiated; to retain it in the sixteenth century was a fate which the Reformation could not yet avoid; but to continue to keep it in Protestantism as a canonical document after the nineteenth century is the consequence of religious and ecclesiastical paralysis.[48]

Harnack clarified that it is not about rejecting the "Old" Testament plain and simple, but about removing it from the Christian canon. The "Old" Testament, he said, "will only be appreciated and valued everywhere for its distinctiveness and importance (the prophets), first when *canonical* authority, which does not belong to it, is removed."[49] Such passages from Harnack are often dismissed by Christians without much thought. And to be sure, Harnack is rightly criticized for his inadequate views of Judaism (though he was an opponent of antisemitism in his time).[50]

In his context, Harnack was not making a point about Jews, but referred to the destructive *Christian* use of "Old" Testament texts. The historian wrote, "If Marcion had reappeared at the time of the Huguenots and Cromwell, he would have met at the very center of Christianity the warlike God of Israel whom he abhorred."[51] Christians have used the Bible to justify colonialism, the crusades, slavery, the displacement and murder of first peoples in Australia and America—the list goes on. In late 2023, "destroy Amalek" has been used in a war with horrific collateral damage inflicted on civilians in Gaza.

Harnack urged the decanonization of the "Old" Testament, but one needs to critically sift *all* of it—Old and New—to selectively decanonize the parts of the Bible that support divine violence.[52] A book like Revelation is in fact

48. Harnack, *Marcion*, 134 (italics removed).

49. Harnack, *Marcion*, 223*, emphasis original ("*erst dann in seiner Eigenart und Bedeutung (die Propheten) allüberall gewürdigt und geschätzt werden, wenn ihm die kanonische Autorität, die ihm nicht gebührt, entzogen sei*").

50. Räisänen, "Marcion," 120–121.

51. Harnack, *Marcion*, 220. See further Kevin Killeen, *The Political Bible in Early Modern England* (Cambridge: Cambridge University Press, 2017).

52. For violence in the New Testament, see Michel Desjardins, *Peace, Violence and the New Testament* (Sheffield: Sheffield Academic Press, 1997); Shelly Matthews and E. Leigh Gibson, ed.

more damaging than Joshua or Judges for the simple reason that it tends to be more widely read. According to Revelation, God has not morally improved since his days as genocidal flood-maker in Genesis (Gen 6–8). In fact, he is depicted as devising even more horrific ways of killing human beings—asteroids, solar heat, drought, even insect-like creatures (Rev 6–11, 15–16). In this text, Christ himself comes, no longer cruciform, but with a sword protruding from his mouth (Rev 19:15).[53]

Admittedly, it is unlikely that self-described mainline Christians will remove bits from both Testaments, even if—practically speaking—they have already excluded many passages from their lectionaries and sermons. In fact, however, this is the first step in effectively descripturalizing parts of the Bible—simply *by not reading them*. Lot's daughters having secret sex with their drunken father (Gen 19) does not normally appear in lectionaries or in stained-glass windows, not to mention the story of how a woman was gang raped to death when visiting an ancient Israelite town (Judges 19). These texts are typically buried under heavy silence, amid dozens of others. Practically speaking, this silence represents an implicit and selective devalorization of biblical passages. If a story is printed in the Bible but never read in church, it is canonical in name only. In many churches today, many passages in the Bible *function* as museum pieces, not as canonical texts. In fact, if the Bible were a space, most of it would be more like an echoing museum than an active playground.

Practically speaking, Marcion's proposal is already being fulfilled among us. Despite the steady stream of the anti-Marcionite rhetoric that continues apace, the implicit processes of decanonization are already moving across the globe. Marcion, to be clear, never recommended that "Old" Testament texts not be *read*, only that they not be read as scripture. Arguably, descripturalization is the key for these texts to be read *more* by Christians, and more critically. Marcion himself demonstrates what it means to read the Bible intensely and critically. One can disagree with his interpretations, but he arguably read Jewish scripture more than most Christians do today—in a time when it was much rarer for anyone to read at all.

Violence in the New Testament (London: T&T Clark, 2005); Susannah Larry, *Leaving Silence: Sexualized Violence, the Bible, and Standing with Survivors* (Harrisonburg: Herald Press, 2021), 183–212.

53. Pieter G. R. de Villiers and Jan Willelm van Henten, eds., *Coping with Violence in the New Testament* (Leiden: Brill, 2012), 185–245.

This very point shows why it is a fallacy to think that, if Christians decanonized select "Old" Testament texts, they would forget the Jewish roots of Christianity.[54] First of all, the Jewish roots of Christianity are clear from virtually all parts of Scripture—so if Christians forget these roots, then pastors and scholars are not doing their job. By releasing their canonical hold on the Hebrew Bible and their identity as the "new Israel," Christians may in fact open new avenues of dialogue with actual Jewish people.

Decanonizing "texts of terror" hardly means that Christians ignore them. Certain texts of the Bible simply become what they already are (as determined by use): deuterocanonical. With this subsidiary status, they can still be the focus of Bible studies, lectures, and courses in Christian churches, seminaries, and universities. Decanonization simply means that certain biblical passages are not read liturgically, or preached on as divinely-inspired sources of truth.

Perhaps, however, one should not stir the pot, and allow the more tacit processes of decanonization to run their course. The violent images of God will presumably fade with years of neglect. But neglect is not enough, for in times of war and crisis, the dark side of Scripture appears from the fog of oblivion in letters of light. Humans are predictable animals: when we feel threatened and raise the ululations of war, we grasp for authorities to back up our calls to violence and revenge. The texts of terror serve as hidden "mind files" that can be pulled out and paraded when it is necessary to justify lobbing missiles and sending snipers. The violent nationalists and militia groups don't need this advantage. Cut out the problem at the root.

Decanonization need not be done with an axe, but with a scalpel. Not everything needs to go, because not everything is theologically unredeemable. Entire books need not be omitted, only passages and verses from *both* Testaments. To agree on what to remove, Christians of all denominations (and none) would have to come together to do very hard, soul-searching work. And of course, they would not agree, and different Bibles would be produced. But different Bibles *are already* being produced and have been for centuries.

When it comes to revising the canon, there is the problem of inertia, but also lack of courage. It should be remembered, however, that God spoke Scripture, not canon. God never said: "this book is in the canon, and this one isn't." Canon lists are entirely human products, representing an ancient—but

54. *Pace* Jürgen Regul, "Die Bedeutung Marcions aus der Sicht heutiger kirchlicher Praxis," in May and Greschat, *Marcion und seine kirchengeschichtliche Wirkung*, 293–311 at 300.

never complete—consensus about what churches took to be scriptural. Accordingly, the canon can always be revised. If a purge was done in the sixteenth century, it can be done today. Most publishers are not afraid to add things to the Bible, such as introductions, blurbs, pastoral admonitions, and study tools. During the 2024 presidential campaign, former President Trump sold a Bible that adds the US Constitution and the words to the song, "God Bless the USA." If parts can be added, they can also be removed.

By not revising the material—including, and even especially, the New Testament material—the Bible will continue to be a factory for justifying militants, and a new crop of "Marcionites" will sprout up in every generation, asking the same old question, "What kind of God is this?" If Christian apologists really had a good answer to the questions raised by biblical texts of terror, they would no longer be asked. For anyone who reads the Bible—who *really reads* it all the way through—troubling questions will continue to bubble up. Christian apologists will continue to sell books defending "hard sayings," but they will never convince the heart. If the canon is revised—patiently, collectively, intelligently—they won't need to.

The violence of the Bible continues to fester in peoples' minds, and they cannot avoid damaging themselves by accepting even a strategic and mitigated version of a violent God. "I may not understand why violence happened, but I trust the God who does."[55] This is a sidestep, a Band-Aid for a bullet wound. There are many things that must be ascribed to divine mystery, but divine violence is not one of them. Why God allows people to do violence is a mystery, perhaps; but the fact that he *commanded* or *incited* it is perversion.

* * *

It is ironic that the very writers who accuse Marcion of being reductionistic are often reductionistic about Marcion. They tend to believe the heresiological clichés about him, the slander, the simplified and canned reports that one finds in heresy catalogues and in modern encyclopedias. Such writers mean well, but they do not seem to realize how smug—not to mention anachronistic and unfair—it sounds to say that Marcion—the church father before the church fathers—is good to think with, but in the end, just plain wrong.

If this book does anything, it should keep researchers accountable as to what can and cannot be confidently stated about Marcion's thought and

55. Kimball, *How (Not) to Read the Bible*, 286.

practice. The standard Harnackian portrait of Marcion as ditheist, docetist, and deleter of Scripture has collapsed. Marcion's supposedly simplistic and one-sided solutions to theological problems are in part heresiological and scholarly inventions.

Of course, Marcion was a selective reader, but it was not as if he did not *know* the passages in which the Judean lord is called compassionate, loving, and merciful. He simply pointed out the inconsistency of a "god" kind to obedient people who keep his covenant, but angry and abusive with those who do not. The larger question here is whether love ought to depend on obedience, and whether the pattern of religion as presented by Paul helps people to rise above a basically transactional relationship with God. This is the perennial challenge within the heart of Christianity.

Marcion's main goal was not to contrast the "Old" Testament with the "New," but to proclaim that something radically new had happened in Christ. "Behold, old things are gone; all things have become new" (2 Cor 5:17). Even if Jesus quoted the "Old" Testament, he took steps to end biblical violence and to transform the image of a violent God.[56] This is a fundamentally Marcionite insight. For Marcion, Christ reveals a God who is truly different from the being represented by "Yahweh." God in Christ is nonviolent. Period. End of story. No ifs, ands, or buts. All the apologists who try to convince themselves and other people that divine justice requires divine violence are in error because they dilute the cruciform gospel of Christ.[57] This is Marcion's message; this is the gospel of the wholly good God.

The time has come to study Marcion anew—not as a heretic, but as a man of history and a church father. It is time to read him in light of his own time and categories, not in light of later heresiological receptions. It is time to give this early Christian his due, to walk a mile in his shoes. If in the end, one accuses the Pontian of binary thinking or simplification, one ought at least to avoid such simplified thinking oneself.

56. Mariottini, *Divine Violence*, 377. Cf. Seibert, *Disturbing Divine Behavior*, 190–207.

57. Mariottini, *Divine Violence*, 375: "in certain situations divine judgment requires violence."

SELECTED BIBLIOGRAPHY

Primary Sources

Adamantius. Der Dialog des Adamantius ΠΕΡΙ ΤΗΣ ΕΙΣ ΘΕΟΝ ΟΡΘΗΣ ΠΙΣΤΕΩΣ. Edited by W. H. van de Sande Bakhuyzen. Leipzig: Hinrichs'sche Buchhandlung, 1901.

Alcinous. *Handbook of Platonism*. Translated by John Dillon. Oxford: Clarendon, 1993.

Apostolic Fathers. Translated by Bart Ehrman. LCL 25. Cambridge, MA: Harvard University Press, 2003.

Aristotle. *The Complete Works of Aristotle*. Edited by Jonathan Barnes. 2 vols. Princeton, NJ: Princeton University Press, 1984.

Arrian. *Periplus Ponti Euxini*. Translated by Aidan Liddle. London: Briston Classical Press, 2003.

Brankaer, Johanna. *The Gospel of Judas*. Oxford: Oxford University Press, 2019.

Cassius Dio. *Roman History*. Translated by Earnest Cary. 9 vols. Loeb Classical Library. Cambridge, MA: Harvard University Press, 1914–1927.

Clement of Alexandria. *Les Stromates*. Translated by Marcel Caster. 7 vols. Sources chrétiennes 30, 38, 278–279, 428, 446. Paris: Éditions du Cerf, 1951–2001.

Cyprian. *Opera Omnia*. Edited by Wilhelm von Hartel. Vindobonae : C. Geroldi filium, 1868-1871.

Cyril of Jerusalem. *Opera quae supersunt omnia*. Edited by W. K. Reischl and J. Rupp. 2 vols. Hildesheim: Olms, 1967.

Dio Chrysostom. Translated by J. W. Cohoon and H. L. Crosby. 5 vols. Loeb Classical Library. Cambridge, MA: Harvard University Press, 1932–1951.

Diogenes Laertius. Translated by R. D. Hicks. 2 vols. Loeb Classical Library. Cambridge, MA: Harvard University Press, 1925.

Ephrem of Nisibis. *Hymnes Contre les Hérésies*. Edited by Edmund Beck and Dominique Cerbelaud. 2 vols. SC 587, 590. Paris: Cerf, 2017.

———. *S. Ephraim's Prose Refutations of Mani, Marcion, and Bardaisan*. Translated by C. W. Mitchell. London: Williams and Norgate, 1912.

———. *Saint Ephrem: An Exposition of the Gospel*. Edited by George A. Egan. Leuven: Sécretariat du CorpusSCO, 1968.

Epictetus. *The Discourses, The Handbook, Fragments*. Edited and translated by Christopher Gill and Robin Hard. London: Everyman, 1995.

Epiphanius. *Ancoratus and Panarion*. 2nd ed. Edited by Karl Holl, Marc Bergermann, Christian-Friedrich Collatz, and Jürgen Dummer. 4 vols. Berlin: Akademie, 1980–2013.

Eusebius, *Histoire ecclésiastique*. Edited by Gustav Bardy. 4 vols. SC 31, 41, 55, 73. Paris: Cerf, 1952–1960.

Eznik of Kolb. *A Treatise on God Written in Armenian By Eznik of Kołb (floruit c.430–c.450)*. Translated by Monica J. Blanchard and Robin Darling Young. Leuven: Peeters, 1998.

Gaius. *The Digest of Justinian*. Translated by Alan Watson. Vol. 1. Philadelphia: University of Pennsylvania Press, 1985.

Galen. *Opera Omnia*. Edited by K. G. Kühn. 20 vols. Leipzig: Knobloch, 1821–1833.

Harris-McCoy, Daniel E. *Artemidorus'* Oneirocritica: *Text, Translation, and Commentary*. Oxford: Oxford University Press, 2012.

Irenaeus. *Contre les hérésies*. Edited by Adelin Rousseau and Louis Doutreleau. 10 vols. SC. Paris: Cerf, 1974.

Jerome. *Commentary on Isaiah*. Translated by Thomas P. Scheck. ACW 68. New York: Newman, 2015.

———. *Epistulae*. Edited by Isidorus Hilberg. 3 vols. Vienna: F. Tempsky, 1910.

———. *Gli vomini illustri: De viris Illustribus*. Edited by Aldo Cresa-Gastaldo. Firenze: Nardini, 1988.

Josephus. Translated by H. St. J. Thackeray. 10 vols. Loeb Classical Library. Cambridge, MA: Harvard University Press, 1926–1965.

Justin Martyr. *Apologiae pro christianis*. Edited by Miroslav Marcovich. Berlin: de Gruyter, 1994.

———. *Apologie pour les chrétiens: Introduction, traduction et commentaire*. Edited by Charles Munier. Paris: Éditions du Cerf, 2006.

———. *Dialogus cum Tryphone*. Edited by Miroslav Marcovich. Berlin: de Gruyter, 1997.

———. *Justin, Philosopher and Martyr, Apologies*. Edited by Denis Minns and Paul Parvis. Oxford: Oxford University Press, 2009.

Lactantius. *De ira dei*. Vom Zorne Gottes. Edited by H. Kraft and A. Wlosok. Darmstadt: Hermann Genter, 1957.

Litwa, M. David, ed. *Refutation of All Heresies*. WGRW 40. Atlanta: SBL Press, 2016.

Lucian. Translated by A. M. Harmon. 8 vols. Loeb Classical Library. Cambridge, MA: Harvard University Press, 1913–1967.

Numenius. *Fragments*. Edited by Édouard des Places. Paris: Belles Lettres, 2003.

Origen. *Homilies on Genesis and Exodus*. Translated by Ronald E. Heine. Washington, DC: Catholic University Press, 1982.

———. *Contra Celsum Libri VIII*. Edited by M. Marcovich. Leiden: Brill, 2001.

Pamphilus. *Pamphile et Eusèbe de Césarée apologie pour Origène*. Edited by René Amacker and Éric Junod. SC 464. Paris: Cerf, 2002.

Papias of Hierapolis. *Esposizione degli oracoli del Signore: I frammenti*. Edited by Enrico Norelli. Milan: Figlie di San Paolo, 2005.

Philo. Translated by F. H. Colson et al. 12 vols. Loeb Classical Library. Cambridge, MA: Harvard University Press, 1929–1962.

Plato. *Complete Works*. Edited by John M. Cooper. Indianapolis: Hackett, 1997.

Pliny the Younger. *Letters and Panegyricus*. Translated by Betty Radice. 2 vols. Loeb Classical Library. Cambridge, MA: Harvard University Press, 1969.

Plutarch. *Moralia*. Translated by Frank Cole Babbitt et al. 28 vols. Loeb Classical Library. Cambridge, MA: Harvard University Press, 1914–2004.

Pollmann, Karla, ed. *Das Carmen adversus Marcionitas: Einleitung, Text, Übersetzung und Kommentar*. Hypomnemata 96. Göttingen: Vandenhoeck & Ruprecht, 1991.

Ptolemy. *Lettre a Flora*. 2nd ed. Edited by Gilles Quispel. SC 24. Paris: Cerf, 1966.

Rahlfs, Alfred, and Robert Hanhart. *Septuaginta, id est Vetus Testamentum graece iuxta LXX interpretes*. 2nd ed. Stuttgart: Deutsche Bibelgesellschaft, 2006.

Rehm, Bernhard, and Franz Paschke, eds. *Die Pseudoklmentinen I: Homilien*. 2nd ed. Die griechischen christlichen Schriftsteller der ersten Jahrhunderte 42. Berlin: Akademie, 1969.

Sextus Empiricus. *Opera*. Edited by Hermann Mutschmann and J. Mau. 4 vols. BSGRT. Leipzig: Teubner, 1912–1961.

Tatian. *Oratio ad Graecos, Rede an die Griechen*. Edited Jörg Trelenberg. Beiträge zur historischen Theologie 165. Tübingen: Mohr Siebeck, 2012.

Tertullian. *Contre Marcion*. Edited by René Braun and Claudio Moreschini. 5 vols. SC 365, 368, 399, 456, 483. Paris: Cerf, 1990.

———. *Opera*. Edited by A. Kroymann and E. Evans. 2 vols. CCSL 2/1–2. Turnhout: Brepols, 1954.

Theophilus of Antioch. *Ad Autolycum*. Edited by Robert M. Grant. Oxford: Clarendon, 1970.

Secondary Sources

Aletti, Jean-Noël. *Without Typology—No Gospels: A Suffering Messiah. A Challenge for Matthew, Mark and Luke*. Rome: Pontifical Biblical Institute, 2022.

Allen, Ansgar. *Cynicism*. Cambridge, MA: MIT Press, 2020.

Aulén, Gustaf. *Christus Victor: An Historical Study of the Three Main Types of the Idea of the Atonement*. Translated by A. G. Hebert. London: SPCK, 1931.

Aune, David. "Luke 20:34–36: A Gnosticized Logion of Jesus?" In *Geschichte-Tradition-Reflexion, Festschrift für Martin Hengel*, vol. 2, edited by Hubert Cancik, Hermann Lichtenberger, and Peter Schäfer, 187–202. Tübingen: Mohr Siebeck, 1986.

Baarda, T. "Marcion's Text of Gal. 1:1: Concerning the Reconstruction of the First Verse of the Marcionite Corpus Paulinum." *Vigiliae Christianae* 42 (1988): 236–256.

Bainton, Roland H. "Basilidian Chronology and New Testament Interpretation." *Journal of Biblical Literature* 42 (1923): 81–134.

Barton, John. "An Early Metacommentary: Tertullian's Against Marcion." In *Reading from Right to Left: Essays on the Hebrew Bible in Honour of David J.A. Clines*, edited by J. Cheryl Exum and H. G. M. Williamson, 38–49. Sheffield: Sheffield Academic Press, 2003.

———. *Holy Writings, Sacred Text: The Canon in Early Christianity.* Louisville, KY: Westminster John Knox, 1997.

———. "Marcion Revisited." In *The Canon Debate*, ed. Lee Martin McDonald and James A. Sanders, 341–354. Peabody: Hendrickson, 2002.

Bazzana, Giovanni. "'Be Good Moneychangers': The Role of an Agraphon in a Discursive Fight for the Canon of Scripture." In *Invention, Rewriting, Usurpation: Discursive Fights over Religious Traditions in Antiquity*, edited by David Brakke, Jörg Ulrich, and Anders-Christian Jacobsen (Frankfurt am Main: Peter Lang, 2012), 297–312.

Beardslee, William A. "De Facie quae in Orbe Lunae Apparet (Moralia 920A-945D)." In *Plutarch's Theological Writings and Early Christian Literature*, edited by H. D. Betz, 286–288. Leiden: Brill, 1975.

Beck, Roger. *The Religion of the Mithras Cult in the Roman Empire: Mysteries of the Unconquered Sun*. Oxford: Oxford University Press, 2006.

Becker, Eve-Marie. "Taufe bei Marcion—eine Spurensuche." In *Ablution, Initiation, and Baptism: Late Antiquity, Early Judaism, and Early Christianity*, vol. 2, edited by David Hellholm, Tor Vegge, Øyvind Norderval, and Christer Hellholm, 871–894. BZNW 176. Berlin: De Gruyter, 2011.

BeDuhn, Jason David. *The First New Testament: Marcion's Scriptural Canon*. Salem, OR: Polebridge Press, 2013.

———. "The Influence of Marcion's Apostolikon on the Gospel of Luke: A Proposal." In *New Perspectives on Marcion*, edited by Paul Allan Mirecki, and Robert D. Royalty Jr., 1–24. Society of Biblical Literature Symposium Series 48. Atlanta: Society of Biblical Literature, 2009.

———. "New Studies on Marcion's Evangelion." *Journal of Ancient Christianity* 21, no. 1 (2017): 8–24.

BeDuhn, Jason David and Mark G. Bilby, eds. "Greek Edition of the First New Testament: ΕΥΑΓΓΕΛΙΟΝ," version 1.2, deposited 2023-10-19.

———. "Greek Edition of the First New Testament: ΑΠΟΣΤΟΛΟΣ." version 1, deposited 2023.

Beker, J. Christiaan. "Christologies and Anthropologies of Paul, Luke-Acts and Marcion." In *From Jesus to John: Essays on Jesus and New Testament Christology in Honour of Marinus de Jonge*, edited by Martinus C. De Boer, 174–182. Sheffield: Sheffield Academic Press, 1993.

Bernard, David K. "The Development of Modalism in Early Church History." *Journal of Early Christian History* 9, no. 3 (2020): 70–84.

Bilby, M. G. *The First Gospel, the Gospel of the Poor: A New Reconstruction of Q and Resolution of the Synoptic Problem Based on Marcion's Early Luke.* Version 4.03, Zenodo, 2020–2024. Published by the author.

Blackman, E. C. *Marcion and His Influence.* London: SPCK, 1948.

Bohorquez, Davinson. "The Cross and the Throne: The Son of Man of Matthew 25:31–46 in Light of the Passion Narrative." *Crux* 58, no. 1 (2022): 20–29.

Brakke, David. *The Gospel of Judas: A New Translation with Introduction and Commentary.* New Haven, CT: Yale University Press, 2022.

Brenk, Frederick E. *On Plutarch: Religious Thinker and Biographer.* Leiden: Brill, 2017.

Bull, Christian H. *Tradition of Hermes: The Egyptian Priestly Figure as a Teacher of Hellenized Wisdom.* RGRW 186. Leiden: Brill, 2018.

Burkitt, F. C. "The Exordium of Marcion's *Antitheses,*" *Journal of Theological Studies* 30, no. 119 (1929): 279–280.

Burns, Dylan. *Did God Care? Providence, Dualism and Will in Later Greek and Early Christian Philosophy.* Leiden: Brill, 2020.

Candy, Peter. "Parallel Developments in Roman Law and Maritime Trade during the Late Republic and Early Principate." *Journal of Roman Archaeology* 33 (2020): 53–72.

Carlson, Stephen C. *Papias of Hierapolis: Exposition of Dominical Oracles.* Oxford: Oxford University Press, 2021.

Carter, Adam. "Marcion's Christology." *Journal of Early Christian Studies* 17, no. 4 (2009): 557–85.

Casey, Robert P. "The Armenian Marcionites and the Diatessaron." *Journal of Biblical Literature* 57, no. 2 (1938): 185–194.

Clabeaux, John J. *A Lost Edition of the Letters of Paul: A Reassessment of the Text of the Pauline Corpus Attested by Marcion.* Washington, DC: Catholic Biblical Association of America, 1989.

Clay, Diskin. "The Philosophical Inscription of Diogenes of Oenoanda." *Bulletin of the Classical Studies* 1 (2007): 283–291.

Collins, John J. *Does the Bible Justify Violence?* Minneapolis: Fortress, 2004.

Coogan, Jeremiah. "Meddling with the Gospel: Celsus, Early Christian Textuality, and the Politics of Reading." *Novum Testamentum* 65 (2023): 400–422.

Cosgrove, Charles H. "Justin Martyr and the Emerging Christian Canon: Observations on the Purpose and Destination of the Dialogue with Trypho." *Vigiliae Christianae* 36, no. 3 (1982): 209–232.

Couchoud, Paul-Louis. "Is Marcion's Gospel One of the Synoptics?" *Hibbert Journal* 34 (1936): 265–277.

———. *The Creation of Christ: An Outline of the Beginnings of Christianity.* London: Watts & Co., 1939.

Cumont, Franz. "Le Zeus Stratios de Mithridate." *Revue de l'histoire des religions* 43 (1901): 47–57.

Dahl, Nils A. "Origin of the Earliest Prologues to the Pauline Letters." *Semeia* 12 (1978): 233–277.

Dassmann, Ernst. *Der Stachel im Fleisch: Paulus in der frühchristlichen Literatur bis Irenäus.* Münster: Aschendorff, 1979.

Davis, Phillip Andrew. "Marcion's Gospel and its Use of the Jewish Scriptures." *ZNW* 112, no. 1 (2021): 105–129.

de Villiers, Pieter G.R. and Jan Willelm van Henten, eds., *Coping with Violence in the New Testament.* Leiden: Brill, 2012.

Den Dulk, Matthijs. *Between Jews and Heretics: Refiguring Justin Martyr's Dialogue with Trypho.* London: Routledge, 2018.

Derrickson, Scott, dir. *The Day the Earth Stood Still.* 20th Century Fox, 2008.

Dillon, John. *The Middle Platonists 80 BCE to AD 220,* 2nd ed. Ithaca: Cornell University Press, 1996.

Drijvers, H. J. W. "Christ as Warrior and Merchant." *Studia Patristica.* 21 (1989): 73–85.

Dungan, David L. *History of the Synoptic Problem.* New York: Doubleday, 2009.

———. "Reactionary Trends in the Gospel Producing Activity of the Early Church: Marcion, Tatian, Mark." In *L'Évangile selon Marc: Tradition et rédaction,* edited by M. Sabbe, 179–202. Leuven: Leuven University Press, 1974.

Ehrman, Bart D. *Lost Christianities: The Battles for Scripture and the Faiths We Never Knew.* Oxford: Oxford University Press, 2003.

———. *Studies in the Textual Criticism of the New Testament.* Leiden: Brill, 2006.

Elliott, J. K. *The Apocryphal New Testament.* Oxford: Oxford University Press, 1993.

Evans, C. A. *To See and Not Perceive: Isa 6.9–10 in Early Jewish and Christian Interpretation.* London: Bloomsbury, 2009.

Flemming, Rebecca. "Demiurge and Emperor in Galen's World of Knowledge." In *Galen and the World of Knowledge,* edited by Christopher Gill, Tim Whitmarsh, and John Wilkins, 59–83. Cambridge: Cambridge University Press, 2009.

Fletcher, Richard. *Apuleius's Platonism.* Cambridge: Cambridge University Press, 2014.

Forness, Philip Michael. "The Anonymous Source for Marcion's Gospel in British Library, Add. 17215: An Identification and Analysis." *New Testament Studies* 67 (2021): 541–559.

Fretheim, Terence E. and Karlfried Froehlich. *The Bible as the Word of God: In a Postmodern Age* (Minneapolis: Fortress Press, 1998).

Fürst, Alfons. *Christentum als Intellektuellen-religion: Die Anfänge des Christentums in Alexandria.* Stuttgart: Katholisches Bibelwerk, 2007.

Gager, John G. "Marcion and Philosophy." *Harvard Theological Review* 77 (1984): 55–56.

———. "Marcion and Philosophy." *Vigiliae Christianae* 26 (1972): 53–59.

Gamble, Harry Y. *Books and Readers: A History of Early Christian Texts.* New Haven, CT: Yale University Press, 1995.

Gathercole, Simon. *The Apocryphal Gospels: Translated with an Introduction*. London: Penguin, 2021.

Gianmarco Cerreti, "Osservazioni sulle fonti sui Συλλογισμοί del marcionita Apelle," *Augustinianum* 62, no. 2 (2022): 297–329.

Gibbon, Edward. *The History of the Decline and Fall of the Roman Empire*, vol. 1. London: ElecBook, 1999.

Gordon, Richard. "Ritual and Hierarchy in the Mysteries of Mithras." In *The Religious History of the Roman Empire: Pagans, Jews, and Christians*, edited by J. A. North and S. R. F. Price, 325–365. Oxford: Oxford University Press, 2011.

Grant, Robert M., ed. *Heresy and Criticism* (Oxford: Clarendon, 1970).

———. *Heresy and Criticism: The Search for Authenticity in Early Christian Literature*. Louisville, KY: Westminster John Knox, 1993.

———. *Letter and Spirit*. New York: Crossroad, 1991.

Gregory, Andrew. *Reception of Luke and Acts in the Period Before Irenaeus*. WUNT 2/70. Tübingen: Mohr Siebeck, 2003.

Hage, Wolfgang. "Marcion bei Eznik von Kolb." In *Marcion und seine kirchengeschichtliche Wirkung*, edited by Gerhard May and Katharina Greschat, 29–38. Berlin: de Gruyter, 2002.

Hägg, Tomas. *The Art of Biography in Antiquity*. Cambridge: Cambridge University Press, 2012.

Harland, Philip A. *Greco-Roman Associations: Texts, Translations and Commentary. II. North Coast of the Black Sea, Asia Minor*. Berlin: de Gruyter, 2014.

Harnack, Adolf von. *Marcion: Das Evangelium vom fremden Gott: Eine Monographie zur Geschichte der Grundlegung der katholischen Kirche*. 2 vols. Texte und Untersuchungen 45.1. Leipzig: J. C. Hinrichs, 1924–1925.

———. *Marcion: The Gospel of the Alien God*. Translated by John E. Steely and Lyle D. Bierma. Durham, NC: Labyrinth, 1990.

Harrison, P. N. *Polycarp's Two Epistles to the Philippians*. Cambridge: Cambridge University Press, 1936.

Harrison, Stephen. *Apuleius: A Latin Sophist*. Oxford: Oxford University Press, 2004.

———, ed. *Apuleius: Rhetorical Works*. Oxford: Oxford University Press, 2001.

Hawes, Greta. *Rationalizing Mythology in Antiquity*. Oxford: Oxford University Press, 2014.

Hays, Richard B. *Echoes of Scripture in the Gospels*. Waco: Baylor University Press, 2016.

Head, Peter. "The Foreign God and the Sudden Christ: Theology and Christology in Marcion's Gospel Redaction." *Tyndale Bulletin* 44, no. 2 (1993): 307–321.

Hill, James H. *The Gospel of the Lord: An Early Version*. Guernsey: John Whitehead, 1891.

Hoffmann, R. Joseph. "How Then Know This Troublous Teacher? Further Reflections on Marcion and his Church." *Second Century* 6 (1987–1988): 173–191.

Hoklotubbe, T. Christopher. "What is Docetism?" In *Re-making the World: Christianity and Categories: Essays in Honor of Karen L. King*, edited by Taylor G. Petrey, 49–71. Tübingen: Mohr Siebeck, 2019.

Jackson-McCabe, Matt. *Jewish Christianity: The Making of the Christianity-Judaism Divide*. New Haven, CT: Yale University Press, 2020.

Janßen, Martina. "'Wider die Antithesen der fälschlich so genannten Gnosis': 1 Tim 6,20 und die Antithesen Markions." In *Frühes Christentum und Religionsgeschichtliche Schule: Festschrift zum. 65 Geburtstag von Gerd Lüdemann*, edited by Martina Janßen. Göttingen: Vandenhoeck & Ruprecht, 2011.

Jülicher, Adolf. *Itala: Das Neue Testament in altlateinischer Überlieferung*. Berlin: de Gruyter, 1954.

Junod, Éric. "Les attitudes d'Apelles, disciple de Marcion a l'égard de l'Ancien Testament," *Augustinianum* 22 (1982): 113–133.

Kelhoffer, James A. "'How Soon a Book' Revisited: ΕΥΑΓΓΕΛΙΟΝ as a Reference to 'Gospel' Materials in the First Half of the Second Century." *ZNW* 95 (2004): 1–34.

Keulen, W. H. and Egelhaaf-Gaiser, Ulrike. *Apuleius Madaurensis Metamorphoses Book XI: The Isis Book*. Leiden: Brill, 2015.

Kimball, Dan. *How (Not) to Read the Bible: Making Sense of the Anti-women, Anti-science, Pro-violence, Pro-slavery and Other Crazy-sounding Parts of Scripture*. Grand Rapids, MI: Zondervan Reflective, 2020.

King, Karen L. "Reconsidering Docetism." In *Nag Hammadi à 70 ans. Qu'avons-nous appris?* Edited by Eric Crégheur et al., 17–30. Leuven: Peeters, 2019.

———. *What is Gnosticism?* Cambridge, MA: Belknap Press, 2003.

Klinghardt, Matthias. "Markion vs. Lukas: Plädoyer für die Wiederaufnahme eines alten Falles." *New Testament Studies* 52 (2006): 484–513.

———. "The Marcionite Gospel and the Synoptic Problem: A New Suggestion." *Novum Testamentum* 50 (2008): 1–27.

———. *The Oldest Gospel and the Formation of the Canonical Gospels*. 2 vols. Leuven: Peeters, 2021.

Knox, John. *Marcion and the New Testament: An Essay in the Early History of the Canon*. Chicago: University of Chicago Press, 1942.

Knust, Jennifer. *Abandoned to Lust: Sexual Slander and Ancient Christianity*. New York: Columbia University Press, 2005.

Lampe, Peter. *From Paul to Valentinus: Christians at Rome in the First Two Centuries*. Edited by Marshall Johnson. Translated by Michael Steinhauser. Minneapolis: Fortress, 2003.

Lane, Jason D. *Luther's Epistle of Straw: The Voice of St. James in Reformation Preaching*. Berlin: de Gruyter, 2018.

Lehtipuu, Outi. "Flesh and Blood Cannot Inherit the Kingdom of God': The Transformation of the Flesh in Early Christian Debates Concerning

Resurrection." In *Metamorphoses, Resurrection, Body, and Transformative Practices in Early Christianity*, edited by Turid Karlsen Seim and Jorunn Øklund, 159–180. Berlin: de Gruyter, 2009.

Lieu, Judith M. *Marcion and the Making of a Heretic: God and Scripture in the Second Century*. Cambridge: Cambridge University Press, 2015.

Lindemann, Andreas. *Paulus im ältesten Christentum: Das Bild des Apostles und die Rezeption der paulinischen Theologie in der frühchristlichen Literatur bis Marcion*. Tübingen: Mohr Siebeck, 1979.

Litwa, M. David. *Carpocrates, Marcellina, and Epiphanes: Three Early Christian Teachers of Alexandria and Rome*. London: Routledge, 2021.

———. "Equal to Angels: The Early Reception History of the Lukan ἰσάγγελοι (Luke 20:36)." *Journal of Biblical Literature* 140, no. 3 (2021): 601–622.

———. *The Evil Creator: Origins of An Early Christian Idea*. New York: Oxford, 2021.

———. *Found Christianities: Remaking the World of the Second Century CE*. London: Bloomsbury, 2022.

———. *How the Gospels Became History: Jesus and Mediterranean Myths* (New Haven, CT: Yale University Press, 2019), 1–21

———. *The Naassenes: Contours of an Early Christian Identity*. London: Routledge, 2023.

Löhr, Winrich. "Problems of Profiling Marcion." In *Christian Teachers in Second-century Rome: Schools and Students in the Ancient City*, edited by H. Gregory Snyder, 109–133. Leiden: Brill, 2020.

Long, A. A. *Epictetus: A Stoic and Socratic Guide to Life*. Oxford: Oxford University Press, 2002.

Lüdemann, Gerd. *Heretics: The Other Side of Early Christianity*. Translated by John Bowden. Louisville: Westminster John Knox, 1996.

Madsen, Jesper Majbom. *From Trophy Towns to City-States: Urban Civilization and Cultural Identities in Roman Pontus*. Philadelphia: University of Pennsylvania Press, 2020.

Marshall, John W. "Misunderstanding the New Paul: Marcion's Transformation of the Sonderzeit Paul." *Journal of Early Christian Studies* 20, no. 1 (2012): 1–29.

Martin, Luther H. *The Mind of Mithraists: Historical and Cognitive Studies in the Roman Cult of Mithras*. London: Bloomsbury, 2015.

Mattern, Susan P. *The Prince of Medicine: Galen in the Roman Empire*. Oxford: Oxford University Press, 2013.

May, Gerhard. *Creatio ex nihilo: The Doctrine of 'Creation out of Nothing' in Early Christian Thought*. Translated by A. S. Worrall. London: T&T Clark, 2004.

———. "Marcion in Contemporary Views: Results and Open Questions." In *Gerhard May: Markion. Gesammelte Aufsätze*, edited by Katharina Greschat and Martin Meiser, 13–34. Mainz: Philipp von Zabern, 2005.

———. "Marcions Genesisauslegung," *Vigiliae Christianae* 24 (1970): 89–98.

May, Gerhard and Greschat, Katharina, eds. *Marcion und seine kirchengeschichtliche Wirkung, Marcion and His Impact on Church History*. Berlin: de Gruyter, 2002.

McGowan, Andrew B. *Ancient Christian Worship: Early Church Practices in Social, Historical, and Theological Perspective*. Grand Rapids, MI: Baker, 2014.

Mitchell, Stephen, and Nuffelen, Peter van, eds. *Monotheism between Pagans and Christians in Late Antiquity*. Leuven: Peeters, 2010.

Moll, Sebastian. *Die christliche Eroberung des Alten Testaments*. Berlin: Berlin University Press, 2010.

———. *The Arch-heretic Marcion*. Tübingen: Mohr Siebeck, 2010.

Moss, Candida R. *Ancient Christian Martyrdom: Diverse Practices, Theologies, and Traditions*. New Haven, CT: Yale University Press, 2012.

Musurillo, Herbert, ed. *The Acts of the Christian Martyrs*. Oxford: Clarendon, 1972.

Navia, Luis E. *Diogenes the Cynic: The War against the World*. Amherst: Humanity Books, 2005.

Nelson-Pallmeyer, John D. *Is Religion Killing Us?: Violence in the Bible and the Quran*. New York: Continuum, 2003.

Nielsen, Charles M. "Polycarp and Marcion: A Note." *Theological Studies* 47 (1986): 297–299.

Nietzsche, Friedrich. *Thus Spake Zarathustra* in *The Portable Nietzsche*. Edited and translated by Walter Kaufmann. London: Penguin, 1954.

Norelli, Enrico. "La Lettre aux Laodicéens: Essai d'interprétation." *Archivum Bobiense* 23 (2001): 45–90.

———. "Marcion et les disciples de Jésus." *Apocrypha* 19 (2008): 9–42.

Olshausen, Eckart. "Pontos: Profile of a Landscape." In *Space, Place and Identity in Northern Anatolia*, edited by Tønnes Bekker-Nielsen, 39–48. Stuttgart: Franz Steiner, 2014.

Panagiotidou, Olympia. *The Roman Mithras Cult: A Cognitive Approach*. London: Bloomsbury, 2017.

Pervo, Richard. *The Making of Paul: Constructions of the Apostle in Early Christianity*. Minneapolis: Fortress, 2010.

Petrey, Taylor. *Resurrecting Parts: Early Christians on Desire, Reproduction, and Sexual Difference*. New York: Routledge, 2015.

Price, S.R.F. *Rituals and Power: The Roman Imperial Cult in Asia Minor*. Cambridge: Cambridge University Press, 1984.

Räisänen, Heikki. *Paul and the Law*. Tübingen: Mohr Siebeck, 1983.

———. *The Rise of Christian Beliefs: The Thought World of Early Christians*. Minneapolis: Fortress Press, 2010.

Reardon, B. P., trans. *Collected Ancient Greek Novels*. Berkeley, CA: University of California Press, 2008.

Regul, Jürgen. *Die antimarkionitischen Evangelienprologe*. Freiburg: Herder, 1969.

Richter, Daniel. "Lives and Afterlives of Lucian of Samosata." *Arion* 13, no. 1 (2005): 75–100.

Rist, Martin. "III Corinthians as a Pseudepigraphic Refutation of Marcionism." *Iliff Review* 26 (1969): 40–58.

Rocca, J. *Galen on the Brain: Anatomical Knowledge and Physiological Speculation in the Second Century AD.* Leiden: Brill, 2003.

Roetzel, C. J. "Jewish Christian-Gentile Christian Relations: A Discussion of Ephesians 2.15a." *ZNW* 74 (1983): 81–89.

Röhl, Ulrike Margarethe Salome. *Der Paulusschüler Markion: Eine kritische Untersuchung zum Antijudaismus im 2.Jahrhundert.* Marburg: Tectum, 2014.

Roth, Dieter. *The Text of Marcion's Gospel.* Leiden: Brill, 2015.

Rothschild, Claire. *The Muratorian Fragment: Text, Translation, and Commentary.* Tübingen: Mohr Siebeck, 2022.

Roukema, Riemer. "Salvation and Victory by Christ's Death and Resurrection in the Ancient Church." *Journal of Reformed Theology* 15 (2021): 304–326.

Schmid, Ulrich. *Marcion und sein Apostolos: Rekonstruktion und historische Einordnung der Marcionitischen Paulusbriefausgabe* (Berlin: de Gruyter, 1995).

Schoeps, H. J. *Aus frühchristlicher Zeit: Religionsgeschichtliche Untersuchungen.* Tübingen: Mohr Siebeck, 1950.

Schüle, E. U. "Der Ursprung des Bösen bei Marcion." *Zeitschrift für Religions- und Geistesgeschichte.* 16:1 (1964): 23–42.

Schweitzer, Albert. *The Mysticism of Paul the Apostle.* New York: Seabury, 1931.

Scott, Thomas McAllister. "Egyptian Elements in Hermetic Literature." PhD diss., Harvard Divinity School, 1987.

Seibert, Eric A. *Disturbing Divine Behavior: Troubling Old Testament Images of God* Minneapolis: Fortress, 2009.

———. *The Violence of Scripture: Overcoming the Old Testament's Troubling Legacy.* Minneapolis: Fortress, 2012.

Shea, Louisa. *The Cynic Enlightenment: Diogenes in the Salon.* Baltimore, MD: Johns Hopkins University Press, 2010.

Smith, Daniel A. *"Seeing a Pneuma(tic body): The Apologetic Interests of Luke 24:36–43." Catholic Biblical Quarterly* 72, no. 4 (2010): 752–772.

Smith, J. Z. *Relating Religion: Essays in the Study of Religion.* Chicago: Chicago University Press, 2004.

Smith, Martin Ferguson. *Diogenes of Oinoanda: The Epicurean Inscription.* Naples: Bibliopolis, 1993.

Still, Todd D. "Shadow and Light: Marcion's (Mis)Construal of the Apostle Paul." In *Paul and the Second Century*, edited by Michael F. Bird and Joseph R. Dodson, 91–107. London: T&T Clark, 2011.

Stowers, Stanley K. "What Does UnPauline Mean?" In *Paul and the Legacies of Paul*, edited by William S. Babcock, 70–77. Dallas: Southern Methodist University Press, 1990.

Tardieu, Michel. "À travers un tuyau: Quelques remarques sur le myth valentinien de la chair céleste due Christ." In *Colloque international sur les textes de Nag*

Hammadi, edited by Bernard Barc, 151–177. Quebec City, QC: Université Laval, 1981.

Trible, Phyllis. *Texts of Terror: Literary-Feminist Readings of Biblical Narrative* Minneapolis: Fortress, 2022.

Tyson, Joseph. *Marcion and Luke Acts: A Defining Struggle.* Columbia: University of South Carolina Press, 2006.

Vélissaropoulos, Julie. *Les nauclères grecs: Recherches sur les institutions maritimes en Grèce et dans l'Orient hellénisé.* Paris: Libraire Minard, 1980.

Vinzent, Markus. *Christ's Resurrection in Early Christianity and the Making of the New Testament.* Burlington: Ashgate, 2011.

———. *Marcion and the Dating of the Synoptic Gospels.* Leuven: Peeters, 2014.

———. "Marcion the Jew," *Judaïsme ancien* 1 (2013): 159–201

———. *Tertullian's Preface to Marcion's Gospel.* Leuven: Peeters, 2016.

Vos, John S. "Das Agraphon 'Seid kundige Geldwechsler!' bei Origenes." In *Sayings of Jesus: Canonical and Non-canonical. Essays in Honour of T. Baarda*, edited by W. L. Petersen, Johan S. Vos, and Henk J. de Jonge, 227–302. Leiden: Brill, 1997,

Watson, Francis. "Pauline Reception and the Problem of Docetism." In *Docetism in the Early Church: The Quest for an Elusive Phenomenon*, edited by Joseph Verheyden, Reimund Bieringer, Jens Schröter, and Ines Jäger, 51–66. Tübingen: Mohr Siebeck, 2018.

Wiles, Maurice. *The Divine Apostle: The Interpretation of St. Paul's Epistles in the Early Church.* Cambridge: Cambridge University Press, 1967.

Wilhite, David E. "Was Marcion a Docetist? The Body of Evidence vs. Tertullian's Argument," *Vigiliae Christianae* 71 (2017): 1–36.

Wilshire, Leland Edward. "Was Canonical Luke Written in the Second Century?" *New Testament Studies* 20 (1974): 246–253.

Wilson, Robert Smith. *Marcion: A Study of a Second-Century Heretic.* London: SPCK 1933.

Wilson, S. G. "Marcion and the Jews." In *Anti-Judaism in Early Christianity*, Vol. 2, *Separation and Polemic*, 45–58. Waterloo, ON: Wilfrid Laurier University Press, 1986.

Winger, Michael. *By What Law: The Meaning of Νόμος in the Letters of Paul.* Atlanta: Scholars Press, 1992.

Woltmann, J. "Der geschichtliche Hintergrund der Lehre Markions vom Fremden Gott." In *Wegzeichen: Festgabe zum 60. Geburtstag von Prof. Dr. M. H. Biedermann*, edited by E. Suttner and C. Patak, 15–42. Würzburg: Augustinus Verlag, 1971.

Zanker, Paul. *The Mask of Socrates: The Image of the Intellectual in Antiquity.* Berkeley: University of California Press, 1995.

Zwierlein, Otto. *Die antihäretischen Evangelienprologe und die Entstehung des Neuen Testaments.* Mainz: Akademie der Wissenschaften und der Literatur, 2015.

INDEX